P9-CCY-725

THE CEO OF THE SOFA

❖

To Sean,
Who's only President

[signature]

Oct 8, 2001

ALSO BY P. J. O'ROURKE

Modern Manners
The Bachelor Home Companion
Republican Party Reptile
Holidays in Hell
Parliament of Whores
Give War a Chance
All the Trouble in the World
Age and Guile
Eat the Rich

P. J. O'ROURKE

THE CEO OF THE SOFA

❖

ATLANTIC MONTHLY PRESS
NEW YORK

Published simultaneously in Canada
Printed in the United States of America

FIRST EDITION

Library of Congress Cataloging-in-Publication Data
O'Rourke, P. J.
The CEO of the sofa / by P. J. O'Rourke.
p. cm.
ISBN 0-87113-825-5
1. American wit and humor. I. Title.
PN6165 .076 2001
818'.5402—dc21 2001035534

Atlantic Monthly Press
841 Broadway
New York, NY 10003
01 02 03 04 10 9 8 7 6 5 4 3 2 1

For Tina, Elizabeth, and Olivia

THE CEO OF THE SOFA

One year in the life of a man who said, "Mind if I put my feet up? I think I *will* take this lying down."

CONTENTS

ACKNOWLEDGMENTS

Poking around in a used-book store a couple of years ago, I came across a beautiful 1875 edition of *The Autocrat of the Breakfast Table* by Oliver Wendell Holmes. I bought it for $1.50. Holmes was once a literary *Pathera leo* of far-heard roar. *The Autocrat,* first published in 1858, was, for half a century, one of the best-loved and most-reprinted American books. As late as the nutty, modernist 1930s Virginia Woolf was comparing *The Autocrat* to "champagne after breakfast cups of weak tea." (A phrase that may explain a lot about Virginia Woolf's mood disorders and literary style, but never mind.)

I hadn't read *The Autocrat of the Breakfast Table* since college. And back then I had read around in it. I'd never read it through. This time I did. The book is a collection of columns from *The Atlantic Monthly* magazine. The conceit is that Holmes lives in a boardinghouse and holds forth to his fellow boarders over the morning meal, which must have lasted rather longer than today's Starbucks-and-a-power-bar-grabbed-on-the-go. The volume's essays, poems, and speculations on widely various topics are presented as the autocrat's monologues with occasional interruptions by such characters as a comely widow, a wisecracking clerk, a dense landlady, and two O.W.H. alter egos, the Professor and the Poet.

Holmes pulled this off with so much wit and charm that there was only one way I could pay his idea the compliment it deserved. I swiped it. And herewith is a collection of my own columns, just not as good and mostly from magazines less august than *The Atlantic Monthly*. Holmes himself said, "A thought is often original, though you have uttered it a hundred times." And he probably uttered that thought again when he handed his book publisher a wad of old *Atlantic* clippings.

I stole the form. I should have stolen the content. As little-known as Oliver Wendell Holmes is today, I could have gotten away with it. The man does not deserve such neglect. Alone among the New England Transcendentalist posse, he merits reading by an adult. Holmes had a broader, better, and more commonsensical intellect than Emerson or Thoreau. He had the humor that Emerson usually, and Thoreau profoundly, lacked. He was far less boring than Melville and wasn't a head case like Whitman. And, most amazingly for a nineteenth-century American intellectual, Holmes was (to speak a thought Holmes wouldn't have uttered once, let alone a hundred times) not full of shit.

The characters appearing in this book are fictional except, of course, for those who aren't, one of whom is not me. I'm completely made up. Muffin and Poppet, however, exist in an even more relentlessly adorable incarnation than what is seen here. Likewise, my wife, Tina. I do have a godson Nick. He's older and possessed of more gravitas than the Nick in these pages. And he doesn't have a crazy older sister Ophelia. He has a normal—although not so normal as to be weird—younger brother, Tom. The baby-sitter, her mother, and the Democrats next door are all imaginary. Although, since we live part of the year in Washington, D.C., there *are* Democrats next door, but we're on good terms—even though both of them are lawyers working for the National Association to Ban Almost Anything (NABAA). Hi, neighbors! And be assured that we have trigger locks on the assault weapons so you can let your nanny bring the kids over for a play date without worrying.

Max Pappas, my young assistant, is also real, which is a good thing since this book really would not be finished or really even started without Max's skills at research, organization, word processing, and diplomatically coaxing the author to put the cork back in breakfast and get to work. As for the Political Nut who shows up at cocktail hour, he is much too real. (And so, God help us, is the book *Guidelines for Bias-Free Writing*.)

Bits and chunks and indeed whole globs of the CEO's monologues have previously appeared in: *Rolling Stone, Men's Journal, Forbes FYI, Forbes ASAP, The Weekly Standard, The New York Times Book Review, The Spectator, The American Spectator, The American Enterprise, The Paris Review, Automobile, Car and Driver, TV Guide,* and even the ancient *National Lampoon.* As the careful reader of the acknowledgments page—if there is such a person—can tell, I am nothing if not a devotee of recycling.

My thanks to these publications for their permission (I assume some more responsible-type person than myself has requested it. Max, where are you?) to reprint this material. Other soliloquies are drawn from a (surely mis-assigned) introduction to a *Men's Journal* book on sport, fitness, and pleasure travel; a letter to Elaine Kaufman on the occasion of her restaurant's twentieth year in business; a monograph about theft of intellectual property (I'm an expert) written for the American Association of Publishers, and a preface to a twenty-fifth anniversary edition of Hunter S. Thompson's *Fear and Loathing in Las Vegas,* which Hunter rejected saying that, while it was certainly a delightful commentary and he thoroughly enjoyed reading it, everything I said about his book was flat damn wrong. (This is why literary criticism tends to concentrate on writers who are either dead or don't have the critic's phone number.)

I owe a debt of gratitude to Oliver Wendell Holmes, but he's not the only one. There's Jann Wenner, proprietor of *Rolling Stone* and *Men's Journal,* who has kept me in daily bread for half a generation even though, for all I knew, Tupak Shakur was an Iranian artificial beverage sweetener; Bob Love, managing editor of *Rolling Stone,* who did the editorial lifting and carrying on most of the longer items in this book; Terry McDonell, who as editor of *Men's Journal* gave me my best essay assignments and who, even better, is the father of my godson Nick; and David E. Davis, Jr., former editor of *Car and Driver* and founder of *Automobile,* who got me started in automotive journalism back when a Hyundai was something you did after too many Budweisers.

Thanks also to Bill Kristol, Fred Barnes, and Andy Ferguson at *The Weekly Standard,* Jean Jennings at *Automobile,* Sid Evans and David Willey at *Men's Journal,* Kim Goldstein at *Rolling Stone,* Patrick Cooke and Thomas Jackson at *Forbes FYI,* Wlady Pleszcynski at *The American Spectator* Scott Walter at *The American Enterprise;* to illustrious copy editor

Janet Baker, fantastic proofreader Don Kennison, outstanding Grove/Atlantic managing editor Michael Hornburg, and to all the other editors, associate editors, editorial associates, proofreaders, fact checkers, and factotums who have been so patient with my Hollywood spelling and Haight-Ashbury work habits. And a special double ration of thanks—with extra grog—goes to Christopher Buckley, editor of *Forbes FYI* (or *Business Fun* as it's called herein). In chapter 5, Chris's part of the dialogue (the funny part) is his own. So are most of the best lines in the rest of the blind (drunk) wine tasting and in the chapter 6 "Who the F— Are They?" section, which was—after a long lunch—Chris's idea. My wife also writes her own dialogue. This is why, my dear, I sometimes leave the room right in the middle of what you're saying. I'm not avoiding a discussion, I'm taking notes.

As long as I'm making a general confession to pilferage, let me confess that I took the Polo-Playing Deaths Memorial Quilt from expert equestrian Molly Vogel and US Airways Church of Christ from brilliant photographer James Kegley. Then there are those jokes that come from who-knows-where and turn up in little bassinets on a humorist's doorstep, so to speak. The humorist is pretty sure he didn't physically produce these jests, but they're awfully cute and he'd hate to leave them out in the cold. E.g., "unauthorized autobiography" is not, I'm almost certain, my progeny. And the quip about Clinton's popularity ratings getting so high that he started dating again definitely belongs to someone else. Maybe it belongs to Al Franken, who is a tremendous wit even if he is a Democrat. I wrote a snarky review of Al's very funny memoir of the Franken presidency, *Why Not Me?* I unfairly twitted Franken with the fact that there was more funny business going on in the Clinton White House than any humorist could invent. Just recompense almost demands that I get caught stealing a joke from Al.

To continue a theme, the cover concept was boosted from a poster by early twentieth-century German architect and graphic artist Ludwig Hohlwein, although in this case it was my wife who had the taste and education to do the shoplifting. The cover was then photographed by James Kegley, a man of genius with portraiture and Job-like patience with other people's children not to mention their grumpy old dad. The cover was designed by the master of cover design Charles Rue Woods, who came to Washington for the photo shoot and ended up doing a stint as Muffin and Poppet wrangler. Enormous thanks to all of these people and their confreres and co-soeurs whom I've failed to mention. And, naturally, a big *much obliged* to publicity wizard Scott Manning, my lecture agent Don Epstein at GTN in New York, my literary agent Bob Dattila, who unaccountably lives in Montana (No, Bob, *I'm* the writer. *I* live in Montana. *You're* back on the East Coast with the mortgage and the kids.), and my publisher and editor Morgan Entrekin. P.S., I'd also like to apologize to the four of you, respectively, for pissing off Oprah, saying "shit" to an audience of nuns, betting the book commission on Kibbles 'N Bits at the Preakness, and making my next project a history of Toledo, Ohio.

THE CEO OF THE SOFA

1

SEPTEMBER 2000

I was just going to say, when I was interrupted. . . .

"Nobody interrupted you," said my wife. "People have tried, but—"

That was a literary reference, dear, the first line from *The Autocrat of the Breakfast Table* by Oliver Wendell Holmes, author of "The Wonderful 'One-Hoss Shay,'" "The Chambered Nautilus," and—

"Other poems used mainly to torture high school students," said my young assistant, Max.

It's a shame the way the classics are treated in our schools, I continued. Holmes was a brilliant aphorist. Americans don't read anymore. Somebody sent me some quotes from *The Autocrat*. Where's that letter?

"Right next to you," said my wife, "under the remote."

Listen to this: *He must be a poor creature who does not often repeat himself. Imagine the author of the excellent piece of advice, "Know thyself," never alluding to that sentiment again.*

"Hmmm," said my wife.

And this: *All uttered thought is of the nature of an excretion. A man instinctively tries to get rid of his thought in conversation or in print so soon as it has matured.*

"Good point," said my wife, flipping through some manuscript pages of mine.

"I printed out the rough draft of your article on the UN 2000 Millennium Summit," said Max, "and I'm almost done with the fact-checking. I just have to go to the UN web site and—"

I stopped him. Max, Oliver Wendell Holmes declares: *All generous minds have a horror of what are commonly called "facts." Who does not know fellows that always have an ill-conditioned fact or two which they lead after them into decent company like so many bull-dogs.*

"You're welcome," said Max.

And, Max, here is Holmes on the subject of computers—a hundred and fifty years ago. He hears about Babbage's mechanical calculating device and foresees the whole pathetic computer age: *What a satire is that machine on the mere mathematician! A Frankenstein-monster, a thing without brains and without heart, too stupid to make a blunder; which turns out results like a corn-sheller, and never grows any wiser or better.* Holmes calls it *the triumph of the ciphering hand-organ.*

"Max," said my wife, "I thought you were going to teach P.J. how to use the laptop."

"I've tried."

Holmes was a man of towering intellect, of wide and deep scholarship—essayist, poet, professor, physician—

"And major babe magnet for Transcendentalist chicks, I'll bet," said Max, "at least compared to Thoreau."

He gave the *Atlantic Monthly* its name.

"What," asked Max, "were they going to call it? *The Cape Cod Nude Beach Express?*"

Holmes anticipated the germ theory of disease. He fathered the great jurist Oliver Wendell Holmes, Jr. He demolished the Puritan doctrine of predestination.

"And thought he was fated to do it," said my wife, the Catholic.

Anyhow, as I was just going to say. . . . What *was* I going to say, dear?

"You were probably going to say, 'Where'd that remote go?'"

Speaking of electronic devices [or electric devices, and I'm not sure I precisely know the difference, although I intend to have Max find out because I'm writing an article for the online magazine *freeSpam* about how the computer is the triumph of the ciphering hand-organ], the other day our daughter, Muffin, announced, "I want a cell phone."

"You're three," said my wife.

"But I love them."

"Ask your father."

I love them too, Muffin. Daddy loves cell phones because Daddy doesn't have a cell phone. Daddy doesn't have a cell phone because Daddy can't see the tiny numbers on the buttons without his reading glasses. And Daddy doesn't have his reading glasses because he left them on the shelf under the Grand Central Station pay phone, which Daddy was using to call you because Daddy doesn't have a cell phone.

And that is what Daddy loves about cell phones—not having one. It makes your father unreachable. Being unreachable is a potent status symbol in the world today. Every dateless pimple nose with a dot.com has a Lexus, a business jet, a weekend house in Phuket, and a cell phone. But, Muffin, you just try getting the Queen of England on the blower. Or try finding the direct-dial number for the president of the United States—unless you're a rich campaign fund-raiser or a fat girl in saucy underwear. And those are two things that I trust you, Muffin, will never be.

[Although, by this time, Muffin had in fact wandered off to watch the Sugared Cereal Channel on TV. And so, come to notice it, had everyone else.]

But as far-too-accessible Bill Clinton has proven, out-of-touch is the important thing to be. Not that anyone would be able to get in touch with me anyway. If I had a cell phone, I'd lose it. I lose everything. I left my first wife in the back of a cab somewhere. And what a great way to be important this is. I'm a big deal because my Zippo slips between the couch cushions, and I once forgot being married. That is so much easier than making a fortune or inheriting a crown.

I also love cell phones because cell phones punish the most discourteous people in the world—phone users—by giving phone users the punishment they deserve—phone calls.

Why does the cell phone always ring while you're having sex? This would be okay if the ringer were set on vibrate and the cell phone were properly located. But it isn't. The cell phone is in the pocket of your pants, which are hanging over the back of a chair next to the bed with your friend's wife in it, that you are hiding under because your friend has just returned, unexpectedly, from a business trip.

"Excuse me?" said my wife from the next room.

Just a joke, I shouted from the sofa. But why does a ringing cell phone take precedence over every other activity in life? People are willing to interrupt anything, including hiding under the bed, to answer a cell phone. During papal audiences, John Paul II probably hears, "*Scuzi, Papa, mia pizza deliverio.*"

Although, in fairness, the situation was as bad or worse before cell phones were invented. Muffin does not remember the pre-wireless era when people had to carry their large desk-model telephones around with them on the street, trailing miles and miles of cord. The result was an alarming tangle. It was this, rather than mismanagement of the economy or Jimmy Carter's incompetence, that caused the well-known malaise of the late 1970s.

And what about Call Waiting? How rude is that? Why not have F— Waiting? That way you could leap up, right in the middle of being discovered by your angry cuckolded friend, and say, "Sorry, my other f— is on the living room couch."

Why do we need cell phones? Why do we *want* phone calls? Think about the phone calls we get. How often do we get the following calls?

"You've won the lottery!"

"It's a girl!"

"Uncle Ned just died and left us a golf resort in Florida!"

No, the cell phone rings and it's "Honey"—you can tell by her voice she's still furious about your friend's wife—"on the way home would you pick up the dry cleaning and a gallon of milk, a package of frozen peas, new linoleum for the kitchen, and an in-ground pool?"

What do we need cell phones *for*? Certainly not to say anything. Especially not in America. Americans are so inarticulate that 411 had to be supplied with a recording—"What city? What listing?"—because the phone company couldn't train operators to say anything but "Huh?" and "Whassup?"

And all those people on their cell phones, to whom are they talking? Men are famously unable to communicate. Women are always on the other line. Parents don't talk to kids these days. Kids say "Huh?" and "Whassup?" You can't call people at work anymore because nobody comes in to the office, and if you try their cell phone you get "no service."

Yet everyone everywhere is always on a cell phone. The best kind come with an earpiece and a microphone built into the wire so that cell phone users don't even look like they're using a cell phone; they look like crazy people raving on street corners. This, of course, is hard on the crazy people who really are raving on street corners and who—instead of receiving sympathy and 25 cents—are assumed to be calling their brokers. Anyway, whomever it is that cell phone users are raving at, it keeps them from raving at me. So I love cell phones.

In fact, I love cell phones so much that I'm getting one. I'm getting a top-of-the-line highly miniaturized cell phone with all the exotic features. I'm buying new reading glasses. I'm programming my cell phone to continuously auto-dial the headquarters of both of the current presidential campaigns. Then I'm going back to New York to hang my cell phone under the tail of a Central Park carriage horse.

"It's for you," said my wife. "Your godson has been elected to the Model UN. He's going to represent all the high school students from his region."

Since when did Darien become a nation? Hello, Nick. Congratulations! And, boy, are you in luck! You know, I've just come back from covering the UN Millennium Summit for *Instant Access Quarterly*. I've got everything you need. Max, would you get my UN piece and all my notes? They're in the file cabinet. Bring the whole drawer. Got a second, Nick?

You should have seen this. I wish I'd taken you with me. You wouldn't have believed it, Nick. One hundred heads of state, forty-seven heads of government, three crown princes, and assorted other eminencies such as Yasir Arafat. It was the largest gathering of world leaders in the history of mankind—*and no one cared.*

Actually, Nick, everyone cared—about the traffic. New York local TV news led, the first night, with stories on the gridlock caused by 1,300 UN dignitary vehicles, including twelve cars just for the president of Georgia. And not even Newt Gingrich Georgia but the somewhat less populous sliver of mountain chaos squeezed between Azerbaijan and the Black Sea. *ABC World News Tonight* began with a Peter Jennings quip about Manhattan traffic jams. The next morning the front-page *New York Times* article noted, in its lead, "Traffic was backed up across the East Side yesterday because of a crush of limousines carrying VIPs everywhere from the United Nations Plaza Hotel to the Bronx Zoo." The latter being the big non-traffic story in the New York press. Denis Sassou-Nguesso, president of the Congo Republic, visited the Congo Gorilla Forest exhibit to see gorillas that come from the Congo where he's president. A global convergence, we-are-one-world moment? Or gridlock on *Planet of the Apes*?

The next morning, a TV news show reported that Bangladesh had a thirteen-car motorcade. This was modest compared to President Clinton's, which, a traffic cop told me, consisted of forty-five vehicles. "And the last two times they were in town," said the cop, "they had accidents." But Bangladesh is a country where 29 percent of the population lives on less than a dollar a day. Figuring the thirteen motorcade cars and drivers at $50 an hour, twelve hours a day, for the four days of the summit, the Bangladesh delegation just took the bread out of the mouths of 31,000 people. Not that I'm accusing the delegation of living large. I saw the entire collection of Bangladeshi Lincoln Town Cars lined up at a Wendy's on Second Avenue.

The indifference with which the Millennium Summit was greeted by everyone except commuters says a lot about present-day global politics. Not to mention what it says about present-day global politicians—this was no confab of Churchills, Roosevelts, Hitlers, Tojos, and Stalins. And what a relief. An excess of international leadership usually results in bullets and breadlines.

Maybe the world—Bangladesh to the contrary—has become rich enough to be bored by global politics. This is good. Politics cause more grief than money. Take the Vietnam War, for instance. How much would the U.S. government have had to pay 47,000 Americans, putting the job out for bid under strict free-market conditions, to go die in Vietnam?

Not that money can't be used to do harm. Ted Turner says he's giving a billion dollars to the UN. Turner's overfunded UN Foundation helped sponsor a convocation of more than a thousand religious and spiritual leaders at the UN the week before the Millennium Summit. Thank God—as it were—I didn't have to cover that. The purpose of this "Millennium World Peace Summit" was, according to the mystical gathering's communications director, "to see how religious leaders can bring the power of their own spiritual traditions to work with UN forces . . . to help reduce conflict." For fear of conflict with the communist Chinese, however, the Dalai Lama wasn't invited. The communist Chinese being atheists, I'd say religious and spiritual leaders are 0 for 1 so far.

But, Nick, I don't want to give you the impression that I don't like the United Nations. I do. I think it's extremely cool, especially the whole black-helicopter New World Order secret-global-government thing. I love it. It'll be like DC Comics' *Justice League International,* except the Security Council members will have superpowers such as the ability to sit through six-hour meetings without going to the bathroom, the ability to figure out what "Document 5: Text of draft optional protocol submitted by the Chairperson (E/CN.6/1997/WH/L.1)" means, the ability to simultaneously translate the click language of the Kalahari bushmen into Farsi, and the ability to fly (business class). And to judge by the crowds in Manhattan's pricier restaurants during the Millennium Summit, UN superheroes will also have *supper* powers. I can hardly wait. I figure a world government run by the UN will be like getting an old, purblind, half-deaf substitute teacher—or like being baby-sat by your fifty-two-year-old godfather when I'm drinking. Have you seen *The Art of War?* Wesley Snipes is a member of a United Nations covert action unit, and he's *completely* out of control.

"Uncle Peej," said my godson, who seemed to be in a hurry, "could you, like, get Max to e-mail this stuff to me?"

Dear Nick,

I was just going to say, when I was interrupted. . . .

Because *The Art of War* had a lot of good chase scenes and explosions, it was with a certain measure of enthusiasm that I went, last week, to the United Nations Media Accreditation and Liaison Unit Media Division/Department of Public Information to get my 2000 UN Millennium Summit press credentials. Except I couldn't find the Division/Department. Though with a name as long as that, you'd think just the size of the sign would give it away. The UN was cordoned off by thousands, maybe tens of thousands, of uniformed officers, security guards, and plainclothesmen, every one of whom was almost, but not quite, too busy and annoyed to point me in the wrong direction. I mistakenly got into the line for the Uganda mission—a long line. Why were people lined up to get into the Uganda mission? To get Uganda immigration visas? Were their own countries so screwed up that they wanted to move to Uganda? Actually, probably, yes.

In due time I found the proper line. It was a much shorter line. In fact, it wasn't a very long line at all, notwithstanding which I stood in it for an hour and fifteen minutes. The Division/Department was bare and stuffy. The only decorations were photocopied flyers Scotch-taped to the wall, bearing such enticing messages as:

MEDI ADVISORY
PHOTO OP
The Presidents of Finland and Namibia,
the two co-chairs of the Summit,
will meet each other for the first time
at 6:20 P.M.

today, 5 September,
in the neck area outside the
Delegates' Lounge

Well, who knows, maybe sparks would fly. (The Delegates' Lounge has a "neck area"?)

The credentials were prepared, waiting for us journalists to collect them. But our names seemed to have been filed according to shoe size, or phase of the moon when application was submitted, or by using the ancient Cretan Linear A alphabet, the key to which has been lost in the mists of time.

UN functionaries were arrayed behind wobbly folding tables. Whenever a journalist approached and asked for credentials, the functionaries would express mild shock and dismay. Such a request came as a complete surprise to them. The functionaries would consult among themselves, agree at last to search for the appropriate document, then plunge into an enormous heap of manila folders and stay there for the rest of the afternoon.

Maybe this is why we don't see so many of those black helicopters. The pilots are probably stuck down at the United Nations Secret Weapon and Unmarked Aircraft Registration and Licensing Division/Department of World Domination while somebody looks for the helicopter keys.

Or maybe the pilots got arrested in some foul-up among the various competing security agencies on hand. There was at least one pack of big-buddies-with-sunglasses for every foreign poobah, plus Secret Service, State Department Security, UN Security, FBI, ATF, NYPD—the works. Forget politicos, this was the largest gathering of guys with radio earpieces sticking out of their jacket collars in the history of mankind. And all of the security people were listening to voices through those earpieces, making them twitch and look around and mutter to themselves. It was like arriving in the midst of a gigantic convention of unusually well-dressed schizophrenics. If these fellows got together and made any treaties and agreements among themselves, we're all in trouble.

It's a shame the police types were too busy to do anything about actual criminals, such as about one-fourth of the world leaders on hand.

The political opponents of Zimbabwe's Robert Mugabe have a knack for conveniently dying, and Mugabe uses the thugs in his political party to terrorize landowners. China's Jiang Zemin is brutal with Falun Gong religious dissidents and murderous in Tibet. Omar Hassan Ahmad Al-Bashir, president of Sudan, leads a genocidal war against Christian and animist tribes in his country. Mohammad Khatami's Iran sponsors worldwide terrorism. Islam A. Karimov is a vicious dictator in Uzbekistan. God knows what Vladimir Putin has been up to in Russia, but it's nothing nice, say the Chechens. Castro is an old butcher from way back. And, in the matter of mopery, sexual misdemeanors, and lurking with criminal intent, there was our own Bill Clinton.

At least the loathsome North Koreans didn't make it. The number-two Pyongyang commie, Kim Yong Nam, and his fourteen wiseguy delegates stopped by—of all the unlikely crime-fighting forces—rude airline personnel. American Airlines wouldn't let the North Koreans onto the Frankfurt–New York flight without pat-downs and luggage inspections. I can just hear the snippy people at the check-in counter: "I'm sorry, but your weapons-grade plutonium must fit in the overhead compartment or under the seat in front of you." By the time Kim Yong Nam et al. got done throwing tantrums, they'd missed their flight. And happy fiftieth anniversary of the beginning of the Korean War to you, too, assholes.

Fortunately I was walking to UN headquarters instead of flying and only had to contend with all the law enforcement agencies on earth and not American Airlines. Thus I was able to saunter into the General Assembly building simply by flashing my credentials. These consisted of one piece of laminated plastic containing blurry print and a picture, allegedly of me, which looked like it was clipped from the middle of a five-dollar bill.

I was just in time to see the fifty-fifth session of the UN brought to order by the newly elected president of the General Assembly, a former prime minister of Finland, Harri Holkeri, who seems like a perfectly nice man despite his Japanese suicide of a name and who can almost speak English. After some opening blandishments, President Holkeri presented the General Assembly with its first piece of serious business under his regime, a plan "to start the General Assembly meetings on time." A fitting proposal, inasmuch as this particular General Assembly meeting was starting twenty minutes late with most of its delegates absent from their seats.

Next order of business was the admission of Tuvalu as a member of the United Nations. Two-of-what? You may well ask. Tuvalu is a former British colony consisting of nine coral atolls halfway between Hawaii and Australia with a land area one-tenth the size of Washington, D.C., and a population of 10,297. My college had fraternity houses larger than that. What's next? Sigma Chi becomes a NATO power? Tuvalu has no crops, no industry, and no known mineral resources. It has no drinking water except what's collected in rain barrels. The economy is based—seriously—on selling Tuvalu stamps to collectors.

The charter of the United Nations states in Article 2, paragraph 1, "The Organization is based on the principle of sovereign equality of all its Members." And no doubt a very good principle this is. But Tuvalu? "If there are no objections . . ." said President Holkeri. And no one in the General Assembly did object or, as far as I could tell, notice.

Having exhausted my interest in the doings of the General Assembly, I wandered into Conference Room 1 in the UN's unimaginatively named Conference Building. Here something called "Dialogue Among Civilizations" was being conducted. Conducted by whom and for what purpose I don't know. Although I do know that "Dialogue Among Civilizations" was Iran's idea and, considering the ideas Iran has had in the past, such as holding scores of Americans hostage, having an eight-year war with Iraq, and sponsoring worldwide terrorism, I figured it would be interesting. I was wrong.

I had missed the morning session where Iran's president, Mohammad Khatami himself, gave a speech that Secretary of State Madeleine Albright called thought-provoking and *The New York Times* called "vague." And I would have missed the afternoon session if it hadn't (notice to President Holkeri) started fifty minutes late. Somebody on the conference podium, I have no idea who, spent a long time proposing a "Question for Conversation," the question being "How do we focus the conversation on dialogue?" Although I was under the impression that conversation *is* dialogue, otherwise social life would be like . . . like sitting in Conference Room 1 listening to the first speaker on the subject of dialogue, who was former UN Secretary General Javier Perez de Cuellar, age eighty, who couldn't find the ON button for his microphone and ,when he did find it, said, "For almost sixty years we are dialoguing here." No, no, Javier, twenty minutes by my watch, although I know it *seems* like sixty years. The former secretary general wanted countries to have "dialogue not only among but within themselves." He said democracy was good for this, although I'll bet the upcoming Bush/Gore debates will argue otherwise.

Then some jerk university professor spoke, asking "Internet companies to act on the basis of something besides self-interest." A novel concept and I can hardly wait for the e-mail notices from AOL telling customers, "We considered improving our online services in order to attract more business and increase our corporate profits, but then we decided, 'Screw that, we're joining the Peace Corps.'"

The next speech was in French, and one of the UN's famous corps of simultaneous translators went to work. She was good. Either that or she just made up stuff and pretended it was what the froggy bozo in Conference Room 1 said. Whatever, the gist was that Western civilization had made the mistake of thinking it was the center of the world just because it was, like, the world center of stuff. This was followed by a pronouncement that "It is the element of the barbarous that everyone must find in his own civilization," which I took to be a suggestion that the delegates hit the lap-dancing bars later on. The bozo then began a declamation upon tolerance: how tolerance begins with sufferance and progresses to the idea that differences are good and progresses further to embrace the realization that "the contrary of a profound thought is another profound thought," this being the definition of tolerance according to the French philosopher Pascal. At which point I ran out of tolerance.

Nick, I've provided you with a taste of UN political and intellectual discourse here, and I sincerely apologize. At least it's better than actually being at the UN in person, the way I was. The place is a dump. The UN headquarters complex was completed in 1952 in the Hanna-Barbera *Jetsons* style of modern, which is now back in vogue—but with light, with color, with irony. At the UN it's with linoleum. There are acres of gray linoleum that seem to have been given a light mopping, once a month, by the same cleaning lady for the past forty-eight years. The Secretariat Building smells of old food. The pole lamps take themselves very seriously.

The chief architect was Wallace K. Harrison, who also designed Rockefeller Center but apparently wasn't feeling so well during the three or four hours it must have taken him to dash off the UN blueprints. Wallace had additional input from Oscar Niemeyer, creator of dreadful Brasilia, and Le Corbusier, who led a lifelong campaign to make the whole world as pretty and comfortable as O'Hare Airport.

Use of bilingual signage in English and French gives the corridors of the UN a sadly Canadian air. One widely posted warning reads, SMOKING DISCOURAGED/VEUILLEZ EVITER DE FUMER, and that says it all about the United Nations, its power and its might.

The dumb slab of the UN Secretariat and the skateboard park shape of the General Assembly are matched with what might be the worst collection of art on earth: A tapestry reproduction of Picasso's *Guernica* full scale, in earth-tone needlepoint; two Fernand Léger murals that appear to be the graffiti tags of a street gang that never learned the alphabet and ran out of spray paint; a painstakingly detailed 660-pound sculpture depicting the construction of the Chengtu–Kunming railroad, gift of the People's Republic of China (tucked away out of sight on the third floor of the Secretariat because it was carved from eight elephant tusks); a huge pistol with its barrel tied in a knot, symbolic of, I guess, the UN's botched peacekeeping missions; an enormous bronze by Soviet artist Evgeny Vuchetich showing an heroic figure beating his sword into what looks like a beaten-on sword; a great big hunk of alloy, vaguely face-shaped, with a hole in its head (a memorial to UN Secretary General Dag Hammarskjöld); and much more, including a thirty-ton pot-metal cast of a sleeping elephant, visible on the way to the UN children's playground, that was partly paid for by donations from the Church of

Scientology and sports a two-foot erection. Bushes have been planted in strategic places.

Everyone connected to the UN must have breathed a sigh of relief in 1987 when the secretary general "informed all the Permanent Representatives of Member States that there would be a moratorium on the acceptance of further gifts."

The United Nations press corps didn't look so good either. Being sent to cover the UN is, for a journalist, not a vote of confidence from the front office. The last—and possibly first—truly dramatic thing to happen at the UN was when Khrushchev pounded his desk with his shoe in 1960. And the main source of drama there was suspense about whether Nikita was too fat to get his shoe back on by himself. Would he have to ask for "foreign aid"? (Ha-ha. A little specimen of General Assembly jokes. Who says the UN has no sense of humor?) This was before most journalists were born but not, alas, before most journalists covering the UN were. Appearances tell the story—the pallor, the jowls, the ill-fitting suit, the self-serious demeanor, the pathetic interest in pointless UN minutiae. And that was just me. You should have seen the others.

Returning to my hotel after Tuesday's UN festivities, I encountered one of the week's few political demonstrations that refused to stay confined to the special political demonstration areas provided. Eighteen Iranian dissidents tried to block First Avenue. This was problematic because eighteen people aren't enough to block First Avenue and also because UN security and New York traffic jams had blocked First Avenue already.

Police dutifully arrested all concerned, using plastic disposable handcuffs. The large bundled loops of polyethylene wrist restraints made the NYPD look like they were about to engage in some idiot craft activity, a postmodern macramé class perhaps, with results to be displayed in the UN Secretariat.

"Khatami," shouted the protesters, "must go! Go! Go! Go!"

"Go Yankees!" shouted a drunk on the sidewalk.

The next morning the General Assembly came to order half an hour late (second notice to President Holkeri), Secretary General Kofi Annan presiding.

Kofi Annan, the man who emerged from Baghdad negotiations in 1998 saying he had "a good human rapport" with Saddam Hussein, was equally optimistic in his agenda for the Millennium Summit. Annan's plan: to ensure that "all children complete a full course of primary education," to "halt and begin to reverse the spread of HIV/AIDS," and to reduce by 50 percent "the proportion of the world's people whose income is less than one dollar a day" (not including, presumably, 31,000 people in Bangladesh). This is to be done by 2015, plus a lot of other stuff such as removing "regulatory and pricing impediments to Internet access," so that, I guess, everybody on the globe can get into the "Living on Less Than One Dollar a Day" chat room.

These are ambitious goals for the UN, considering the organization's previous achievements.

The United Nations set off the 1948 Arab–Israeli war with an arbitrary partition of Palestine that told everybody in the Middle East where to go. Then the UN got blindsided by the Korean War and let a too-enthusiastic Douglas MacArthur be sucker-punched by the Red Chinese, who had meanwhile squashed Tibet while the UN wasn't looking.

The United Nations hopped up and down and yelled "phooey" during the 1956 Suez crisis and sat with its collective thumb up its butt while Russia invaded Hungary the same year.

In 1960 the UN sent troops to shoot Africans because Katanga province wanted to secede from the former Belgian Congo, even though Chapter I of the UN Charter mandates "self-determination of peoples" and even though the former Belgian Congo was in a state of anarchy so that, in reality, Katanga was seceding from nothing. But later the UN would stay home, maxing and relaxing, while Nigeria slaughtered and starved the Biafrans because that was "an internal matter."

The United Nations let its peacekeepers be used as doormats in the 1967 Six-Day War, the 1973 Yom Kippur War, the 1974 Turkish invasion of Cyprus, the 1982 Israeli invasion of Lebanon, and in many other places where UN peacekeepers were so careful about keeping peace that nobody was given any.

The United Nations just fumed and sputtered during the war in Vietnam and didn't even do that when the Soviet Union crushed Czechoslovakia in 1968. The UN membership stared at the General Assembly hall ceiling and whistled "Dixie" while Tutsis committed genocide on Hutus in Burundi and gazed out the window and picked its nose while Hutus committed genocide on Tutsis in Rwanda.

The United Nations gave Idi Amin a pass while he expelled all the Asians from Uganda and ate a bunch of the rest of the people there. The United Nations couldn't go out—had to wash its hair—during the Khmer Rouge horrors in Cambodia.

The UN let George Bush chop the wood and carry the water in the Persian Gulf, screwed the pooch in former Yugoslavia, and ran like a spanked Cub Scout out of Somalia. I could go on, and the UN doubtless will.

Nor was it an encouraging sign when Kofi Annan began his remarks to the Millennium Assembly by announcing that a mob of Indonesian militiamen had overrun a United Nations refugee office in West Timor, killing three of the UN staff. A minute of silence was observed, and—with no disrespect for the dead intended—maybe that minute should have been extended for a decade or two. Even former U.S. ambassador to the UN Adlai Stevenson, a noted internationalist and strong United Nations proponent, once complained to the State Department, "Do I have to stay here for more of that yak-yak? It doesn't mean a thing."

Speaking of yak-yak, the format for the Millennium Summit General Assembly meeting was this: Every single UN member nation would have five minutes to make a speech, delivered by its chief of state, head of government, or senior UN delegation member—a marathon of natter lasting from 9 A.M. to 6 P.M. for three days.

President Clinton commenced the blathering with orotund Clintonisms: "The international community must take a side, not merely stand between the sides or on the sidelines." With a side of fries.

Next was the president of Equatorial Guinea whose name is on the tip of my tongue. Let's see, maybe it was Teodoro Obiang Nguema Mbasogo. Or maybe not. My *World Almanac* is three years out of date, and Equatorial Guinea may have experienced a number of coups and revolutions since then. Anyway, What's-his-face said, "The growth of some nations is based on exploitation of others." Although nobody I know has made a bundle by exploiting Equatorial Guinea. I checked with my stockbroker and I know *I* haven't.

After that came the president of Guatemala, who said, "Cultural diversity is an asset." Interesting words from a country that spent most of the eighties in a civil war, trying to kill off its culturally diverse Indians.

Then it was Mohammad Khatami's turn, he of First Avenue blockage and Dialogue Among Civilizations fame. Khatami praised democracy (of which there is a very funny sort in Iran) and called for democracy (although whether the Iranian type or the regular kind he did not say) to be extended to the operations of the UN.

Nicaragua's president protested the exclusion of Taiwan from the United Nations. (I suspect a certain amount of business investment and/or foreign aid has arrived in Managua from Taipei recently.) He pointed out that there are twenty million people in Taiwan who are not represented at the UN, but he refrained, diplomatically, from mentioning the contrasting case of Tuvalu.

Vladimir Putin touted disarmament—something his country had already begun on a unilateral if unintended basis with the submarine *Kursk*.

If the foregoing speeches sound absurd, it's important to remember that absurdity is integral to the United Nations. The allies in a war against Nazism founded the UN, which, on the anniversary of *Kristallnacht* in 1975, passed a resolution declaring "Zionism is a form of racism" under the auspices of a secretary general, Kurt Waldheim, who was a Nazi.

A doddering Franklin Roosevelt thought that the naive United States, enervated Britain, corrupt and impotent Nationalist China, and Stalin's gulag of a Soviet Union would be the world's "Four Policemen." And quite a plot for *NYPD Blue* that would be. FDR insisted on holding the preliminary 1944 United Nations conference in Washington, even though it was August and air-conditioning hadn't been discovered, and nobody in his right mind was in Washington—not that the arrival of the UN delegates changed that. The location for the conference, the Dumbarton Oaks mansion in Georgetown, was suggested by young State Department official and communist spy Alger Hiss, and, gee, I wonder if Stalin somehow managed to get microphones planted in the caucus rooms. British representative Sir Alexander Cadogan (who *did* happen to be in his right mind) called the meeting "a foretaste of hell."

Absurdity is written right into the United Nations Charter. Says the preamble, "armed force shall not be used, save in the common interest." What possible "common interest" united still-imperial Britain, rich goofy America, the sleazeball Chiang Kai-shek, and a U.S.S.R. intent on world revolution? The only thing the United Nations is suited for, according to its charter, is an invasion from Mars. This, despite numerous books and movies on the subject, has been slow coming. Then there's the UN's Universal Declaration of Human Rights, adopted by the General Assembly in 1948, which starts out worthy and high-minded in Article 1: "All human beings are born free and equal in dignity and rights," but by Article 24 has degenerated into "Everybody has the right to rest and leisure, including . . . periodic holidays with pay." I took mine as soon as Putin shut up.

Sure, I'd love to be able to say I listened to all 189 member nations' speeches plus the extras from the League of Arab States, Conference of Presiding Officers of National Parliaments, Sovereign Military Order of Malta, and so on. This would be a great *Into Thin Air* Everest-climb kind of brag about my ability to endure pain and hardship, but I was starting to lose circulation in my hind end. While I might be willing to sacrifice a frost-bitten finger or two to stand on the roof of the world, I was not about to leave my butt cheeks at the UN.

I had lunch in the United Nations cafeteria instead. They have bagels there—with butter. No cream cheese. No lox. Just butter. At the UN they put butter on their bagels. No wonder these people can't achieve peace in the Middle East.

Don't get me wrong, Nick. It's not that the UN doesn't do good things. There's the Office of the UN High Commissioner for Refugees (UNHCR), which provides food, shelter, and—sometimes—protection to thousands of displaced persons. Never mind that those persons were displaced by wars and civil disturbances that the UN failed to do anything about. And the UN's World Health Organization (WHO) did help stamp out smallpox, but meanwhile WHO was also spending $55 million a year in Europe, where people catch colds, and only $36 million for "integrated control of tropical diseases" in the Third World where people die. Then there's the United Nations Children's Fund (UNICEF) that gives primary health care, nutrition, and education to young people and also tried to give American kids UNICEF donation cans to replace trick-or-treat sacks on Halloween, which made lots of children furious at their liberal parents and I, for one, think that was a good thing.

All in all, the UN has about 38,500 people working for more than seventy-five agencies, programs, and organizations devoted to making the earth wonderful, including the International Court of Justice (in case anyone gets caught jaywalking in Antarctica or something) and the Universal Postal Union (Tuvalu asks, Please buy our stamps), and also including the World Bank, which goes around giving money to countries for half-baked development schemes, and the IMF, which goes around taking the money back.

The UN also gets Fidel Castro out of Cuba now and then, for which the Cubans are no doubt thankful, although Fidel did not seem to be. He gave a blistering speech in the General Assembly, calling the UN a "worn-out institution" and railing against "the inequality in the distribution of wealth and knowledge." (You *could* go learn something, Fido. Sorry. I forgot. You banned the books.)

Castro laid into everybody—"There is nothing in the existing economic and political order that serves the interest of Humankind"—and everybody loved it. He was the only speaker who got enough applause to make Kofi Annan use his gavel—Kofi being unemployed during the other 188 speeches. Then Castro went out on the town and had a fine time being serenaded by 2,000 American supporters at Riverside Church and shaking hands and making small talk with Bill Clinton at a UN lunch. One shudders to think what these two were saying to each other:

"Can't believe you got custody of the Elián kid, you wacky bearded maniac, you."

"*Compañero,* I hope that was not a Cuban cigar you used on the fat *puta.*"

And the speeches went on. In double dose, too, since there was a bonus head-of-state-level open-to-the-media meeting of the Security Council.

Clinton kicked off again, forty minutes late (third notice to President Holkeri), and trotted right into a crowd-pleasing play: "This idea of relieving debt, if the savings are applied to the well-being of people, is an idea whose time has come."

Third World debt relief was certainly on a lot of Third World minds at the Millennium Summit. Whether its time has come, however, depends on if you are owed or if you are owing. I hope my bank doesn't decide it's part of the Third World. (It already answers phone queries as if it were.) I don't want to hear that the balance in my checking account has been "relieved."

And while we're on the subject of debt relief, let us not forget the $1.8 billion debt in back dues the UN says that the United States owes. Oh-oh, we're going to get ourselves posted in the UN clubhouse and lose our tee time on Saturdays.

Congress has agreed to pay about half of that $1.8 billion, contingent upon the UN making organizational reforms to clear up problems such as the fact that, due to red tape, it takes about 461 days to hire a single staff person at the UN and that, due to accounting "errors," there was a $6.3 million overpayment in staff allowances for the UN Iraq–Kuwait Observation Mission. The UN says the reforms have been made. They're in a manila folder. And someone at United Nations Dues Assessment and Membership Development Unit Reform Division/Department of Accounts Receivable is looking for them now. Congress has permission to give my share of the $1.8 billion to Aromatherapists Without Borders.

But most of the plenipotentiaries at the Millennium Summit were willing to forgive America for owing lots of money to the UN—as long as America gives lots of money to them. As Castro put it, after lambasting the world's rich, orderly, and nice countries, "It is their moral obligation to compensate our nations for the damages caused throughout the centuries."

King Mswati III of Swaziland called upon the Millennium Summit "to correct the imbalance of wealth and social standards," except, of course, such social standards as having an all-powerful hereditary monarch.

President Eduard Shevardnadze of Georgia, whose twelve-car motorcade had been helping tie up New York, told the members of the international financial elite who were currently stuck in traffic to "release poor and developing countries from the fetters of debt. This breakthrough would equal that of the victory over the Cold War." (Or maybe even equal to finding an on-duty cab at rush hour in Manhattan.)

And Jeremiah Manele, chairman of the Solomon Islands delegation, baldly stated, "Solomon Islands . . . needs your assistance."

But, said Batyr Berdyev, Minister for Foreign Affairs of Turkmenistan, "no assistance, be it from international organizations, individual countries, or financial centers, should be conditioned by an infringement of sovereign rights." So, your assistance with no strings attached, please.

And also, please, forget about the *United Nations Development Program Poverty Report 2000,* which puts much of the blame for global poverty on bad government—something Turkmenistan, with an authoritarian regime and an unreformed state-run economy, should know plenty about.

Why would 150 heads of state and chief executives come all the way to UN headquarters just to say, "Give me dollars"? It's a mystery, though not much of one. Consider how ineffective it would be for a UN delegate to squat on a New York sidewalk with a letter typed on official stationery reading, "My boss will work for money."

Fleeing endless importuning speechification, I went to the "Daily Briefing by Spokeswoman for the Co-Chairs of the Millennium Summit and Spokesman for the Secretary General. Media Advisory: Moved to Room 226." The first part of the briefing was devoted to an explanation, by the Spokesman for the Secretary General, of how the briefing had been scheduled to be in Conference Room 2 but had been moved to Room 226 because of scheduling conflicts, but then, due to a switch in venue for a press conference with the prime minister of Israel, the briefing was supposed to be moved back to Conference Room 2 but hadn't been. The full-time UN correspondents were taking notes on this.

A ministerial-level round table on globalization issues had been held that morning, said the Spokeswoman for the Co-Chairs of the Millennium Summit. But the proceedings, she said, were off the record.

A petition for cancellation of world debt with an enormous number of signatures attached was being presented to the UN today by the music star Bono, said the Spokesman for the Secretary General, mispronouncing "Bono."

My mind wandered. And by now, Nick, I'll bet yours has too. The UN Charter begins, very sweetly, with the words, "We the peoples of the United Nations determined to save succeeding generations from the scourge of war." But there's a flaw in this conception: that succeeding generations won't *want* war. The history of all *pre*ceding generations tells us otherwise. So does observation of humanity after it's had three drinks. Humans like peace? Weren't any of the people at the founding of the United Nations married? Actually, Dag Hammarskjöld, the first significant UN Secretary General, wasn't. This led to a certain amount of sniggering about his private life. But he seems to have been simply an overgrown, idealistic twelve-year-old. Hammarskjöld filled his journals with such adolescent maunderings as "the mask you put on with such care so as to appear to your best advantage was the wall between you and the sympathy you sought. A sympathy you won on the day when you stood there naked."

The UN has proven itself about as good at bringing peace to the world as the average naked twelve-year-old. The wars go on in spite of—indeed, sometimes because of—the 27,000 UN troops on peacekeeping duty around the globe. Kofi Annan wants to expand the scope and mandate of this UN army. The Annan-endorsed "Report of the Panel of United Nations Peace Operations" talks about "the fundamental ability to project credible force" and "robust rules of engagement." According to the report, "Member states should . . . form several coherent brigade-size forces, with necessary enabling forces, ready for deployment." Annan envisions a United Nations rapid-reaction corps with soldiers drawn from all and sundry countries, prepared to fight for peace at any time. Your dog, your cat, the mice in the walls, and the squirrels in the yard get together in case the tropical fish act up.

Speaking of squirrels, the next morning Jimmy and Rosalyn Carter were having breakfast in the greasy-spoon coffee shop two doors from my hotel.

Now I am a man with few firm principles regarding conduct in international political affairs. But I do know, from past experience, that any international affair that attracts the attention of Jimmy Carter—Panama Canal giveaway, Iranian hostage-rescue disaster, Moscow Olympic boycott, Sandinista takeover in Nicaragua—is something with which I want nothing to do. Rosalyn seemed to agree. She looked completely pissed off about being at the Millennium Summit or maybe about being at that lousy coffee shop, probably both.

A woman who'd been sitting near me returned to her tablemates with a Carter-autographed paper napkin. "He was kind of distant," she said to her friends about our most ex- of ex-presidents.

Not distant enough for me, Nick. I went back to my room, packed my bags, and—traffic being what it was—dragged my luggage on foot to Grand Central Station, where I took the first train up to your house and mixed myself a drink that filled your mother's Waterford crystal rose vase.

2

OCTOBER 2000

Anything in the mail, dear?

"A note from your godson. He says, *Thanks for an awful lot of information about the UN. I've decided to go out for football instead.*"

Good kid—considering he grew up in a neighborhood where they fill their squirt guns with Perrier. Not much of a letter writer, though. Well, never write anything in a letter that you wouldn't shout from the housetops.

"Which is why," said my wife, "all we ever hear from our friends and relatives is *Help, I'm trapped on a roof.*"

Anything else in the mail?

"A children's video catalog—*The Chipmunks Sing the Ring Cycle,* and a feature-length Disney cartoon based on Edvard Munch's *The Scream,* and something called *Winona and the Werehumans,* 'The touching story of a little girl and her pack of warm, caring wolves. But when the moon is full they turn into terrifying hairless creatures that litter.' And a check from *Blather* magazine."

Good.

"Two hundred and fifteen dollars for your story, 'Chewing-Mouth Dogs Bring Hope to People With Eating Disorders.' You know," said my wife, "maybe I should open one of those theme restaurants like Hard Rock Cafe or Planet Hollywood—The Freelance Writer's Buffet. Decorate it in pine-board-and-cement-block bookshelves, davenports found on the street, orange-crate end tables, and bare lightbulbs. Paper the walls with rejection slips, of course. The menu . . . let's see . . . 'tomato soup' made with ketchup packets stolen from diners, weenies cooked on the end of a fork over open stove burners, and cold pizza crusts. *Specialité de la maison:* cheap domestic beer. Cocktail napkins could be printed with things actually written by freelance writers, or with the titles of unsold magazine articles like your 'High Tech's Next Big Wave—Lifeguard Laptops.' Then, to lure the tourists, I'd get a really famous freelance writer such as, um. . . .

Yes? I said.

"Sebastian Junger. Except I'm afraid he has a bar of his own already."

Hmmm. Is that our Charles Schwab statement?

"Don't look in there," said my wife.

NASDAQ acting up again? It seems that "Quick, turn on CNBC, oh, God, how's NASDAQ doing?" is replacing "Whassup?" as the universal American salutation. And people were only saying "Whassup?" because "Yo" had been sold as a ticker symbol to a Silicon Valley start-up making software to generate pointless e-mail messages, send them to everyone you know, scan the lame answers, and compose inane replies—*www.litzon.com/nobodyhome*.

"As I recall," said my wife, "you got in on the initial offering. And I really wouldn't open that Charles Schwab statement. You know what the doctor said about stress and your acid reflux."

Right you are. I resolutely swore off looking at our investments on Friday, April 14, 2000, which ended one of the worst weeks in the history of U.S. stock exchanges up to that time. Mark my words, when they write the story of the twenty-first century's financial collapse, the books will all begin with April 10 through April 14, 2000. It will be called Black Monday-Tuesday-Wednesday-Thursday-Friday. Maybe I'll call it that myself. Make a note in our 2001 calendar, honey: P.J., write book: *How the Financial Collapse of 2001 Happened.*

What a week that was. NASDAQ went down 25.3 percent, and 7.3 percent was trimmed from the Dow. More than $2 trillion worth of New Economy stock market cash turned out to be, ha-ha, "virtual." As *Webster's* says, the money was "existing in effect or essence though *not in actual fact.*"

"Italics added by your wife," said my wife, "who called Charles Schwab and told them never to let you buy anything again as long as you live."

Personally, I said, I think the New Economy looked even more "virtual" before NASDAQ took its first fall. On March 27, 2000, Cisco Systems became the most valuable corporation in the world. The stock shares of Cisco were worth $555.6 billion that day—$502.9 billion more than it would have cost to buy General Motors. And what does Cisco Systems make? Certainly not profits; the company's P/E—its price/earning ratio—was a whopping 216.

"I know what a P/E is, dear."

It's best thought of thus: If you had a lemonade stand in your front yard and your profits were $5 on a warm Saturday, would you expect to be able to sell your lemonade stand to a younger sister for 5 x 365 × 216 or $394,200? Not unless she planned to lap-dance for the neighborhood dads.

"A very unlikely idea, considering my younger sister has an MBA from Stanford."

By way of comparison, I said, during the allegedly insane boom of 1929, Dow Industrials had an average P/E of 19. But I was asking what Cisco Systems makes. Um, systems? . . . Systems of the, uh, Cisco kind? . . . Maybe Max knows. Hey, Max, what the hell does Cisco Systems make?

"Routers," shouted Max from the next room, where he was using the computer to unload something or off-put it or whatever the term is.

Routers. Cisco makes the little thingamadoodle that sends my godson Nick into the Radiohead chat room all night. This, as opposed to General Motors, which makes an entire damn car. In fact, GM makes 8,677,000 cars a year, including the fuel-injected four-speed red Corvette convertible that used to be catnip to the sweeties before the sweeties became more interested in how much Cisco Systems stock one owned.

"Stock you sold at the bottom," said my wife. "And I'd rather have a BMW Z8."

Anyway, it served the sweeties right when, between March 27 and April 14, 2000, Cisco shares went down 27 points—a $173.5 billion decline. And that was nickels dropped under the couch cushions compared to what happened at Microsoft. Microsoft shares went from a peak price of almost 120 in December 1999 to 74 in the mid-April 2000 blowout. And they're down to 50 now and headed Greenspan-knows-where.

Bill Gates owns about 15 percent of the company. He's lost more than $53 billion, so far. I go Columbine when US Airways misplaces my suit bag. What on earth is the appropriate response to losing $53 billion? Does Gates get mad at his own computer operating systems for providing the tools for the programmed trading that cost him 53 supersize? Does he pull a Ted Kaczynski and go off the grid? It's going to be hard to run that cyber-house in Redmond on car batteries.

"Mrs. O," shouted Max from the next room, "I warned you not to get him started on the New Economy."

"I thought I'd hidden the Charles Schwab statement," said my wife.

"Now," said Max, "he's going to give the whole speech he wrote for the Buried Krugerrands Investment Society."

In reality, what Bill Gates does, I continued, is rush to Washington to kiss the enormous behind of President Clinton at something called the White House Conference on the New Economy, held, with apposite timing, last April. Bill Clinton spent the conference taking credit for the way American business had been going like a cat that sat in the cherries jubilee. Never mind that the stock market began its rise during the first Reagan administration and had been climbing ever since with the exception of a setback in 1987 (caused, I think, when one of those enormous chintz window treatments that were popular back then fell on some important yuppies and they smothered). And never mind that while Clinton was boasting about the New Economy, the New Economy was in a dash to the fire exit triggered by an antitrust lawsuit brought by Clinton's Justice Department against the guy sitting next to Clinton.

As I understand it, this lawsuit was based on the fact that if you use Microsoft's built-in web browser, you have to click your mouse once, but if you want to use another company's web browser you have to—call Morley Safer—click twice. And there in the Monica Lewinsky seat was poor (or, at any rate, $53 billion poorer) Bill Gates, probably thinking to himself, *If I take* another *$53 billion and donate it to Hillary's Senate campaign, maybe I'll . . .*" Get indicted. That's usually what happens to people who do the Clintons a favor.

Well, Gates is not going to get any sympathy from me, and neither is Cisco Systems or any other part of the New Economy. What is the New Economy? It's "smart appliances." Oh, joy, our toaster can talk to our fridge, expressing such deep thoughts as "Leggo my Eggo." The New Economy is the Internet, which puts all the fools on earth in close personal touch. Matt Drudge used to be a guy in LA who didn't know from beans. Now those beans aren't known from everywhere on the planet. The New Economy is *www.matchedsocks.com*. All I have to do is enter the bar code for the missing half of my hosiery pair and I'll get a readout—"caught under the agitator in the Maytag"—for a monthly fee. The guys who thought this up became paper billionaires at age twelve. How young are the high-tech moguls? There's a sign on the door at most New York investment banks: NO SHIRT, NO SHOES, NO IPO.

The web is just a device by which bad ideas travel around the globe at the speed of light. And on April 17 and 18, they did. The same investment community that decided tech stocks were wildly overvalued on April 14 decided they were wildly undervalued on April 17. That is what's significant about April 2000. NASDAQ crashes on Friday, and the next Monday NASDAQ has its highest point gain ever except for the point gain it has on Tuesday, which is even higher. We've entered a world of bungee valuations. We can't even slide into a comfortable recession with stock prices in a reassuring decline because, while we're going broke and losing our jobs, half the time the markets are up. Go figure. But don't do your figuring on a computer—the whole high-tech field is obviously insane. And if you think people were angry during the Great Depression, wait and see how they feel when NASDAQ leaps to 10,000 while they're standing in breadlines.

"Although," said my wife, "it will be croissant lines, these days."

If you ask me, the problem is nobody wanted to be the prick who burst this bubble. Nobody, that is, except me and every other journalist in the universe plus Alan Greenspan. The chairman of the Federal Reserve has serious concerns. He's in charge of the nation's money supply, and he's worried that what the stock markets have been doing is, basically, printing a bunch of fake money with things like CISCO SYSTEMS STOCK CERTIFICATE printed on the front instead of FEDERAL RESERVE NOTE. Meanwhile, journalists just know that the Great Depression sold a lot of newspapers. Also we're mad about buying Cisco Systems on March 27, 2000, and selling on April 14.

"The New Economy is like the Dutch tulip-bulb mania of the 1630s!" we journalists say in unison, with our usual brilliant individuality of mind. Hardly an op-ed piece about the New Economy gets to paragraph three without reference to the wild rise and fall of 370-year-old Netherlandish tuber prices. A book is already out on the subject, *Tulipomania,* by Mike Dash. And of course—what's a mania if the maniacs aren't in on it?—there's a web site: *www.bulb.com/historymyth/romp.html.* Boning up on seventeenth-century flower crazes in Holland has become the journalism Year 2000 equivalent of listening to the Linda Tripp phone tapes.

"The New Economy is like the Dutch tulip-bulb mania of the 1630s!" I said to friends of mine who are economists and actually know something about these things.

"No," they said, "it isn't." And I suppose, come to think of it, they had a point. Try streaming video on a tulip bulb or using it to store your income tax files. If my godson spent all night in his bedroom chatting with tulip bulbs, that would be a worry. Also, if you look up the history of the tulip craze, you'll find it happened in the middle of an enormous expansion of the Dutch economy between the 1620s and the 1670s and that tulips didn't much affect this expansion one way or the other. Bulb speculation was for the rubes and boobs—more Beanie Babies than Microsoft. Besides, just how much of our economic model do we want to base on people in wooden shoes with their fingers stuck in dikes?

Last spring I went to talk to William Niskanen, chairman of the Cato Institute think tank, PhD in economics from the University of Chicago, and acting chairman of the President's Council of Economic Advisors eighteen years ago, when the U.S. boom began. "'New Economy' is a journalists' term," scolded Niskanen. He told me that what I was actually talking about was the "digital effect," which is not something that Steve Jobs and Steve Wozniak were plugging dikes with in their garage.

The Internet is "flattening organizations," said Niskanen. All those expensive middle-management types are being fired because nowadays the CEO of Taco Bell can be in direct communication with his employees simply by logging on and e-mailing the zitty kid behind the counter in Dayton: *Time to nuke some more Chalupas.*

The web means "fewer intermediaries between buyers and sellers," said Niskanen. The guy in the horrible sport coat who rooked me on the car lot has been replaced by me, in virtual plaid, rooking myself electronically.

"The net," said Niskanen, "is reducing the need for agglomeration," this being what economists call getting up in the morning and going to work. Someday soon we'll be able to convert all of America's office parks into homeless shelters for automobile salesmen and Taco Bell vice presidents. And we can convert all of America's warehouses, too. Another important (if not exactly Buck Rogersish) thing the digital effect does is control inventory. According to the Congressional Joint Economic Committee, U.S. inventory-to-sales ratio went from over 2.7 in 1990 to under 2.4 in 1997. This is the kind of statistic that turns us civilians glassy-eyed but gets a big whoop out of economists because it means that products no longer experience a sort of adolescence on the wholesale shelves, just hanging around uselessly. Products now get up and go directly to buyers. Plus, Niskanen explained, computerization means greater manufacturing flexibility, leading to wider product variety. A new Nike shoe style every ten minutes. And Muffin will just have to have them.

"Is this a *good* thing?" I asked.

"Heretofore," Niskanen said, "many economists have been skeptical about computers increasing productivity." It seems that from 1870 to 1973 productivity in the United States increased annually by an average of 2.3 percent. Then computers arrived and—think Hal in *2001: A Space Odyssey*—productivity growth dropped to an average of 1.3 percent for the next twenty-two years. This was known as Solow's Paradox, named after MIT economist Robert Solow, who said, "You can see the computer age everywhere but in the productivity statistics." Of course Solow wouldn't have thought this was paradoxical if he'd ever walked around an office watching what people do on their computers: play solitaire, send pointless e-mail messages, and check their high-tech stocks (ticker symbol YO). But the supervisor finally caught them. Or something. Anyway, productivity has been rising at an average rate of 3 percent a year since 1996.

Niskanen believes that the introduction of a valuable new technology *reduces* productivity, sometimes for decades. Innovations are a shock. This must have been literally true with the introduction of electricity. Imagine all the would-be high-tech moguls of the nineteenth century grasping a live wire in each hand and reducing their productivity to a burnt crisp. Niskanen thinks we're over that, and the digital effect will now bring tremendous growth.

"I tend to be an optimist," Niskanen told me. His main worry is not overvalued New Economy stocks but government intervention in that New Economy, which, said Niskanen, "is still vulnerable to bad policy mistakes."

The Microsoft antitrust case comes to mind. We don't want to find ourselves saying a twenty-second-century equivalent of "Good thing we broke up Ford Motor Company, otherwise where would America's draft-horse industry be?"

I also went to see Stephen Moore, Cato Institute's director of fiscal policy studies and a former senior economist at that source of inventory-to-sales ratios, the Congressional Joint Economic Committee. Moore agreed with Niskanen about the danger of government intervention. But he didn't think the government had the guts to do much of it. Moore said, "Bubbles burst because of, one, protectionism; two, tax increases;

three, bad monetary policy; and four, welfare state expansion." There's no danger of numbers one, two, and four unless the vegans-with-face-tattoos vote gets a lot larger. As for number three, Moore pointed me to a passage in Bob Woodward's 1994 inside-the-Clinton-administration book, *The Agenda:*

> Clinton's face turned red with anger and disbelief. "You mean to tell me that the success of the program and my reelection hinges on the Federal Reserve and a bunch of fucking bond traders?"...
>
> Nods from his end of the table. Not a dissent.

"Politicians are impotent today," Moore told me, beaming. He explained that the free market is running the world. "Libertarian. Self-organizing. Democratic. It votes every minute." Governments, he said, "get immediate rewards for good policy, immediate punishments for bad policy. This is new. Even the Europeans are getting their act together."

Moore didn't think the high-technology field is insane. "If we want to have a share-the-wealth economy," he said, "the only way to do this is to have people own things." America is supposed to have a very low rate of savings, but, Moore explained, buying stock doesn't count as saving. While the Japanese were getting tiny Christmas Club interest payments and free toasters, Americans were investing. "We've created twenty trillion dollars in new assets," said Moore. "The other day I was driving by a construction site, and there were four guys in hard hats sitting on an I-beam reading *The Wall Street Journal*. Don't underestimate the intelligence of ordinary people. I'm skeptical of the skeptics. Are you," he asked me, "smarter than the millions of people who are voting with their money?"

"As a matter of fact ..." I said. And then I thought about our stock portfolio—ticker symbol YO. "So this *isn't* a bubble?"

"Well," said Moore, "I'm not fully convinced by these Internet stocks. The more they lose, the more they sell for. I wouldn't buy NASDAQ."

So this *is* a bubble.

Not that a new economy can't be both real and a bubble at the same time—ask people who invested in Packard, Studebaker, Hudson, Nash, Cord, Duesenberg, Stutz Bearcat, Pope Toledo, Baker Electric, and Stanley Steamer.

Anyway, of course this is a bubble. The indications are clear. The mine shaft canaries are giving away their little mirrors and perches and birdseed cakes and scratching farewell notes on the newsprint in the bottom of their cages. When NASDAQ hit the 5000 level for the first time on March 9, 2000, 20 percent of its value was made up of companies that didn't even exist in 1998, and three-quarters of those companies had no earnings at all. And observe the progress that New Economy companies are making. NASDAQ darling Amazon.com had almost $610 million in sales in 1998, losing $124.5 million. By 1999 sales had grown to more than $1.6 billion. Resulting in profits? No. Resulting in losses of $720 million. The Amazon.com business philosophy: Lose a little on every sale and make it up in volume. Meanwhile, the rats have been donning life jackets and signing up Kate Winslet to play them in the upcoming film *NASDtanic*. Between November 1999 and February 2000, Internet executives sold some $48 billion worth of their own stock in their own companies. This was approximately six times the usual rate of insider selling. Drugstore.com's founder sold 150,000 shares at $23. Two months later the stock was at $9.88. MicroStrategy insiders sold $80 million worth of stock shares shortly before the stock dropped 62 percent in one day. And former surgeon general and all-around killjoy C. Everett Koop made $3 million selling shares of drkoop.com at $9 in February. The stock went to $2.31 in April. Have a cigar, Doc.

"There is nothing so disturbing to one's well-being and judgment as to see a friend get rich," said American economist Charles Kindleberger. And this disturbance has come at an inopportune moment of general affluence. Said English economist Walter Bagehot, "At particular times a great deal of stupid people have a great deal of stupid money." High-tech investing has reached the men and women at the bottom of the fad chain. Joseph P. Kennedy used to claim that he got out of the 1929 stock market when the shoeshine boys started giving stock tips. The day after NASDAQ reached 5000, *The Wall Street Journal* had a story citing, approvingly, an old lady who walked into the office of her conservative Coral Gables financial planner and berated him for "missing the boat" on high-tech stocks. "I think the world is changing," she said. "It's very possible there's a new economy." Three days later *The Washington Post* printed a story, also approving, about a group of young people who had placed second in the "Maryland–DC student stock market game"—the young people being inmates of the Montgomery County Detention Center. The *Post*'s famously behind-the-curve gossip column had already run an item about StockGift.com, a bridal registry where newlyweds can pick out things from the equity market that they'd like to have around the house.

There's an old joke that Alan Greenspan is said to tell. A man gets a tip on an obscure stock. He calls his broker and says, "Buy me a thousand shares of XYZ." The next morning the man opens *The Wall Street Journal* and sees that XYZ has gone up. He calls his broker and says, "Buy me another thousand shares of XYZ." The next morning he opens *The Wall Street Journal* and XYZ has gone up again. He calls his broker, "Buy me *another* thousand shares of XYZ." The third morning XYZ has gone up yet again. The man starts to think, *Let's not get greedy here*. He calls his broker and says, "Sell me out of XYZ." And the broker says, "To *who*?"

No one is more high tech than Esther Dyson. She is the chairman of the Internet Corporation for Assigned Names and Numbers, author of the book *Release 2.0: A Design for Living in the Internet Age,* and a member of the President's Export Council Subcommittee on Encryption. She sits on the board of directors of the Electronic Frontier Foundation, Scala Business Solutions, E-Pub Services, iCat, and many other New Economy corporations and is president of Edventure Holdings, which hosts tech conferences and publishes a newsletter devoted to "complex adaptive systems and the transformation of artificial intelligence into commercial technology." That phrase might as well be in Russian as far as I'm concerned, but that's okay because Esther Dyson is fluent in Russian, too.

I phoned Esther Dyson two days after NASDAQ reached 5000. "So when is this bubble going to burst?" I asked.

"I thought it would have happened by now," she said.

Not that Dyson doesn't believe in the New Economy. "I think the Internet economy is real," she said. That, however, is the problem. Dyson explained—the way William Niskanen had—how computers make an economy more efficient. But she pointed out that "when an economy becomes more efficient, it's *harder* for investors to make money. They can't spot the inefficiencies." Investors get rich by noticing things that are undervalued, buying low and selling high. "An efficient economy means capital and machinery are selling for the lowest possible price," said Dyson. "In an efficient economy like this the only thing left with value, the only thing that's unique, is the human being. An efficient economy is good for people."

And that was a relief because, although I may be flummoxed by technology, confused about economics, and useless as an investor, I am absolutely, indubitably, purely, and completely a people.

"Good for good people," said Dyson.

"Oh," I said.

Of course I could be wrong, I said to my wife. Maybe this New Economy will just keep expanding forever. "All the old rules seem to be obsolete," said former labor secretary Robert Reich at that White House Conference on the New Economy. Sometimes short, annoying guys who suck up to powerful people know things. I'll have to check and see how Truman Capote did in the sixties stock market. Maybe the NASDAQ troubles are just a blip. Maybe we'll all keep getting richer and richer until everybody in America is a billionaire. And how weird will that be? Nobody will care about money anymore, just sex. I'll have to sleep with the guys at the car wash to get the interior vacuumed.

"You could get a job," said my wife.

I have a better idea: a new book project. One of those success-in-business things that are always on the best-seller lists. It's the management secrets of mothers with toddlers.

"And how, exactly," said my wife, "did you research this?"

Chris Buckley and I had a long lunch. He thinks I should call it *Kid Pro Quo*. Here's my opening paragraph:

In the 1970s there arrived in the American workplace something that would change the business world forever. This thing would prove more important than Arab oil embargoes, dim-bulb Carter-era monetary policies, or even the desktop computer. It wore lipstick. Although only if it wanted to.

"There were no Dress-Down Fridays when I was at Nasser and Stein," said my wife. "However, we did consider *Dumb*-Down Fridays for certain clients who were freelance writers."

And then, I said, I go on to say: that until about 1978 the majority of adult female Americans did not have jobs, not even when they were supposed to during World War II. Why is a matter of debate. Sexual discrimination, social tradition, and lack of economic opportunity doubtless played their parts. Although my own opinion (and I have known a number of adult female Americans personally and am married to one) is that women decided to go to work because they felt like it.

Anyway, the results have been spectacular. The Independent Women's Forum, a nonpartisan pro–free market think tank very much devoted to having women do what they feel like doing, has collected statistics on the subject. Between 1960 and 1994 women's wages increased ten times faster than men's. Females are currently starting businesses at twice the male rate, and women-owned enterprises are growing more quickly than the overall economy. In 1973 only 11 percent of corporations had women on their boards of directors; now 72 percent do. In 1970 the legal profession was 95 percent male. Today there's a 29 percent chance that your wife's divorce lawyer will be . . .

"Your wife," said my wife.

Some professions are, in effect, controlled by women, who make up 51 percent of editors and reporters, 66 percent of PR "men," and 62 percent of the psychologists telling us to get over it about the Mrs. making more than we do. Even the federal government's Glass Ceiling Commission, created by the Civil Rights Act of 1991 to bird-dog the remaining boys-only boardrooms, had to admit that women are getting along all right. The commission conceded that the two economic sectors expected to grow most at the beginning of the new century—service/trade/retail and finance/insurance/real estate—are well on their way to becoming hen parties.

No ethnic subculture or immigrant population has ever swept capitalism off its feet the way women have. The last time any group rose so quickly to the top was when men first got jobs and the only competition was from woolly mammoths.

What accounts for the distaff triumph? Of course, as every son, brother, boyfriend, and husband knows, women are smarter than we are. But it can't be only that. Looking around at my fellow males I realize *everything* is smarter than we are—the copy machine, for instance. And, when I was working, the copier never got promoted ahead of me. Although, as I recall, it did have a nicer cubicle.

The fact is, women possess a certain body of arcane knowledge, an eons-old set of complex skills, an ancient esoteric understanding that no one else has. This profound wisdom and well-learned craft is shrugged off by the ignorant (i.e., me) in the single dismissive phrase *good with kids.*

Or I used to shrug it off. But one day I came home from New York and was fuming into my martini about childish articles editors, infantile managing editors, and a publisher who was a spoiled brat, when what should my eyes behold but—a spoiled brat. *My* spoiled brat. There was my daughter Muffin, age two and a half, in the middle of the living room shouting *no,* kicking the furniture, and otherwise acting like every corporate executive since the great Ice Age Inc. takeover of Woolly Mammoth Ltd. in 11,000 B.C.

Then you, my dear, breezed into the room and did something involving a sippy cup and a Barney tape. Peace reigned. During that reign of peace I had a brilliant insight. Well, brilliant for a man.

Women are successful in the business world because the business world was created by men. Men are babies. And women are . . . *good with kids*.

So if I want to be successful in the business world, I need to be good with kids too. But how to go about this? Well, I could undertake to become principal care provider for Muffin. But there's our daughter's welfare to be considered. I have no idea how many Ring Dings and packages of beer nuts a toddler needs each day. And are diapers supposed to be changed three times a week or only twice?

I could ask you, honey, how to be good with kids. You're certainly good with the one who is, at the moment, contentedly singing along with a fuzzy *Tyrannosaurus rex*. (I'll bet Microsoft wishes it could get the Justice Department to do this, although, actually, in that case the *Tyrannosaurus rex* is Janet Reno. Which shows there is an exception to the good-with-kids rule; Janet would scare the hell out of Muffin.) You also rose higher on the corporate ladder than I ever did, before you resigned to run our wholly owned subsidiary of Toys "Я" Us. But would you tell me? Does Apple tell Microsoft? (Actually Apple *does* tell Microsoft, now that they're married—but you know who wears the pants in that family. And in mine.)

Instead, what I decided to do was buy books about raising children. But not just any children. Not babies—anybody with a dairy farm, a chain of rug-cleaning establishments, and 200,000 shares of Procter & Gamble can raise a baby. And not teens—raising teens is the business of the police and the National Association of Television Broadcasters' Code of Standards and Practices. I bought books about the most crucial and difficult periods in child raising: the God-Awful Ones, the Terrible Twos, the Threes That Are So Bad There's No Name for Them. I bought books about raising the variety of kid that I am absolutely clueless about raising: ours.

Of course, I chose books that were written by women. I remember the disaster that ensued when a generation of parents listened to Dr. Benjamin Spock. Trying to gain management acumen from Spock's ultrapermissive *Baby and Child Care* would result in running a brokerage house full of people in bell-bottoms eating peyote and handing out stock certificates for free on the street. I also wanted books that received high marks from women readers, so I had Max consult the Average Customer Review page at the Amazon.com web site, looking for things like: *I am still using the "respectful" techniques I learned from this book.* (Note the sly use of quotation marks.)

Here's what I picked.

- *1,2,3 . . . the Toddler Years: A Practical Guide for Parents and Caregivers* by Irene Van der Zande (Santa Cruz Toddler Care Center, 1995), 184 pages, $11.95.
- *Parenting Your Toddler: The Experts' Guide to the Tough and Tender Years* by Patricia Henderson Shimm and Kate Ballen (Perseus Books, 1995), 227 pages, $12.00.

- *Your One-Year-Old: The Fun-Loving, Fussy 12- to 24-Month-Old* by Louise Bates Ames, PhD, Frances L. Ilg, MD, and Carol Chase Haber (Dell, 1982), 178 pages, $11.95.

Was I imagining it or did the lady at the bookstore cash register look suspicious? "My wife is going to a Theta reunion in Bloomington, Indiana," I said, "for the *whole weekend.*" I placed a concealing copy of *Sports Afield* in my shopping bag and slipped home. I opened *Your One-Year-Old* at random and . . . the shock of recognition was so severe that the vermouth bottle almost dropped from my hand. Listen to these excerpts from the chapter titled "Characteristics of the Age":

- He seems to want *everything,* to prefer everybody else have nothing.
- A busy little person. Though much of his activity is purely . . . bumbling around from one spot to another.
- Almost anything may attract his attention, and then he almost seems to have to respond, without rhyme or reason.
- Extremely self-involved. He relates to others if and when it pleases him.
- All too likely to put on a full-fledged temper tantrum over what may actually be only a minor frustration.
- Can be seen as enchanting if the viewer appreciates an almost total egocentricity.

Is that not the most brilliant description of management ever limned? Consider the management in the Clinton White House. What had I been doing wasting my time reading *What Flavor Is Your Poison Pill?* and *The 137,240 Secrets of Highly Concise People*?

And women's sagacity does not stop at mere keen observation. The books I bought wade right in and tell you how to deal with the president of the United States or, for that matter, a regional director of sales and marketing.

"You control him," says *Your One-Year-Old,* "by controlling the surroundings and by just not having too many things around that will get him into difficulty." Interns, for one.

"If you do use language to motivate him," the book continues, "keep it very simple, and use words of one syllable only." The most famous boss-motivating monosyllable is, naturally, the *Yes*. But its opposite, the *I will get right back to you on that,* works too, because, as *Your One-Year-Old* says, "he has such a very short attention span." And try "Your golf game looks real good," and "You've lost weight." *Your One-Year-Old* points out that "Whatever gives comfort is worth its weight in gold." Naps are also suggested. They worked with President Reagan.

The three books are full of good advice about how to make people who think they're in charge think they actually are. Never ask your boss a yes-or-no question. "*No* becomes his favorite word even when he wants to say *yes,*" states *Parenting Your Toddler*. "He quite typically says 'no' instead of 'yes,' 'down' instead of 'up,'" notes *Your One-Year-Old.* "There's almost always a way to give . . . a choice," vouchsafes *1,2,3 . . . the Toddler Years*. "Notice that these questions are all offered in the form of closed questions." And the latter book goes on to give examples, one of which, since we're using President Clinton as our specimen awful boss, is rather too pertinent:

> "Do you want to wear your red pants or your blue pants?" It's important before asking the question to decide what choices we're willing to live with. Open questions such as "What do you want to wear?" lead to answers we may not be willing to accept, like, "Nothing!"

The closed question—it is so easy, so obvious, and yet every one of the Joint Chiefs of Staff forgot to ask Bill Clinton, "Do you want to stay out of the Balkans or not get involved in former Yugoslavia?" The problem is, the Joint Chiefs are guys.

The books are equally savvy about temper tantrums. Says *Your One-Year-Old,* "The less they bother you, chances are the less frequently they will occur. It is not much satisfaction to play to an uninterested audience."

Parenting Your Toddler gives six rules for dealing with tantrums:

1. Don't punish.	("I quit.")
2. Don't reward.	("I quit. Sob. Sob.")

3. Don't bribe. ("I'll quit if you ask me to.")
4. Don't placate. ("You don't really want me to quit, do you?")
5. Don't leave the room. ("I quit. F— you.")
6. Don't have a tantrum yourself. ("I quit. F—you. I'm suing.")

Then the text goes on to posit a strategy worthy of Napoleon, if Napoleon had been a woman. But he wasn't, so he wound up getting fired and hanging out at the day care center on St. Helena. And the strategy is: Just name the feelings that caused the tantrum. "Once your toddler calms down, explain in short sentences why he gets angry."

Let's try using the example that *Parenting Your Toddler* gives, about putting crayons away, with some minor modifications to fit Napoleon's case. "General Wellington and General Blucher, you got really mad when I said it was time to put Louis the Eighteenth away. It's okay to be angry; next time you can tell me this. You can say, *Napoleon, we get mad when you escape from Elba*. I will listen to you. And you know that no matter how mad you get at Napoleon, somebody stinky is always going to run France."

Just naming things seems ridiculous to a male. But think how often females make it work around the house: *Because I'm your mother* or *Oh, no, you don't, you're a married man.*

Equally effective for dealing with tantrums, and with almost all other lousy executive behavior, is a technique that women invented at a very early date—distraction. "Not right now, Adam, I've got to go fig-leaf shopping. Why don't you have an apple instead?" Or, as *Your One-Year-Old* puts it, a "new and interesting object if offered may prove to be a satisfactory substitute for the thing he really wanted. Or a total change of scene . . . may help him forget his frustration." Hence the importance of the business jet, which, you'll recall, came into use in the middle seventies just when large numbers of women were gaining influence over America's executive suites. If the corner-office carpet apes get completely out of control, put them on the G-5.

Besides sage advice, the books contain a variety of real-life anecdotes to help me better understand how corporate and professional life looks to women. It looks like a play date gone horribly wrong. Thanks to the following item from *Parenting Your Toddler,* I now know everything about telecommunications networks and am ready to go toe-to-toe with the sharpest gal in the industry:

> Lily walked into her friend's house and her eyes immediately lit upon a beautiful new doll. Lily quickly said, "Joan, I'll share your new doll." Joan, who obviously had heard that sharing was a good thing, replied, "Oh, yes, we'll share the doll." Lily then grabbed the doll and ran into a corner with it, saying, "Now, we are sharing."

I suppose women thought men would never read these books. Or women thought these books would be read only by the kind of man who bikes to his job at the organic food co-op—not a threat to promotion. Anyway, women didn't work very hard at putting their percipience into code. Even a board chairman could crack it. Examine the following passage, allegedly about biting, from *1,2,3 . . . the Toddler Years.* First, however, we will substitute *account supervisor* for "eighteen-month-old," *new executive assistant* for "four-year-old sister," *Palm Pilot* for "doll," and *vice president of account services* for "Mama."

> Account Supervisor Kenny stood quietly watching his new executive assistant. It's possible to guess at the sort of thoughts going through Kenny's head. "I wonder about this girl here. I know what she looks like . . . I know what she smells like . . . but what does she taste like? I'll just find out. . . . Wow, she made a big noise! And she dropped that Palm Pilot she never lets me play with. Uh-oh! Looks like the vice president of account services is real mad at someone. . . . Who, me?"

You members of the business sisterhood, I said to my wife, should be more careful about putting your secrets into print. Or at least you should make a pretense of actually using these books to raise kids. I've noticed you never look at them. When anything untoward happens in our house you call your mother. "Mom," you say, "I'm having a terrible problem with bedtime. It's just, *No, no, no! More bottle! More bottle!* Nothing seems to work. What did you used to do?"

"And," said my wife, "my mother says, 'I used to hide your father's gin.'"

3

NOVEMBER 2000

So the Fairy Godmother waved her magic wand and Cinderella's rags were suddenly transformed into a fabulous ball gown, and upon Cinderella's dainty bare feet there appeared a pair of beautiful glass slippers. That can't be right. One good polka and she'd smash them to bits. If Cinderella steps on broken glass she's going to cut the heck out of herself and bleed all over the handsome prince's ballroom floor and the prince is going to have to call 911. Emergency services will never get there before midnight. Fiberglass must be what's meant or Plexiglas or one of those clear plastics like they're making Nikes out of nowadays. So what Cinderella was really wearing was probably a big pair of lumpy athletic shoes, and that must have looked strange with the fabulous ball gown. But never mind. The Fairy Godmother waved her magic wand again and changed a pumpkin into a magnificent carriage. Of course you can change a pumpkin into a carriage, but it's still going to retain a basic pumpkinishness. It was kind of wet and slimy inside. The way the pumpkin we carved for Halloween was. There were seeds all over the carriage floor. And Cinderella smelled like a big pie when she got out. Which, incidentally, is not a bad way to get a man. The Fairy Godmother waved her magic wand one more time and changed the mice in Cinderella's kitchen into a team of splendid carriage horses. But they had a terrible gait and tended to scurry down the street too close to the buildings, scraping off a lot of pumpkin-colored carriage paint. And they bolted whenever they sniffed cheese.

"Mommy!" screamed Muffin "I hate this story!"

"Better let me put her to bed," said my wife. "You go down and entertain the neighbors. And, please, honey . . ."

[My wife was referring to the fact that I think the neighbors are Democrats. They look like Democrats—the same kind of shoes as Cinderella. And they smell like Democrats. That is, using smell as a transitive verb. When I light a cigar they wave their hands in front of their faces and pretend to cough. Not that I mind having Democrats in the house occasionally, when they own a snowblower I'm going to need to borrow. The problem is the Political Nut who lives around here. He can't keep his mouth shut. And the Weather Channel says it's going to be a severe winter.]

Well, both the presidential candidates suck, I said, attempting to put the Democrat neighbors at ease with an even-handed show of bipartisanship. So I guess the real campaign issue is which candidate gives us more looty for our booty?

That would be George, I continued. Big juicy tax cut from him. A family of four earning $35,000 would have their federal income tax reduced to the nice round sum of 0. And the top tax bracket would be lowered from 39.6 percent to 33 percent. Whee . . . but wait. Family of four making 35K. These days that's two parents mopping the floor at Target or a single mom waiting tables at Hooters, and those people are going to vote Democratic anyway. The $1,500 tax relief George W. is promising will not exactly let you Democrats build cathedral-ceilinged great rooms with hot tubs and decks onto your trailer homes. No offense, of course. That's a perfectly nice fake colonial you've got next door. Anyway, for you better off, it will take only about $150,000 a year to get into Bush's 33 percent category. One hundred fifty long is nice money, but not Wild Willy Gates income territory. So there you are, doing good, working hard, making America strong and prosperous, and the government's getting a third of your pay. Is the government doing a third of your job? Is the government even doing a third of your laundry? If one of you is feeling romantic and the other is tired, does the government take care of foreplay? When you go to Hooters, is the government tending bar, making one out of three margaritas on the house?

Gore, on the other hand, I said, has a dog's breakfast of little tax cuts allegedly aimed at poor people. These involve 401(k) matching funds, 401(j) "lifelong learning" accounts, and other things that, if poor people could understand all the mathematical and regulatory complexities entailed, would qualify the poor people for top executive posts and they wouldn't be poor. They would be voting for George W. Bush to get their tax bracket down to 33 percent.

Gore's tax plan is based on Gore's ideas about America's silicon-injected economy. Actually, the ideas of both candidates on America's economy can be summed up briefly as "Hot damn! How'd that happen? Wow! Cool! Now let's ruin everything."

Gore believes that wrecking America's economy is best accomplished by paying down the national debt a little while spending the hell out of the gross national product, whereas Bush believes in spending the hell out of the gross national product while cutting taxes somewhat.

Medicare prescription benefits are one way to cure the burn that boom times have caused in the government pants pocket. Gore has a specific and detailed Medicare Rx plan that would be horrendously expensive. Bush lacks the specifics and details but has the horrendous expense thing well in hand. And neither candidate wants to lick the frozen pump handle of means-testing. We give billions of Medicare dollars to retired people such as yourselves, and a lot of you are not standing at highway intersections with cardboard signs reading HOMELESS AND COLOSTOMY BAG IS FULL. Average household net worth for Americans over sixty-five is more than a quarter of a million dollars. You two could kick in a little something for your doctor bills. It is not like you're saving for a jet-ski.

And by the way, I've about had it with this "greatest generation" malarkey. You people have one stock market crash in 1929, and it takes you a dozen years to go get a job. Then you wait until Germany and Japan have conquered half the world before it occurs to you to get involved in World War II. After that you get surprised by a million Red Chinese in Korea. Where do you put a million Red Chinese so they'll be a surprise? You spend the entire 1950s watching Lawrence Welk and designing tail fins. You come up with the idea for Vietnam. Thanks. And you elect Richard Nixon. The hell with you.

Just kidding. Actually it's the hell with *me*—since I'll be the old person when the Social Security chain letter runs out of suckers. "Put your name at the bottom of the list. Mail a check for $1,200 to everyone over sixty-five. Break this chain and you'll never be elected to national political office."

There is no money in the Social Security trust fund, and there never was. Money is a government IOU. Government can't create a trust fund by saving its own IOUs any more than I could create a trust fund by writing *I get a chunk of cash when I turn twenty-one* on a piece of paper. Social Security is just such a piece of paper, except it says, *I get a chunk of cash when I turn sixty-five, the government promises*. Consult American Indians for a fuller discussion of government promises.

Of course, what Al and George want to do to the economy is not all bad. Or else it is. This depends on your definition of bad and whether you two were running with the nose-ringers at the last WTO meeting—metaphorically speaking—or whether you were boarding up your Starbucks shop. Bush and Gore are both free-traders and both are opposed in this by organized labor, environmentalists, human rights activists, and Pat Buchanan kooks, a weird coalition of people who don't understand economics and people who don't understand economics at all. Gore says he'd be the better proponent of free trade because the UAW Joe—soon to be José—Six-Pack is a Democrat and all the bunny-huggers love *Earth in the Balance*. Bush argues that at least he isn't a lickspittle traitor to everything he's ever believed in, and thus a George W. administration would be better trusted by Paddy B. and the left-wing hootenannies.

Bush and Gore also agree on what a wonderful thing technology is. And both men mean to get a clue about it soon. They do know it should be used only to do good. Bush is against pornography on the Internet. Gore is in favor of the V-chip. And Bush wants to open American borders to immigration by high-tech workers. This is great because it means more curry take-out restaurants and exciting Pakistani cab-drivers. You Democrats should like it too. You're running low on Chinese spies at the Los Alamos nuclear laboratory.

Gore is supposed to be tech-savvy. But there was that awful moment last March on *CNN Inside Politics* when Al told Wolf Blitzer, "During my service in the United States Congress, I took the initiative in creating the Internet." And Socks the Cat invented the mouse thing.

The candidates are putting this technology to wonderful use, too. Just click on algore2000.com or georgewbush.com. My heart goes out to the young, underpaid, politically infatuated campaign staffer who has to type this garbage. Here's the key to your dad's gun cabinet, kid. Use your toe if you can't reach the trigger with the barrel in your mouth.

Bush and Gore are educated idiots, members of the Lucky Sperm Scholarship Society, a small privileged class of elite Americans who have shoe-size IQs and the best educations that money, power, and influence can buy. If George W. Bush and Al Gore had grown up on my block in Toledo, Ohio, they wouldn't have gone to Yale and Harvard. They would have gone to Kent State. Easy to picture them there circa 1970—Al picking up on the hippie thing a little late, ordering his bell-bottoms from the Sears catalog, and George W. in a *real* National Guard unit, shooting Al.

At algore2000.com, you get page after page of identically formatted lame brags about how Al has got all the answers—with matching titles that maybe Tipper or somebody thought would be cute:

VICE PRESIDENT AL GORE

- FIGHTING FOR AFRICAN AMERICANS
- FIGHTING FOR THE JEWISH COMMUNITY
- FIGHTING FOR ARAB AMERICANS
- FIGHTING FOR WOMEN
- FIGHTING FOR WORKING FAMILIES

- FIGHTING FOR SMALL BUSINESSES
- FIGHTING FOR NATIVE AMERICANS
- FIGHTING FOR ASIAN PACIFIC AMERICANS

That's a lot of fighting, Al, for a guy who got shot at less on his Vietnam tour than he would have if he'd gone to Kent State. And what if the blacks hate the Jews and the Jews hate the Arabs and the Arabs treat the women lousy? This fighting could get out of hand.

Web site georgewbush.com is almost as bad, although quieter. But then, George W. has things to be quiet about, such as his environmental record in Texas now that Houston has overtaken Los Angeles as the most smog-putrid city in the nation. George supports greater state-level control over environmental policies. That might prove to be a problem with certain states such as—mmm, Texas. Gore, on the other hand, has spent the past eighteen months in Redwood National Forest living in a tree named Luna. Or that's what he told Wolf Blitzer.

Both Gore and Bush favor the use of ethanol—just what the world is crying out for, a fuel that's more expensive than gasoline and that, when you get done planting, harvesting, fermenting, and refining it, generates more pollution. Neither Bush nor Gore would do much about America's excrement-oriented farm policies that give manure loads of money to giant agribusinesses while making sure Willie Nelson always has a role saving the small farmer who's crapped out because he can't grow any good shit to sell to Willie.

Speaking of which, I hope you two aren't looking for bold moves on the drug legalization front. The candidates don't even mention it. My assistant, Max, tells me that a search for MARIJUANA yielded no results on either Bush or Gore's web site. I wonder if, three decades ago, a search for marijuana in Bush or Gore's bachelor pads would have yielded the same results. These guys are reputed to have done some "flying on instruments." But Gore was shameless enough to say, in a speech last spring, "We fought for and won the biggest antidrug budget in history, every single year. Now we can see the results of that strategy." We sure can. Heroin is cheaper than a carton of cigarettes, and you hardly ever get carded when you're scoring smack.

And, speaking of things that will kill you, don't go voting Democratic just because you think Gore will give you life without parole. See "Working to Reduce Crime and Punish Criminals" at algore2000.com, and read Al's boast about how the 1994 Crime Bill expanded the death penalty for federal law-breaking. Vice presidents, however, don't get a chance to invoke the death penalty very often—and a good thing, considering such past VPs as Dan Quayle, Spiro Agnew, LBJ, and Richard Nixon. Meanwhile, "Lethal-Injection George" has left us with little doubt about where he stands on this issue, having turned Texas into the "Gurney Journey State."

And how about death penalties for people who haven't done anything because they aren't born yet? Republicans are still against abortion, or so their platform says. But from the way that actual Republican candidates toe-dance when they address actual abortion questions, it's clear that Republicans have finally gotten it through their thick skulls that even Republican women want abortion to be available at least as an option under certain circumstances. These certain circumstances involve Republican men. Republican women sometimes get so desperate that they sleep with us, and then the women wake up the next morning thinking, "Ohmigod. What if I'm . . . ?"

You Democrats are pro-abortion but you don't want to come right out and say, "It's great to kill babies, especially the babies of poor uneducated teenage girls, babies that are just going to grow up to be . . . Democrats." So Gore supports abortion but will make it stop. While Bush is against abortion but will let it continue.

Watch the candidates pull the same trick on gun control. Gore is in favor of gun control, but when he was in Congress he voted for the NRA-backed 1986 Firearm Owners' Protection Act and against both a fourteen-day waiting period for handgun purchases and a federal requirement that serial numbers be put on guns. Bush is opposed to gun control, but he wants to put more controls on guns by raising the minimum age for handgun possession from eighteen to twenty-one and aggressively enforcing the existing gun laws—that Al Gore voted against.

On affirmative action, Bush rises to the level of Baloney King. According to georgewbush.com, the candidate "Supports 'affirmative access' to open the doors of opportunity." Although for pure fatuousness, it's hard to match Al Gore on Stronger Families: "We need policies that value real families—that let parents balance work and family, and make our schools, hospitals, and communities more friendly to families' needs."

What am I supposed to say when I hear candidates talking like this? "Oh, no, Al. We need policies that value *pretend* families. You be Mommy and I'll be Daddy when he comes home with a load on: 'Where is that bitch?' We need policies that keep parents working all night at Hooters while the kids eat dry Ramen noodles out of the Styrofoam cup, policies that make our schools, hospitals, and communities into one big Knife and Gun Club."

And what about gay rights? If you're gay, Al Gore will let you get into the military. George Bush will let you get out. You choose.

Let's see, what campaign issues haven't we discussed? There's education. They're both for it. Bush supports vouchers that would let children get away from the meatheads and troublemakers in the public school system. This may not work. Most children *are* meatheads and troublemakers. Gore is against vouchers. The Gore position is, "I'm living proof that your child is not too dumb to go to St. Albans. Now help me make sure you can't afford to send him there."

And there's foreign policy. Both Bush and Gore believe we should have one. That gives the edge to Bush, since it's almost impossible to have a worse foreign policy than the Clinton/Gore one of kissing China's butt while bombing their Belgrade embassy, kicking Russia's butt while giving them piles of money, and sending American soldiers to stand around and scratch their butts in Somalia, Bosnia, Haiti, and Kosovo. It's almost—but not completely—impossible to have a worse foreign policy than that. George's dad, with the help of Dick Cheney, came pretty close in Iraq. Saddam Hussein sends his thanks for ten great years of remaining in power.

"Where are the neighbors?" asked my wife.

Oh, they left a while ago. The missus didn't seem to be feeling well, mumbled something about a pain in the ass.

My wife sighed. "Well," she said, "at least this election will be over and done with next Tuesday."

"What the heck are you doing?" asked my young assistant, Max.

I'm reading Hillary Clinton's book, the one she published in 1995, *It Takes a Village*. We never listen to what people we can't stand are saying. Now that she's going to be a senator, I want to know what she thinks.

"Spare me."

It takes a village to raise a child. The village is Washington. You are the child. There, I've spared you—from having to read it. And I don't recommend that you do so. Nearly everything about *It Takes a Village* is objectionable, from the title—an ancient African proverb that seems to have its origins in the ancient African kingdom of Hallmarkcardia—to the acknowledgments page, where Mrs. Clinton fails to acknowledge that some poor journalism professor named Barbara Feinman did most of the work. Mrs. Clinton thereby unwisely violates the first rule of literary collaboration: Blame the co-author. And let us avert our eyes from this Kim Il Sung–style dust-cover photograph showing Mrs. Clinton surrounded by joyous youth-of-many-nations.

The writing style is that familiar modern one so often adopted by harried public figures speaking into tape recorders. The tone is Xeroxed family newsletter, the kind enclosed in a Christmas card from people you hardly know:

> One memorable night, Chelsea wanted us to go buy a coconut. . . . We walked to our neighborhood store, brought the coconut home, and tried to open it, even pounding on it with a hammer, to no avail. Finally we went out to the parking lot of the governor's mansion, where we took turns throwing it on the ground until it cracked. The guards could not figure out what we were up to, and we laughed for hours afterward.

Hours? However that may be, let us understand that what we have in *It Takes a Village* is a Christmas card with ideas, "a reflection of my continuing meditation on children," as Mrs. Clinton puts it. And we need only turn to the contents page to reap the benefits of her many hours spent in philosophical contemplation of puerile ontology: "Kids Don't Come with Instructions," "Security Takes More Than a Blanket," "Child Care Is Not a Spectator Sport," "Children Are Citizens Too." Bold thoughts. Brave insights.

"Children," says Mrs. Clinton, "are like the tiny figures at the center of the nesting dolls for which Russian folk artists are famous. The children are cradled in the family, which is primarily responsible for their passage from infancy to adulthood. But around the family are the larger settings of *paid informers, secret police, corrupt bureaucracy, and a prison gulag.*"

I added the last part for comic relief, something *It Takes a Village* doesn't provide. Intentionally.

The profound cogitations of Mrs. Clinton result in a treasure trove of useful advice on child rearing. "The village needs a town crier—and a town prodder," she says. I shall be certain to propose the creation of this novel office at the next city council meeting. I'm sure my fellow citizens will be as pleased as I am at the notion of a public servant going from door to door at convenient hours announcing, as Mrs. Clinton does, "We can encourage girls to be active and dress them in comfortable, durable clothes that let them move freely."

Mrs. Clinton has swell tips on entertaining toddlers: "Often . . . a sock turned into a hand puppet is enough to fascinate them for hours." There's that "for hours" again. I suppose even the briefest period spent in the company of Mrs. Clinton might be described that way. She's good on keeping older kiddies fit, too: "If your children need to lose weight, help them to set a reasonable goal and make a sensible plan for getting there." And what parent would not applaud Mrs. Clinton's suggestion "to explain to the child in advance what the shots do, perhaps by illustrating it with her favorite dolls and stuffed animals." Plus, this is an excellent method of educating offspring about sexual abuse and, perhaps, capital punishment. Don't call the Senate if the kid refuses to be left alone in the room with Fuzzy the Bunny.

Mrs. Clinton also taps the expertise of—what else to call them?—experts. "The Child Care Action Campaign . . . advises that 'jigsaw puzzles and crayons may be fine for preschoolers but are inappropriate for infants.'" And Ann Brown, the chairhuman of the Consumer Product Safety Commission, is quoted opining that "baby showers with a safety theme are a great way to help new and expectant mothers childproof every room in their homes." Oh, honey, look what Mom got us—a huge bouquet of rubber bands to put around all the knobs on our kitchen cabinets!

But *It Takes a Village* is so much more than just a self-help book for morons. Mrs. Clinton lets us in on her deepest personal sorrows. "Watching one parent browbeat the other over child support or property division by threatening to fight for custody or withhold visitation, I often wished I could call in King Solomon to arbitrate." One trembles at the thought of the lawsuits the Children's Defense Fund would bring against old Sol for endangering the welfare of a minor, bigamy, and what Mrs. Clinton calls "the misuse of religion to further political, personal, and even commercial agendas."

Mrs. Clinton explains, however, that church is good. "Our spiritual life as a family was spirited and constant. We talked with God, walked with God, ate, studied, and argued with God." And won, I'll warrant. "My father came from a long line of Methodists, while my mother, who had not been raised in any church, taught Sunday school." Interesting lessons they must have been. I myself am a Methodist. But Mrs. Clinton apparently belongs to the synod from Alpha Centauri. "Churches," she says, "are among the few places in the village where today's teenagers can let down their guard and let off steam." She says that, in her Methodist youth group, "We argued over the meaning of war to a Christian after seeing for the first time works of art like Picasso's *Guernica*, and the words of poets like T. S. Eliot and e. e. cummings inspired us to debate other moral issues." I can only wonder if any of those words were from "one times one" by cummings:

a politician is an arse upon
which everything has sat except a man

But Mrs. Clinton can't be stupid. Can she? She has a big long résumé. She's been to college, several times. Very important intellectuals like Garry Wills consider her to be a very important intellectual, like

Garry Wills. Surely the imbecility of *It Takes a Village* was a calculated, cynical attempt to soften the First Lady's image with ordinary Americans. Mrs. Clinton chose a thesis that can hardly be refuted: *Kids—Aren't They Great?* Then she patronized her audience, talked down to them, lowered the level of discourse to a point where it could be understood by the average—let's be frank—Democrat. This was an interesting public relations gambit, repositioning the dragon lady to show how much she cares about all the little dragon eggs. But if the purpose of *It Takes a Village* was to get in good with the masses, then explain this sentence on page 182, "I had never before known people who lived in trailers."

Is the First Lady a dunce? Let us marshal the evidence:

STUPIDITY

ARGUMENTS CONTRA	ARGUMENTS PRO
President of her class at Wellesley	It was the sixties, a decade without quality control
Involved in Watergate investigation	So was Martha Mitchell
Partner in most prestigious law firm in Arkansas	Examine phrase "most prestigious law firm in Arkansas"
Went to Yale	Went to Yale
Married Bill	Married Bill
Won the New York Senate race	Won the New York Senate race

There are times in *It Takes a Village* when Mrs. Clinton seems to play at being a horse's ass, when she makes statements such as "Some of the best theologians I have ever met were five-year-olds." Mommy, did they put Jesus on the cross before or after he came down the chimney and brought all the children toys?

But some kinds of stupidity cannot be faked. Says Mrs. Clinton, "less developed nations will be our best models for . . . home doctoring." And she tells us that in Bangladesh she met a Louisiana doctor "who was there to learn about low-cost techniques he could use back home to treat some of his state's more than 240,000 uninsured children." A poultice of buffalo dung is helpful in many cases.

Mrs. Clinton seems to possess the highly developed, finely attuned stupidity usually found in the upper reaches of academia. Hear her on the subject of nurseries and preschools: "From what experts tell us, there is a link between the cost and the quality of care." And then there is Mrs. Clinton's introduction to the chapter titled "Children Don't Come with Instructions":

> There I was, lying in my hospital bed, trying desperately to figure out how to breast-feed. . . . As I looked on in horror, Chelsea started to foam at the nose. I thought she was strangling or having convulsions. Frantically, I pushed every buzzer there was to push.
>
> A nurse appeared promptly. She assessed the situation calmly, then, suppressing a smile, said, "It would help if you held her head up a bit, like this." Chelsea was taking in my milk, but because of the awkward way I held her, she was breathing it out of her nose!

The woman was holding her baby upside down.

But let's not confuse stupid with feeble or pointless. Stupidity is an excellent medium for vigorous conveyance of certain political ideas. Mrs. Clinton is, for instance, doggedly antilibertarian. She says the "extreme case against government, *often including intense personal attacks on government officials and political leaders* [emphasis added by an extremist, me], is designed not just to restrain government but to advance narrow religious, political, and economic agendas." That crabbed, restrictive screed the Bill of Rights comes to mind.

There is no form of social spending that Mrs. Clinton won't buy into—with my money. "I can't understand the political opposition to programs like 'midnight' basketball," she says. And no doubt the Swiss and Japanese, who owe their low crime rates to keeping their kids awake until all hours shooting hoops, agree.

And Mrs. Clinton is oblivious to the idea that the government programs she advocates may have caused the problems the government programs she advocates are supposed to solve. "Whatever the reasons for the apparent increase in physical and sexual abuse of children, it demands our intervention," she says. But what if the reason *is* our intervention?

Only the lamest arguments are summoned to support Mrs. Clinton's call for expansion of state power. She uses a few statistics of the kind that come in smuggy faxes from minor Naderite organizations, like "135,000 children bring guns to school each day." She recollects past do-goodery:

> In Arkansas we enlisted the services of local merchants to create a book of coupons that could be distributed to pregnant women. . . . After every month's pre- or postnatal exam, the attending health care provider validates a coupon, which can be redeemed for free or reduced-price goods such as milk or diapers.

In 1980, Arkansas had an infant mortality rate of 12.7 per 1,000 live births, almost identical to the national average of 12.6. As of 1992 the Arkansas rate was 10.3 versus a national average of 8.5.

Mrs. Clinton talks long and often about "the harsh consequences of a more open economy." So unlike the lovely time people are having in North Korea. Mrs. Clinton thinks that "one of the conditions of the consumer culture is that it relies upon human insecurities to create aspirations that can be satisfied only by the purchase of some product or service." A private-school education for our kids, maybe. And she quotes approvingly from the book *The Lost City* by Alan Ehrenhalt, a doofus: "The unfettered free market has been the most radically disruptive force in American life in the last generation."

Yet, at bottom, Mrs. Clinton cannot really be called a leftist. Mrs. Clinton doesn't dislike business, as long as business is done her way. She gives examples of corporate activities that statists can cozy up to. For instance, "A number of our most powerful telecommunications and computer companies have joined forces with the government in a project to connect every classroom in America to the Internet."

If you want to put a name to these stupid politics, you can consult the *Columbia Encyclopedia*, the article that begins "totalitarian philosophy of government that glorifies state and nation and assigns to the state control over every aspect of national life." Admittedly, the totalitarianism in *It Takes a Village* is of a namby-pamby, eat-your-vegetables kind that doesn't so much glorify the state and nation as pester the dickens out of them. Ethnic minorities do not suffer persecution except insofar as a positive self-image is required among women, blacks, and Hispanics at all times. And there are no brownshirt uniforms other than comfortable, durable clothes on girls—in earth tones—and no concentration camps, just lots and lots of day care. Nonetheless, the similitude to a certain ideology exists. The encyclopedia article points out that this ideology "is obliged to be antitheoretical and frankly opportunistic in order to appeal to many diverse groups." "Elitism" is noted as is "rejection of reason and intelligence and emphasis on vision." Featured prominently is "an authoritarian leader who embodies in his [or her!] person the highest ideals of the nation." The only element missing from *It Takes a Village* is "social Darwinism." It's been replaced by "Social Creationism," expressed in such Mrs. Clinton statements as "I have never met a stupid child."

It Takes a Village is what *I* call a good read, said the Political Nut who lives around here. Neville Chamberlain made a famous mistake by not bringing a copy of *Mein Kampf* with him on the plane ride to Munich.

The Political Nut flipped through *It Takes a Village*. Hillary says, he quoted, "Children have many lessons to share with us." And on page 153, there's a swell lesson some children taught Hillary:

> When my family moved to Park Ridge, I was four years old and eager to make new friends. Every time I walked out the door, with a bow in my hair and a hopeful look on my face, the neighborhood kids would torment me, pushing me, knocking me down, and teasing me until I burst into tears and ran back in the house.

Or the Senate, said the Political Nut.

The Political Nut was back a few days later, carrying a stack of bumper stickers, PRO-CHOICE—ON LAND MINES, that he'd ordered from a classified ad in the back of *Waco Digest*. I know, said the Political Nut, how to fix this presidential election stalemate. My wife escaped upstairs, as she often does when the Political Nut is around. There are, he continued, a number of Americans who shouldn't be voting. The number is 48 percent, to judge by the total Al Gore popular vote. Or maybe the number is 65 percent, that being the *ABC News* poll tally of Americans who supported the forced removal of Elián González from Miami. We need a method to prevent these people from ever going to the polls again. Such an idea is not, I assert, antidemocratic. At this moment our democracy is filled with enthusiasm for minority culture, minority rights, and minority political expression—anti-Castro Cubans always excepted. So who will gainsay a pronouncement that the majority sucks? Speaking of which, there was once talk among conservatives and Republicans—back when the terms weren't mutually exclusive—about building a "New Majority." I was skeptical.

Lord Acton said, "At all times sincere friends of freedom have been rare, and its triumphs have been due to minorities that have prevailed by associating themselves with auxiliaries whose objects often differed from their own; and this association, which is always dangerous, has sometimes been disastrous, such as, for instance, when the GOP gave free Confederate flags to all $50-plus George W. Bush donors." Although I believe Lord A. implied rather than actually stated that last part. Also, I'm from East Yoohoo, Ohio, went to a state college, and rarely make it past the level of "Who's buried in Grant's Tomb?" when Regis Philbin is on the air. Therefore, I am closer to the national median than most of my right-wing pals and realize, better than they, that—do what we will with school vouchers, merit pay, core curricula, and killing the leaders of the teachers' unions—half of America's population will be below median intelligence. The trick answer, by the way, is Ulysses S. Grant *and* his wife, Julia.

But how to go about limiting suffrage? Literacy tests are in bad odor due to misuse by the white-trash illiterates of the South—all of them Democrats, let it be noted. Numeracy tests would be more to the point anyway, since, according to a May 14, 2000, *New York Times* clipping I have here, one quarter of America thinks that buying lottery tickets is a better retirement plan than saving or investing. But the trouble with math is that people like Hillary Clinton always got the good grades in it.

Poll taxes in federal elections are banned by the Twenty-fourth Amendment. Repealing a constitutional amendment is time-consuming. It took fourteen years to repeal the prohibition amendment, and repeal might not have happened even then except the country got a good look at Eleanor Roosevelt and then everybody needed a drink. Anyway, if we're going to repeal amendments, the Nineteenth, giving the vote to women, would be a better choice. The girls went 60 percent for Hillary Clinton and 54 percent for Al Gore.

There was an ominous thumping on the ceiling.

However, the Nineteenth Amendment is sacred and inviolable and stay-at-home mothers voted heavily for George W. Bush, said the Political Nut, loudly enough to be heard in the bedroom above.

Besides, we sincere friends of freedom, he continued, should be ashamed of ourselves, proposing to improve the land of freedom by restricting ditto. If a better electorate is wanted, we lovers of laissez-faire should do the right thing and buy one. American votes have always been sold on a wholesale basis, from the Homestead Act of 1865 to present proposals to give free AndroGel testosterone rubs to horny Medicare geezers. Let us open the business to the retail trade.

Votes, vote options, vote futures, vote derivatives, and shares in vote mutual funds will be purchased through NASDAQ, auctioned on eBay, or bought off the shelf at Sam's Club. You may sell your vote on the street corner or—during a recount in Florida—at Sotheby's. We'll each get one vote per political contest in our district, same as ever. But now we will be truly free to use that vote as we see fit and won't be forced to waste it with a Charlton Heston write-in for Ann Arbor city council.

The advantage to the poor is obvious. Come the second Tuesday in November, instead of Maxine Waters, they get food—or something, and anything would be easier to stomach than Maxine. The rich benefit as well. You RNC maximum contributors will receive real and actual power and not just an autographed photo of Tom Delay shaking your hand while his eyes work the room.

When the vote is deregulated and electoral majorities can be bought and sold without bureaucratic interference, the result will be governance on the corporate shareholder model. Will this be an improvement? Let us compare Congress to the Justice Department's case against Microsoft.

No one is trying to break up the House of Representatives because it's been too successful.

Of course, there are potential drawbacks to an open market at the polls. Rich liberals might spend all their money gaining control of America. But look around. They control it already. What's the dif? And if rich liberals spend all their money, they won't be rich enough to be liberals anymore.

Vote vending would be good for the economy. Here is an enormous new business enterprise with a customer base of almost 200 million people and practically zero start-up costs. More than 130 million potential customers are already "registered"—signed up for their slice of the American dream. Referendum buying would also force American politicians to learn at least something about economics—knowledge they have resisted acquiring for 224 years. Furthermore, plebiscite marketing gives the nation's campaign fund-raisers an incentive to enter rehabilitation programs, get well, and find honest jobs.

Most importantly, having a wide variety of useful and attractive ballots readily available at our local mall is the best way for us ordinary middle-American voters to enter the political arena and put our two cents in—two cents being about what our votes were worth this fall, everywhere except Florida.

4

DECEMBER 2000

How was your trip?" my wife asked. [I was returning from Las Vegas, where I had given an address to the National Association of People Without Enough to Do (NAPWETD).]

"I like it when Daddy goes away," said Muffin, clutching the martini-shaker plush toy I bought her at the airport gift shop.

Something is going on in Las Vegas that I don't understand, I said.

"Something besides blackjack and whether to draw on sixteen when the dealer is showing a face card?" asked my wife, who is of a mathematical turn of mind.

Las Vegas is one of the most peculiar cities in the world, I said, but apparently that's not enough. Las Vegas has decided to become all the world's other peculiar cities, too.

The gambling capital already has Paris Las Vegas and New York New York. In the Nevada version of the City of Lights, waiters never mock you for ordering in the local lingo. If something smells like a smoldering Doberman, you can safely call the fire department; it's not an existentialist smoking a Gauloise. And at New York New York you experience a wonderful, heartwarming phenomenon that the native Gothamite will never know: parking.

So far so good with the urban impersonators on the Strip, I said. Although one might prefer that the cities chosen were cities that really needed replacing, not to mention roulette and girlie shows. I suggest Dayton Ohio Las Vegas and Tehran Tehran.

But now there's something much more ambitious in the middle of the desert—Venice. A fellow named Sheldon Adelson has built The Venetian resort and casino. And according to its brochure, when Adelson announced his plans for The Venetian, he said, "We're not going to build a 'faux' Venice. We're going to build what is essentially the *real* Venice." This has given me a great idea for a magazine article: "Venice *vs.* The Venetian."

Anyone who can make a bagel and a lot of noise can create a convincing New York. And Paris as we know it today is mostly a recent fabrication. It's the product of urban renewal in the 1870s when the French government undertook an innovative program of slum clearance by killing all the members of the Paris Commune. But Venice is another matter—heir to Byzantium, progenitor of Marco Polo, patron of Titian, and inspiration to Lord Byron, who

Look'd to the wingèd Lion's marble piles,
Where Venice sate in state, throned on her hundred isles!

And they should get that wingèd lion treated, because marble piles sound very painful.

Anyway, there is a mystery to Venice, a soul, an essence—quite a strong essence on a hot August day when the tide is low in the Adriatic. Phew!

I actually met Sheldon Adelson when I visited The Venetian. I told him, "You didn't get the smell right."

"Can't do everything," he said. Although he certainly has tried. Pulling into the Ducal Palace's driveway, you can see St. Mark's Square, the clock tower with its clockwork Moors, the twin columns topped by St. Theodore and the winged lion of St. Mark that needs Preparation H, the Campanile, the Sansoviniana Library, the Ca' d'Oro palace, the Bridge of Sighs, and the Rialto. This is a lot more than you can see from the original Ducal Palace's driveway, especially since it doesn't have one.

Considering the desiccated landscape around Las Vegas, a city with an average rainfall of 4.2 inches a year, I would have thought Sheldon Adelson faced a major obstacle to building "the *real* Venice." After all, what was the main physical feature causing Venice to be Venice? Barbarians, as it turns out. Venice is built on a mudbank in the middle of a lagoon and is up to its Venetian blinds in water because of barbarians. Attila the Hun chased the Italians out there in A.D.453. So Sheldon Adelson was in luck. Las Vegas is filled with barbarians, particularly the kind who wear black socks and sandals and T-shirts and shorts to restaurants at night and leave their baseball caps on during dinner.

What is it with Americans? America's malls are full of clothing stores. America does almost nothing but shop. Then why are Americans dressed like Muffin when she's allowed to choose her own clothes? Except much fatter. Italians don't look like this. You don't catch Italians going into the Basilica di San Marco in flip-flops and a halter top with extra butt hanging out of their Speedos. But I digress. Venice *vs.* The Venetian. Is Venice as romantic as I remember it being, after nine Bellinis at Harry's Bar? Will video poker ever inspire a novella by Thomas Mann? Would it be easier to read than other Thomas Mann stuff? I'll provide the answer in my article. About the Bellinis, I mean. I could care less about Thomas Mann.

Now some people might think that Venice *vs.* The Venetian would be no contest. After all, Venice is the most romantic city on earth. I remember—when you and I were first married, dear—an evening in one of those beautiful mahogany *motoscafo* water taxis, coming back from Harry's to the Excelsior Hotel on Lido Beach. . . .

"It might have been a heck of a night," said my wife, "if you hadn't had nine Bellinis and wound up hanging over the gunwale."

Yes. Well, anyway, as you've pointed out, Venice *can* be handicapped in a contest with the Venetian. And actually I think you and I did another good job of handicapping it, last year, when we returned by car (we weren't thinking *that* through) in the middle of winter with a two-year-old in tow.

Then there's the matter of taking one's wife to Venice at all. Nothing personal, darling. It's just that wives *will* want one of those Murano glass chandeliers that's the size of a sailing dinghy even though our dining room ceiling is less than eight feet high, and this would leave all the handblown dangling glass chandelier stuff dragging in the butter dish. . . .

"The butter dish that was the *only* thing you'd let me buy in Murano. And which you broke by stubbing out a cigar in it," said my wife.

Plus there's the matter of getting a chandelier into the overhead bin on the return flight, I said. Furthermore, Murano chandeliers cost as much as . . . as much as the water-taxi fare from where the autostrade runs out of dry land to the dock at the Gritti Palace Hotel. And let's not talk about what the Gritti Palace costs. A phone number. That's in dollars. The trail of zeros from the Italian lire hotel bill spilled off one receipt page and filled two others.

However, we did have a good time last year, even though there is practically nowhere in Venice that you can push a stroller without going into the drink or carrying it up and down the stairs on those cute little bridges, Venice being woefully behindhand in Americans with Disabilities Act compliance.

And you can't take the toddler out of the stroller because Italians are too nonchalant—or too short on tort lawyers—to put guard rails along the canals. Also, the balusters on the cute little bridges are spaced so far apart that toddlers are tempted to run a quarterback draw even on fourth down and ten. You recall the one time we did let go of Muffin's hand, in the middle of St. Mark's Square? A Japanese tourist handed the child an open bag of bird feed, and ten thousand filthy pigeons reenacted the climactic ten minutes of Alfred Hitchcock's *The Birds* on our baby daughter's head. Don't order squab in Venice—or, come to think of it, for God's sake, *do*.

Las Vegas was a very different experience. For one thing, I was alone. And I had a good-sized wad of cash—a financial windfall resulting from your failure to buy a Murano chandelier. [Hint to husbands wishing to avoid chandelier purchases: When you go to the Murano glass shops take a two-year-old. And turn her loose. This is expensive, but not as expensive as the chandelier. Your wife won't have time to buy anything anyway because all three of you are going to get the bum's rush from every glass shop on the island.]

But is The Venetian "essentially the *real* Venice"? For a Venice that's on the wrong continent, in the middle of a dust bowl, and was built last year, The Venetian is surprisingly authentic. The Campanile, for instance, is fake, but so's the one in really real Venice. The original Campanile, completed in 1173, collapsed in a heap in 1902, and a replica was constructed in its place.

The Venetian's architectural unity is marred by a large, ugly, modern parking garage. Ditto Venice's. The Autorimessa Comunale is on the Piazza Roma, and getting a space in it is more of a crap shoot than anything in Las Vegas. Then there's Giorgio Armani, Dolce & Gabbana, Donna Karan, and Calvin Klein. Are these brands for sale along the Grand Canal in Venice or along the Grand Canal in The Venetian? Both. Plus The Venetian's Grand Canal is not only indoors, it's on the second floor. I'd like to see Venice's famed Renaissance architect Jacopo Sansovino pull that off. Not that I'd let him try. When Sansovino was building his namesake Libreria Sansoviniana in 1545, the roof fell in and Sansovino went to prison for a while. Nevada has too many tort lawyers for Sheldon Adelson to let something like that happen. And Adelson's Libreria Sansoviniana is not, like Sansovino's, filled with musty old books that you aren't allowed to touch. It contains Madame Tussaud's Celebrity Encounter. You aren't allowed to touch things there either, but who'd want to touch a wax Wayne Newton?

However, back to the Grand Canal. The gondolas don't actually go anyplace in the indoor version, just back and forth. But they don't actually go anyplace in the outdoor version—just around in circles until your wallet is empty and your head is ringing with a pidgin English rendition of "That's Amore." And the American tourists in the Las Vegas gondolas look less uncomfortable than the American tourists in the Venice gondolas because, in Las Vegas, the gondolier isn't some sneering foreigner in suspiciously tight pants; he's a nice out-of-work actor or musician who feels just as dumb in the gondola as you do. Furthermore, the water in the Las Vegas Grand Canal is clean, chlorinated, and shallow. And if you do fall in, so what? There are enough coins on the bottom to play the slots for hours.

Most of the things that aren't authentic about The Venetian's Venice are, like the smell, an improvement. The ten thousand filthy pigeons of St. Mark's Square have been replaced with fifty trained white doves that are released for a brief flyby, on the hour, from 1 to 4 P.M. In the Grand Canal food court you can get—as opposed to authentic octopus in its own ink—pastrami with mustard on rye.

The suite we had at the Gritti Palace was half the size of the single I stayed in at The Venetian. The Venetian's room decor was not equal to the gilded ceiling mirror and ormolu bidet rococo of the Gritti, but I didn't mind. And I would have minded even less if I'd had, as we did in Italy, a two-year-old girl along. The walls of our rooms at the Gritti were certainly covered with enough paintings of the very naked mythological type. "Where their clothes go, Daddy? What's that? What's that? What's *that*?" And the Las Vegas Rialto Bridge has—bless those tort lawyers again—metal bars between the balusters to keep toddlers from getting a first down in the clean, chlorinated lagoon.

Las Vegas gambling is a terribly vulgar affair, of course. I certainly thought so after losing all my Murano savings at blackjack. But maybe some better-bred, more white-shoe sort of games of chance could be developed to suit the refined taste of those who appreciate nine Bellinis at Harry's Bar. Sending the children to Brown and betting that they don't become communists is a possibility, as is marrying chorus girls without getting prenuptial agreements.

And the entertainment at The Venetian C2K nightclub wasn't very good. A "tribute show" featured some guy who did pop music impressions, including all the stages of the Elvis career. But it could have been worse. An Italian doing impressions might have run through all the popes.

So, darling, our next European vacation is going to be spent in the Mojave. And yet . . . and yet . . . there's something about the damp, smelly, expensive Venice of old. Maybe it's the gleam in your eye (although I suspect that's the Murano chandelier), or maybe it's the thought of what Shakespeare's *The Merchant of Las Vegas* would be like.

ACT I, SCENE III
Shylock to Antonio:
If you repay me not on such a day,
In such a place, such sum or sums as are
Express'd in the condition, let the forfeit
Be nominated for an equal pound
Of your fair flesh. . . .
Enter "Porsche," scantily dressed.
A *pound* of flesh? Here's *a hundred and sixteen pounds!*
With a pair of D-cups! And get a load of these gams!

Talking Points for a Discussion Between My Wife and Me About Whether to Spend Our Next Vacation in Venice or Las Vegas

VEGAS	vs.	VENICE
Wear authentic straw hats	GONDOLIERS	Wear leather jackets and talk on cell phones
Yes	SEAT BELTS IN GONDOLAS?	*Scusi?*
Too many	TORT LAWYERS	Not enough
Too many	ELVIS IMPRESSIONS	Not enough
Too many	WAX WAYNE NEWTONS	Not enough
Connects shopping mall with parking garage	BRIDGE OF SIGHS	Provides Byron's view of wingèd lion with painful itch (*Childe Harold's Pilgrimage* Canto IV, stanza 1)
Yippie-ki-yay!	RODEO IN TOWN?	No, but a big roundup was under way with police corralling Nigerian hawkers of knockoff Prada bags
No	"KOOKED CLUMS IN FRIED PAN" ON MENU?	*Si, buono!*
Script for *Viva Las Vegas*—asks existential question, "Who was Elvis impersonating?"	KEY LITERARY WORK	*Across the River and Into the Trees*—portrait of the artist when he's over the hill and into the Bellinis
Death in Las Vegas—late-in-life Thomas Mann attempts a second career as a stand-up comic at the Dunes	KEY LITERARY WORK YET TO BE WRITTEN	*Fear and Loathing in Venice*—machine-gun-toting carabinieri make short work of Raoul Duke and his Samoan attorney
Don't know	DRAW ON 16 IF DEALER HAS FACE CARD SHOWING?	*Non capisco*

Making out our Christmas list? I said to my wife, who was making out our Christmas list.

"Yes."

[My wife has chosen the Christmas presents ever since the year we gave her parents a vacation trip. The "See Ireland's Back Roads Like You've Never Seen Them Before" holiday package, on which I got a very good price, featuring a glass-bottom-bus tour.]

I'll browse through the mail-order catalogs, I said, and make helpful suggestions. Look, here's a miniature closet from the gift shop at the New York Museum of Affordable Two-Bedroom Apartments. And check this out: the *It Takes a Village Catalog,* with quotes from Hillary Clinton about each product. We'll have to get a "Socktapus" for the neighbors' children. It turns eight used men's dress socks into a creative toy.

"I believe the neighbors' children are in their forties," said my wife.

That's okay. Hillary Clinton says, "Often a sock turned into a hand puppet is enough to fascinate them for hours."

The World of Remainders Bookstore, I continued, has an interesting offer: "Buy two of our books and we'll pulp one for free." They've got a wide selection of Frappaccino Table Books. *The Worst Golf Courses in the World* is only $4.95, in color. Your dad would like that. You should see the water hazard at the Marianas Trench Club. And the ninth hole at the Grozny Par-3 has tank traps all around the green. *The Illustrated Guide to Adventure Bowling* would be good for your sister. She likes the outdoors. There's an amazing photograph on the cover of a guy making a 7-10 split on the north face of K-2. Speaking of which, the *X-Treme Sports Company Catalog* has a family road luge for $395. Dad sits up front, Sis and Junior ride outrigger, Mom's on the brake. Could be fun when we have another kid. Says it's been highway tested from the Rockies to the Alps and is safe up to speeds of seventy miles per hour. They're also offering a wheelchair-access Stairmaster.

I see *Bad Dog Pet Supplies* is trying to broaden its market. They're having an introductory sale on Bulgari shock collars, "perfect for wives who range too far and so beautiful and chic she won't be able to resist wearing it." Shocks can be adjusted from "reminder buzz" to "mortal" and programmed via cell phone to operate worldwide.

Wait, here's my favorite, the *Long-Pig Specialty Food Catalog*. They've got a new line of naturally sugar-sweetened desserts "for that saccharine flavor without harmful chemical additives." And baby beluga whale veal straight from Japan. And an entire section on cooking with popcorn. Orville Redenbacher's Deluxe Turkey Dressing "lets a small bird feed the whole family." The popcorn-stuffed grape leaves look exciting, not to mention the ravioli. Did you know we can give a gift membership to the Lunch Meat of the Month Club? January is Vietnamese Puppywurst. And there's a resort in Idaho where you can dig your own potatoes. The Midwest "Gor-Met" Basket of Cheer includes Ice Cheese from Wisconsin, canned Baloney-O's—you don't see those on the East Coast—and Liquid Chicken. Mom used to use that for baking cookies. Then there's the Grub-to-Go products from famous restaurants, such as the Tort Sauce they serve at the Ms. Steak chain, where all the waitresses are dressed as lawyers; the toothpick-flavored after-dinner mints from Doe's Eat Place in Little Rock, and the House of Blues' unique blue-flavored frozen yogurts: blue-point oyster, bluefish, or Bluebonnet Margarine with real oleo added. Here's something that might be good for New Year's Eve, a Piñata Colada Kit that lets you hang from the ceiling while drinking blindfolded. And a perfect stocking stuffer for Muffin, little jars of Baby Soul Food—mashed chitlins with grits, strained catfish and collard greens, hog jowls in hominy. Did you know that *Long-Pig* carries genuine Jamaican Goatmeal? Oatmeal with natural goat flavoring. I'll bet my godson's vegan sister would love that. Only goat droppings are used, so no actual goats are exploited while obtaining their flavor.

But I'm afraid my wife missed that last helpful suggestion, having left the room rather hurriedly.

The Political Nut who lives around here came in just then, as he tends to do when my wife goes out. This year, for Christmas, he said, I think I'll buy everybody a copy of Pat Buchanan's new book about the American Indian, *I Have My Reservations*. Serves 'em right for giving the popular vote to Al Gore.

You know, the Political Nut went on, I'll bet a lot of people think I'm upset by all the legal challenges to George W. Bush's victory in Florida. Nope. I'm too excited about Hillary Clinton's win in New York. Gosh, I wanted Hillary to get that Senate seat—the one Pat Moynihan had for years until he misplaced it after a long lunch. Is it too late to send five dollars to Hillary's campaign fund? Make that ten dollars, because she got gypped on the $1.7 million house in Chappaqua. From Whitewater to Castle Grande to Palestinian statehood, Hillary has always been dumb about real estate. And a lot of other things. And why not? If you think about it, she's just another Suzy Loser with endless man troubles living in public housing at the taxpayer's expense. What's she know? Actually, I can answer that question because I watched her television interviews, listened to her speeches, and read her appalling newspaper columns.

Fortunately a U.S. Senate seat was open. The Founding Fathers, in their wisdom, devised a method by which our republic can take one hundred of its most prominent numskulls and keep them out of the private sector, where they might do actual harm. At any given moment a full five score of America's largest corporations are being spared Paul Wellstone as CEO. This could be the entire secret of America's economic advantage over western Europe and Japan. Let Hillary loose in the free enterprise system, and the New York Stock Exchange winds up like Madison Savings and Loan. Our 401k's will be invested in Arkansas pea patches.

And I'm glad that Hillary was elected, because this is fitting punishment for a person who has made a fatuous claim to be a mover and shaker, who believes she is a political colossus, and who thinks the earth trembles from her great progressive strides. Into the tar pit of the Senate with you, you soon-to-be-extinct mastodon of Poli Sci, you fossil in pants suit. Let's watch you squeal and bellow as you sink helplessly to the very bottom of the seniority system ooze.

Furthermore, putting Hillary in the Senate keeps Rudolph Giuliani out.

"She didn't run against Giuliani," said my wife, emerging from the powder room with a cold washcloth pressed against her forehead. "Giuliani dropped out when he got sick. He has prostate cancer."

Just like Vince Foster! said the Political Nut. This is the kind of thing that happens to everybody who crosses the Clintons. I'm being watched myself. Just the other day I found a piece of paper in the pocket of my new Dockers that said INSPECTED BY NO. 4. Giuliani wasn't needed in the Senate. Rudi is a cold, angry, vengeful martinet of a man—exactly the person that we 263 million Americans who don't live in New York City want that town to have as its mayor. Rudi's what New Yorkers have deserved for years. I hope he recovers and stays mayor forever—if not of New York, then of some other horrible city. Seattle leaps to mind. Ah, the Nose Ring Leash Law of 2003.

But saving the economy, bugging Soho twits, and bringing snot-bobbers to heel are mere fringe benefits to a Hillary election. The real prize is a guaranteed six years of Hillary in high-profile public exposure. Consider what this means to Republican fund-raising efforts. That little smirk of hers, that faint suggestion of a self-cherishing pout, is worth thirty million a year to the GOP, easy. Here is a woman who can give $30 million to fight the good fight without—literally—lifting a finger. A small change in the shape of her pie hole, and we're rich.

We're rich. And we're smart. Suddenly we're thinking critically again. The theatrical craft, the special effects, the stage business of the New Democrats made us almost forget that liberalism has a plot. Hillary's role is to remind us of the scheme: Liberals plan to take everything and give it to bad actors as a reward for talking crap. Speaking of bad actors, we've lacked a villain. Pickled, lardy Ted won't do. Jeering Ted Kennedy is like making fun of Falstaff at the end of *Henry IV, Part II*. Lady-Macbeth-in-a-headband, however, will more than suffice. And what's that she's trying to get off her hands? Bill, probably. Those hands of Hillary's will be busy in any case. Rest assured, no mulligatawny of social legislation will be served up in the Senate without Hillary's thumb in the soup bowl. She has ideas about everything—education, minimum wage, earned-income tax credits, college tuition, Social Security, Medicare, the national debt, and making "a mean tossed salad," just to mention a few of the subjects I recall being touched upon during her campaign kickoff speech. Hillary has ideas the way Arkansas has cars on blocks. Ideas are to Hillary what sex is to her husband—something to be had indiscriminately and often and the results of which, thank goodness, go right down the drain. And every time Hillary gets one of these ideas she starts exercising the smugness muscles with which the Liberal face is so richly endowed. Her mouth compresses in a suck-purse grimace. Her lips form a simper of sanctity. And then—oh, man, it's triple cherries on the campaign chest slots!—treasure just comes tumbling into the laps of the prudent and the wise.

"Um," said my wife, "anything good on TV tonight?"

The Political Nut picked up the cable guide. There's *Amal and the Oslo Peace Process, No Room at the Homeless Shelter, or The Grinch Who Stole Kwanza—and Your VCR.*

"Still working on Christmas Eve?" said my young assistant, Max.

I'm rewriting famous tragedies for Democrats, I said. I figure that, after the tragedy Democrats suffered in the Supreme Court, they need a little cheering up.

"Do they?" said Max. "Hillary just got an eight-million-dollar book contract with Simon and Schuster."

Yes, but Pope John Paul the Second got eight-point-five million, and he's pro-life. Anyway, I want to do something to help the healing process begin. At the moment, Democrats are doubtless feeling that tragedy, as an artistic form, does not respect the public will. Therefore I've fixed *An American Tragedy* by Theodore Dreiser. Reproductive rights have been preserved by courageous moderates in a narrowly divided Congress. Roberta Alden is able to obtain an abortion. She sues Clyde Griffiths for sexual harassment in the workplace. Roberta's lawyer is the local heiress—and former Griffiths love interest—Sondra Fichley. Fichley saw Theodore Dreiser interviewed on TV by Diane Sawyer, read *An American Tragedy,* became a feminist, and went to law school.

Faust, a sensitive adolescent who is suffering painful alienation caused by the pressures of conformity in a materialistic society with suburban sprawl, is able to connect to other lonely teens who worship Satan through Internet chat rooms. Thus a nurturing sense of community is fostered. Faust decides to sell his soul to the Devil. His single-parent mother is supportive, and society respects his alternative spirituality. The Pew Charitable Trust endows a chair in Satanism at the Harvard School of Divinity. Faust (that's *Doctor* Faust, now, thank you) writes a best-selling book, *Hades in the Balance,* which is turned into a critically acclaimed series on PBS.

Oedipus Rex thinks he has killed his father and married his mother. Of course he does. At some level, all men in Western cultures believe this. Fortunately Oedipus and Jocasta go into therapy, work on communicating, and avoid a prolonged custody battle over the Sphinx after their divorce. Since health care reform has been recently enacted in Thebes, Oedipus is able to get his crippled feet reconstructed, thereby raising his self-esteem and leading him to form a better-adjusted relationship with his new partner. The Riddle of the Sphinx, by the way, is: "What requires extensive government programs as a child and an elder but needs to pay a lot of taxes in between if he's a white male?"

Because multiculturalism is taught in Algerian schools, Camus's "stranger" understands the oppressive nature of French colonial rule in North Africa. He becomes politically committed and moves to Paris, where he causes the downfall of Adolf Hitler's vast right-wing conspiracy by writing poems, plays, and novels.

Anna Karenina leaves her husband to pursue a career with the military but discovers that proper day care is not available for her child. She almost throws herself under a train. Her support group stages an intervention. Anna decides to run for an open Duma seat in a distant oblast. She introduces needful legislation protecting children's rights.

In *A Tale of Two Cities* (now set in Washington, D.C., and Austin, Texas), David Boies regains his legal reputation by using DNA evidence to obtain Sidney Carton's release from death row. Carton becomes a tireless advocate for abolition of capital punishment and the WTO. The whole world has a revolution that brings social justice to all.

It is in the works of Shakespeare, however, where I've found the most fruitful material for rewrites. Perhaps this is because Shakespeare, like the modern Democratic Party, has certain identity issues that I feel we should honor. A critical reading of Shakespeare's texts leads me to believe that the Bard of Avon was a minority-college-student-male-inner-city-soccer-mom who belonged to an ecology-friendly labor union.

I need hardly say that Lear receives appropriate medication (for free, with Medicare prescription benefits) and realizes that Goneril and

Regan are strong independent women with lives of their own who are members of the "sandwich generation" that finds itself burdened by both child- and elder-care responsibilities. When Cordelia gets back from her fellowship year in France studying textual deconstruction, she helps Lear find a cheerful assisted-living facility. The Fool is symbolic of HMOs.

Hamlet understands the Freudian implications of seeing his father's "ghost." With the help of a sympathetic mental-health professional recommended by Polonius, Hamlet comes to terms with his true feelings for "Uncle" Claudius, who subsequently leaves Gertrude. Hamlet and Claudius are married in Vermont. Ophelia's attempt to drown herself is recognized as a plea for help. She has an eating disorder.

Thanks to timely intervention by the president of the United States (a Democrat), the Capulets and Montagues are engaged in negotiations that lead to mutual respect and understanding. Meanwhile, UN peacekeeping troops have brought calm to the streets of Verona. Romeo and Juliet engage in some youthful sexual experimentation, normal for their age. Fortunately, Mr. Laurence, a former Catholic friar who now heads the local chapter of Planned Parenthood, has instituted a program providing free contraceptives at Romeo and Juliet's high school. A citywide midnight basketball league rescues Mercutio and Tybalt from gang involvement. But Juliet's nurse spends many sleepless nights in her quest for universal health care because, tragically, 35 percent of Verona's citizens still lack adequate medical insurance.

Affirmative action helps Othello achieve a high position in the Venetian political system, where he works to achieve economic fairness and the elimination of prejudice based on race, gender, and sexual orientation. Othello's leadership is undercut when Iago gains a majority in the Venetian House of Representatives. Othello almost wins the following election but has his victory stolen from him by means of politically manipulated ballot undercounts in a southern peninsula of Venice. Now, *that's* a tragedy.

5

JANUARY 2001

Tonight is the actual beginning of the new millennium, I said. [We journalists are great repositories of such knowledge.]

"I notice nobody's going on about Y2.001K bugs," said my wife, looking up from a long list of New Year's resolutions headed "P.J."

I could have told the world nothing would happen. In fact, I probably did tell the world nothing would happen. Let me look through my article clippings. After all, you know what computers do?

"I *do* know," said my wife. "But *you* had better ask Max."

What they do is count. They count very fast. But that's all they do. So here we have a machine, all it does is count, and someone tells me it can't count to 2000? *I* can count to 2000.

"Given enough time," said my wife.

There is some deep-seated need in humans to believe things are awful, I said.

"Also," said my wife, "a deep-seated need to pay the rent. My guess is that Y2K was a tidy little moneymaker for obsolete computer experts about your age. They'd been out of work for years until they hit upon the idea of saying, 'Oh, my gosh, back when we were making all those punch cards for Univac, we forgot to put in the number after 1999.'"

We always were a resilient generation, I said.

"Bill Clinton, for example," said my wife.

He was the perfect *fin de siècle* president. The end of a century is notoriously an era of decline and dissolution. And in this case it was the *fin de* whole thousand years. We wrapped up a Mauve Decade for all time, mooning the ages with our big hairy *ars gratia artis* of Platinum Card bonus-upgrade dilettantism, high-yield neurasthenia, and heavily leveraged degeneration of manners and morals. Awful decadence reigned. "It is made up," said the awfully decadent poet Paul Verlaine, "of carnal spirit and unhappy flesh and of all the violent splendors of . . . the collapse among the flames of races exhausted by the power of feeling, to the invading sound of enemy trumpets."

"Or," said my wife, "the sound of George W. Bush trying to speak in public."

We were bored and surfeited, I said. We sought strange forms of sensuality. Pretty darn strange, to judge by the president, the fat girl, and the sink in the Oval Office pantry. The 1990s were the time of the ten-cent conscience brandishing the twenty-dollar cigar. Corruption was considered a mere luxury, mere luxury was had in dreadful excess, and dreadful excess was . . . just dreadful. Also excessive. Our institutions crumbled. Right and wrong lost their meanings. Men wore shorts in public. Young women from good families got tattooed on parts of their bodies that young women from good families didn't used to know they had. Aerosmith was still on tour. Decay was all I saw before me. I saw a pale, unhealthy overripeness. I saw flaccidity. I saw—

"Yourself in the mirror with your clothes off," said my wife.

I'll almost miss the decadence, I said.

"What decadence?" asked my wife.

All those nights we stayed up till dawn.

"The baby was teething."

* * *

Oh, well. It was an era of decline and dissolution, anyway. Unfortunately the dissolute thing that was going downhill was me. It was ever thus—at least since the first century B.C., when porky, middle-aged blowhard Horace wrote, "The age of our parents, inferior to that of our grandparents, brought forth ourselves, who are more worthless still and destined to have children still more corrupt."

People over fifty always think things are going to heck in a handbasket, or in one of those Prada backpacks, or in something. The world has been collapsing for more than two thousand years. Either the world was once a very wonderful place with a long way to fall (of which there is no historical evidence) or people my age are full of crap. They certainly were in the late 1800s, when decadence and Paul Verlaine were last being denounced.

The scholar Richard Gilman, in his scholarly book *Decadence: The Strange Life of an Epithet,* points out that there was nothing actually decadent about the French *décadents*. Verlaine, Rimbaud, Huysmans, and Baudelaire were sometimes preposterous and often creepy, likewise their English confreres Oscar Wilde and Aubrey Beardsley. But decadence (from the medieval Latin "to fall away") means decrepitude, debilitation, senescence. These words do not describe *Les Fleurs du Mal*, *The Picture of Dorian Gray*, and the illustrations in the *Yellow Book*. The art of the *fin de siècle* before this one was alarmingly vigorous and shockingly new—*and* preposterous and creepy, but more from the bumptiousness of callow youth than from the dissipations of jaded age.

What the artsy types were up to was a rebellion against the cuteness-loving, happy, upright, optimistic bourgeoisie of the nineteenth century. Paul Verlaine was bugging the squares. This is what Dr. Dre, Pokémon, and Calista Flockhart have been doing to me, with notable success. And everything else is bugging me, too. I'm at that stage in life where everything does. I call it *decadence* because I'd like to think that all of creation is turning into a superannuated poop at the same rate as myself.

But if I take my acid reflux medicine and blood pressure pills and look at life with a gimlet eye (vodka gimlet, make that a double), the world appears to be a healthy young place.

The human race has not decayed. People are longer-lived and more prosperous than they've ever been and are breeding like gerbils. Some of my querulous age-mates feel that's a bad thing and, taking an example from elsewhere in order Rodentia, claim people are breeding like lemmings. I don't know. If the earth's population ever runs off a cliff, it will probably be because we've all decided to take up hang gliding at the same time.

Perhaps the environment has been degraded. It's certainly fashionable to say so. But I have always held with writer Larry L. King that "The world would be a better place if it was half-dark, indoors, and air-conditioned." Set up the high-resolution digital TV in the McMansion great room, and, lo, it's coming true. Meanwhile, species extinction is sad, in a way, but it's nonetheless pleasant to go get the paper in the morning without being bothered by pterodactyls. And a mastodon would wreck the lawn.

Western civilization is full of vim, expanding on all fronts and doing lots better than any other civilization has lately. Contrast it, for instance, with the civilization of the Plains Indians. Our friends don't come back from abroad complaining that London is jammed with families in feathered headdresses dragging travois through Piccadilly Circus or that Rome is full of franchised restaurants serving fast dog.

And business and industry flourish, or at least I hope they will, if the Fed cuts interest rates enough.

As for culture, I'm sure there's plenty extant. I don't happen to understand it. But that's the point. If artists wanted to be understood, Raffi and the lady who writes the poems for the "With Deepest Sympathy" greeting card line would be our most revered cultural figures.

I find no evidence that we've been living in a particularly tired or desiccated period. The epoch is pressed by the eager swellings of fecundity and tumescence—albeit with help from little blue pills and in vitro fertilization for forty-five-year-old career women. It is a green and growing day. We sojourn midst a riot of vigor.

I guess. And yet there's a whiff of rot in the air. Putrefaction wasn't absent from the millennium's end. Something stinks. One doesn't need to be a geezer using a dial phone to call the truant officer on Britney Spears to think that decadence is real.

If we examine the spirit, the essence of the twentieth century, it's surprising how much of that zeitgeist has already become nouvelle cuisine for worms. Most of the woolly concepts and great slobbering ideals that ran wild through the past hundred years—chewing the slippers of custom and ruining tradition's rug—are now roadkill on the path to the future or buried behind the intellectual garage with phrenology, Zoroastrianism, and the rest of mankind's dead mental pets.

We are surrounded by the decomposing remains of things that, just a few years ago, seemed so modern. *Modern,* for example—the word is now mainly used on tags at yard sales to increase the price of ugly lamps. Modern lamps were the product of Modern Design, which was the product of Modern Art, a product that turned ugly because its producers thought art should constantly change. Art quickly ran out of things to change into that weren't stupid. The modernists believed that artistic creativity—like the manufacture of kitchen appliances or flint spear points—should progress. This is like believing that sex appeal should progress. Sandra Bullock has a marvelous behind. Now if only she could grow a third buttock.

Modern designers responded to modern artists by making furniture that was comfortable for people with three buttocks—and nobody else. And modern architects cooperated by building homes and offices of such astonishing ugliness that random drools of paint on canvas, bum-punishing armchairs, and light fixtures from yard sales looked good inside, by comparison. This was all visionary stuff in its day. This was how we were all going to live. This was the future. Now it's the decor theme of retro martini bars.

As went the visual arts, so went the others. John Cage, Philip Glass, and the rest of the Atonal Def Crew proved that, if you abandon rhythm, melody, harmony, and so forth, you get noise; anyone with a toddler and a piano in the house could have told them this. Dance became so silly that tap shoes and Irish bog stomps are being taken seriously. Theatergoers grew bored enough waiting for Godot that they didn't mind when Andrew Lloyd Webber showed up. Modern prose stylists, taking possession of the vast and fabulous mansion that was the nineteenth-century novel, burned the house down to get the nails. And poets? Comparisons being odious, only a comparison will do to illustrate the odium of modern poesy.

Here is Robert Frost, last of the antiques, celebrating the inauguration of old-fashioned high-binder John F. Kennedy:

Some poor fool has been saying in his heart
Glory is out of date in life and art.
Our venture in revolution and outlawry
Has justified itself in freedom's story
Right down to now in glory upon glory.

Not Keats, perhaps, but not bad, and with interesting use of the dactyl and amphibrach in the final tercet.

Now here is Maya Angelou, foremost of the contemporaries, at the inauguration of that most modern of all presidents, Bill Clinton:

A Rock, A River, A Tree
Host to species long since departed
Marked the mastodon,
The dinosaur, who left dried tokens
Of their sojourn here
On our planet floor.

No rhyme, no meter, and it's about dinosaur turds. Maya Angelou, celebrating the most solemn and momentous ritual of the republic, can think of nothing to write about except dinosaur turds—and that mastodon who'd be playing the devil with our dethatching and reseeding if it weren't, like modern poetry, mercifully extinct.

The works of Ms. Angelou do, however, prove that art does not progress. And it's good to have that proven. Because the modern progressive art of the twentieth century was just a come-on, a shill, a barker for a whole brain circus of much larger and more dangerous modern progressive ideas.

Fascism, for one. What was that about? Only a generation ago this political movement almost conquered the world. Now we have to look it up in an encyclopedia to find out what it was. Fascists must have been reactionaries because that's the other word we always called them when we were calling the draft board fascists in the 1960s. And yet, in the 1920s and 1930s, fascists considered themselves way-modern and a hot source of progress. They had admirers ranging from Charles Lindbergh and the Duke of Windsor to that arch instigator of modern poetry Ezra Pound, who was jailed for treason and not, alas, for his verse.

Fascism sought to bring people together, to heal the fragmentation of society, to remedy the alienation that the individual feels in the ruthlessly competitive atmosphere of the free market. But, at the same time, fascism wanted to preserve and improve all the material benefits of industrialism and trade. So far it sounds—as I've pointed out before—like a New Democrat's campaign platform. But instead of recounting votes in Palm Beach County, Mussolini, Hitler, Franco, and Tojo believed they could accomplish their aims with mindless patriotism, genocide, and secret police. It didn't work.

Neither did communism. Communism was the notion that, if you took everything away from people and made them go sit in Siberia, people would behave like perfect little angels. Communism was hell's own time-out, Mom being Joseph Stalin. It fizzled when permissive parent Mikhail Gorbachev put a VCR and some *Blue's Clues* tapes in Yakutsk so the little gulagers wouldn't cry.

The wonder is that communism lasted so long. But, then again, modern poetry lasted a long time too. Communism appealed to the kind of progressive intellectuals who liked to read dinosaur-turd sonnets while sitting on Bauhaus ass-crampers inside Le Corbusier terrariums lit by yard-sale lamps. They could dig the modern literature and design because it seemed so dumb that anybody—even a progressive intellectual—could do it. And the same went for thinking the large thoughts behind communism. Everyone knows that life ought to be fair and that God's a lousy guy for not making it happen. Everyone should get what everyone else gets. And, if everyone gets broke, hungry, and dead, well, fair's fair.

Then there was communism's weak-tea sister, socialism. Socialists maintained that we shouldn't take all the money away from all the people since all the people don't have money. We should take all the money away from only the people who make money. Then, when we run out of that, we could take more money from the people who . . . hey, wait! Where'd you people go? What do you mean you're "tax exiles in Monaco"?

And last, and most dead, but not quite sure whether to lie down, is liberalism. Liberals believe that bad things are bad. Except for people. There are no bad people, just bad things that people do. Such as start wars. That's a bad thing. A very bad thing. There's nothing worse than war. Unless it's the war in Kosovo where liberals saved a bunch of people's lives or would have if those people hadn't gotten killed first. That was a good thing. Liberals, even the liberal draft-dodgers in the Clinton White House, agreed that the war in Kosovo was a good thing. Liberals believe that good things are good. Prosperity is a good thing. There's nothing better than prosperity. Unless the prosperity is in the alienated suburbs where "smart growth" has not been practiced. Then it causes teenagers to kill everyone in their high school. Which shows that weapons are a bad thing. A very bad thing. Unless the people who *didn't* dodge the draft use the weapons in Kosovo when the people who did dodge the draft tell them to.

Since the time of Jimmy Carter, liberals have been chasing their tail, and, last heard, they'd caught it and begun eating and had chewed their way up to the back of their own ears.

The ridiculous abstractions of the twentieth century were not, however, limited to the artistic and the political. The social sciences plagued almost the whole hundred years. It wasn't until we were in college and looking for gut courses so we could slide through senior year that we realized Anthropology is just travel writing about places that don't have room service, Sociology is journalism without news, and Psychology is peeking into your sister's diary after your parents have sent her to rehab. Freudian psychology was more interesting but, unfortunately, it was past its sell-by date before I started searching for an easy B in a class that met after 11 A.M.

As for why our folks shipped Sis to Silver Hill, Sigmund Freud held that the whole problem with everything in life is that we want to boff the 'rents. What was this guy snorting? In point of fact, Sigmund *was* whacked on blow most of the time. Go down to the Jacuzzi at the assisted-living facility and take a look at Mom and Dad in their swimsuits. No. Way.

Psychology, of course, is not an issue anymore. We discovered that if you're crazy you can take drugs. Unless you're crazy *because* you've been taking drugs. In that case you can stop taking drugs and start taking other drugs.

Philosophy is not an issue anymore either. Amazing to think that people once took philosophy seriously. They would sit around Plato's symposium for days at a time asking each other, "What is truth?" while Plato ran his hand up under their togas. But philosophy topped out with Existentialism.

It must have been a great moment, in that Paris café with a bunch of French guys who were one Pernod over the line, when suddenly Sartre (or maybe it was Camus) said, "I'm me! Here I am! This is now! And here I am right now being me!"

There were, I believe, further developments in twentieth-century philosophy, but the class was at 9 A.M. and mathematical symbols were involved, and getting a B would have meant breaking into the professor's office and stealing the exam.

There was also a sort of general informal philosophy afoot in the twentieth century. This came into full blossom in the 1960s. The dictionary word for it is *antinomism*, although we usually say *whatever*. The basic idea—assuming there was a basic idea, which there wasn't—was *anything goes*.

Everything went. And when it went it didn't go well. The wild, prophetic voices of the sixties can still be heard muttering in doorways and begging with paper cups. And the nonconformists long ago exhausted the supply of stuff with which not to conform. They've been reduced to wearing tongue studs.

The rest of us got over it, the same way we got over sexual liberation when we found out that the viruses were having all the reproductive fun. We got over feminism, too. At least you women did—the moment you were hired for those prestigious jobs that only men used to have. It turns out work sucks. I don't know what women thought we were doing at the office all day. Maybe we needed a double vodka gimlet when we got home because we were tuckered out from all the prestige. Furthermore, women discovered that, even if they were running the State Department, they still had to take care of the kids. Not that we men didn't want to help, but if you leave us in charge, the rug monkeys wind up with their mouths diapered, watching the Spice Channel instead of *Sesame Street*, and when they open their school lunches there's a Tickle-Me Elmo with mayo between two slices of rye.

The forces that drove the twentieth century are now driving off the ends of the earth. The nationalism that caused the wealthiest and most sophisticated nations to sacrifice ten million of their citizens in World War I now causes an occasional Slobodan Milosevic. The religious zealotry that once shook empires now shakes Afghanistan, the Gaza Strip, and the New Hampshire presidential primary. Even capitalism teeters since we entered the information age. These days a successful business depends not on an enormous accumulation of capital but on an enormous accumulation of—if I properly understand what Charles Schwab has been telling me—bullshit.

Things were rotten at the end of the old millennium. But that's okay. They were rotten things. The bullshit of capitalism, the offal of fanatic beliefs, the moldy fruit of goofball thinking—they're compost now. Mix the offscourings of the twentieth-century mind with the loam of human hope and effort and you get fertile soil and a badly strained metaphor.

Like most annoying older people who don't have a life, I garden. I know about these things. Think of the garden bed out back as being enriched with theories, conceits, abstractions, and orthodoxies that had been festering in a large, wilted heap since the modern era ran out of steam about the time *Sgt. Pepper* was released. And bursting from this garden covered in organic spoil there teems, in wild abundance, a new and vigorous crop of . . . Christina Aguilera, Compassionate Conservatism, and PalmPilots.

Weeds! Damn weeds! Just like in my real garden. Nothing but useless, ugly weeds spreading everywhere, as high as my head. Decline and dissolution? I wish. I've got to go get the brush hog and a fifty-gallon drum of Agent Orange.

* * *

"Honey, that's ridiculous. There's a foot of snow outside," said my wife, who I don't think had been listening closely.

Well, all the more reason not to go to the neighbors' New Year's Eve party, I said.

"That and the fact that we weren't invited and they aren't speaking to us."

You don't mind staying home, do you? I consider New Year's Eve to be the Special Olympics of inebriation. I thought we'd just sit here, build a fire, and I'd do a little research on the article I'm writing about how to get drunk.

"Well," said my wife, "even if *I* drive, I'd probably flunk the Breathalyzer just from kissing you at midnight."

Puritans! I said. America is plagued by puritans. It always has been plagued by puritans. Take the Puritans, just for instance. Within a year of landing at Plymouth Rock they had dragged the poor Wampanoag Indians to one of those family Thanksgivings full of religious aunts, Rotarian uncles, and Donna Shalala–type girl cousins all eating overdone turkey, with no booze in the log shelter and nothing worth popping in the bathroom medicine cabinet. And I'll bet the meal was timed so that the Wampanoag tribe missed the Michigan/Michigan State kickoff. Then there was the eighteenth-century Great Awakening, the nineteenth-century Revival Movement, twentieth-century Prohibition, and now cable TV advertisements for Buns of Steel.

These puritans are ruining my essay on how to get hit by a whiskey truck with grace, style, and wit. I meant to address important questions such as: When is it appropriate to get drunk? (When you're sober.) When is it appropriate to sober up? (When you come to and find a soda straw in the empty windshield-washer-fluid reservoir of your car and your dog is wearing a negligee.) Are there things you shouldn't say with three sheets waving in the wind after letting go of the water wagon with both hands while having a brick under your hat? ("I do.") Then there were the myriad matters of technique: When making a dry martini you can use, as an emergency vermouth substitute, more gin—obvious when you think about it. And so forth.

Alas, health, fitness, and self-approval are in vogue. A man who drinks in a healthy, fit, and self-approving manner will mix vodka with yogurt and get tangled in the Nautilus machine trying to kiss his own ass. Thus I am compelled to skip the do's and don't-you-dare's, the how-to's and here's how's. Instead I must explain *why* readers should knee-walk into the attached garage of the psyche, tear the MADD bumper sticker off the Oldsmobile of their superego, make John Barleycorn their designated driver, and weave across both lanes of life with nothing on but their fog lights.

Metaphorically speaking, my dear, of course.

Do it for the sake of humanity, I say. Lushes are morally superior to uninebriated people. Compare, for example, drunken impromptu bar fights to soberly calculated professional wrestling matches in terms of the adverse effects upon society. Are children taught that violence is normative by cartoon network shows based on hooch-sodden donnybrooks in Boston's South End? Are the poor economically exploited by product endorsements from enraged Micks with noses like Rose Bowl floats? Are there any action figures in the toy stores depicting O'Rourkes with a fat lip and a shiner? Did my rum-dum cousin Kevin, who's got an attempted manslaughter conviction, run for president on the Reform Party ticket?

Beerjerkers, mug blots, and pot wallopers are careless and bad-tempered, it's true. But consider the greatest evils of history. Is "careless" the word you'd use to describe Auschwitz? Was the Rape of Nanking something Tojo did instead of kicking the cat? It's smoking in bed versus the firebombing of Dresden. Real evil requires the kind of thoughtful planning that is hard to do when you're wearing the soup tureen on your head and trying not to let your wife notice you're taking a leak in the potted palm. The worst people always have an abstemious streak. Hitler was a teetotaler. What if he'd been a soak? What if Himmler and Göring emerged from the Reich Chancellery asking each other, "How do we persecute the *gnus*?" Real evil also requires lying, and *in vino veritas.* "Adolf, you really oughta shave that booger broom." A drinking man couldn't have written *Mein Kampf*. Give Shicklgruber a couple of silly milks, you get *Turn Your Head and Kampf*. And think of all the suffering that mankind would have been spared if the *Communist Manifesto* said, "Workers of the world, it's Miller Time."

* * *

"Maybe," said my wife, removing the empty martini shaker, "you should switch to wine."

Speaking of which, I said, there's a problem with wine writing. That is, there's a problem worse than wine writers' using "fleshy," "supple," or "elegant" when they aren't writing about . . . well, about you, my dear.

Recall your first childhood savor of the vintner's art. Perhaps it was the swig out of the cooking-sherry bottle, or the sip at dinner from the would-be sophisticate parent, or a glass of first aid administered by a Methodist grandmother who thought there was no excuse for drink in the house except to treat such conditions as croup, rheumatism, lumbago, and having a grandson who, at 11:30 P.M., insisted there was something under the bed. Anyway: ugh.

To innocent tongues the grandest *cru* smacks of Spic and Span used instead of sugar in the Kool-Aid. Wine—indeed, all booze—tastes horrid. This is because of the alcohol. Alcohol's flavor is so bad that no one would ever drink an alcoholic beverage—unless, of course, it contained alcohol. Hence the problem with wine writing. Despite all the hooey about attack and finish, fruits and flowers, round robust length upon palate, and the Robert Parker hundred-point scale, we are swallowing the stuff to get high.

That was why, last week, Chris Buckley and I embarked on a Blind (Drunk) Wine Tasting.

"And I," said my wife, "had to get a sitter and come collect you and take out the toddler seat and fold down the back part of the SUV because you and Chris were too dizzy to sit up."

We're both deeply grateful for your efforts. And it has paid off with an important, if I do say so myself, article for *Business Fun*. Here's the rough draft of my introduction:

A wide variety of wines were sampled, ranging from the reputedly splendid to the allegedly pitiful. Selection of the better stuff was done by V, proprietor of a quietly chic potables emporium in Washington, D.C. Lesser plonk was chosen on the basis of weird names and ugly labels. Additional expertise came from the pages of Hugh Johnson's *Pocket Encyclopedia of Wine,* 1999 edition. This book was chosen because it is wide-ranging, authoritative, concise, and the only wine guide for sale at the local card and gift shop.

The blind tasting was conducted in two rounds. The first commenced at 3:45 P.M., with both participants well lunched and purely uninebriated. The second round began at . . . . well, no one remembered to consult the time, but it was much later, after all of the No. 5 and most of the No. 7, described below, had been consumed.

There was no spitting into little cups. A hefty gulp of every wine was taken and then some, in many cases. Palates were cleansed with bites of liver pâté and puffs on Monte Cristos.

Chris (or perhaps it was I) claims to recall—from some comparative lit class taken a generation ago—that when the Babylonian gods sat in assembly they thought it incumbent upon themselves to debate each judgment twice—once sober and once blitzed. A good idea, and never better than when judging wine.

"I'm surprised you remember that much," said my wife.

We were taking notes, I said. Max has typed them up. We'll present the tasting comments verbatim—more or less, since the notes begin to become illegible even before the Lynch-Moussas is reached in the first round. Here's what Max has been able to decipher so far:

1. Los Vascos

Les Domaines Barons de Rothschild (Lafite)
Cabernet Sauvignon, 1997
Chile, $8.99

V's comments: "A more Californian than Bordeaux taste."

Pocket Encyclopedia of Wine: Two stars (out of four); no vintage info. Wines of Los Vascos are "fair but neglect Chile's lovely fruit flavours in favour of firm structures." Of Chilean wine generally: "Its problems . . . above all [are] old wooden vats."

Sober Tasting

C.B. (*whose wife once took a wine-tasting course, sloshes wine around, holds it up to light, and explains that if the wine sticks to the side of the glass it has "legs"*)

P.J. (*looks skeptical*)

C.B. Good legs, jejune nose, almost flippant. Acidic in a bad way.

P.J. What the man said.

C.B. Nicotine bitterness; deep, almost asphalty finish.

P.J. Bark mulch undertones.

Drunk Tasting

P.J. Bland, sweet-smelling, not evil.

C.B. But pretty evil.

P.J. Blandly evil.

C.B. Box wine or Livingston Cellars

P.J. Box.

Conclusion (after labels had been revealed): Old wooden vats.

2. Livingston Cellars

"Burgundy" (no vintage)
Modesto, California, $3.99

V: "It's made by Gallo. They took their name off."
PEW: E&J Gallo, one to two stars. Livingston not rated separately. "Having mastered the world of commodity wines (with eponymously labeled 'Hearty Burgundy,' 'Pink Chablis', etc.) . . . is now unleashing a blizzard of regional varietals."

Sober Tasting

C.B. No legs, no nose.

P.J. No tits.

C.B. Tutti-frutti (*he spits it out*).

P.J. (*who does not spit it out*) Yuck.

Drunk Tasting

C.B. Really bad.

P.J. A new flavor of candy that Lifesaver decided not to market.

C.B. Flunks the "stuck with boring relatives" test. Flunks the "altar boy communion wine" test. That is, flunks the "time when you'll drink anything" test. I'm not sure it would be transubstantiated if consecrated.

P.J. My guess is Skouras.

C.B. Really *Greek,* or Livingston, or box wine. It's exotically bad.

Conclusion: When the varietal blizzard strikes, don't duck into a wine bar.

3. Codice

Rioja, 1997
Spain, $7.49

V: "Bordeaux method with Tempranillo grape. A bit lighter, tarter than California wines. Wood flavor, rusticity."
PEW: "Spain and Portugal joined the EU (and, as far as most of their wine is concerned, the twentieth century) only thirteen years ago."

Sober Tasting

C.B. Okay legs, chlorine nose.

P.J. YMCA pool.

C.B. Better than it tastes.

P.J. Huh?

C.B. Daring to be really bad, but not quite managing.

Drunk Tasting

P.J. Fruity smell.

C.B. If fruit were a medicine.

P.J. Drinkable.

C.B. Acceptable, complex. Ariel or Livingston Cellar.

P.J. (*who, not long ago, had been to Spain, where he swilled Rioja and was thus cheating*) Codice.

Conclusion: CB's mistaking Codice for Ariel dealcoholized wine —a subconscious plea for the Twelve-Step Program?

4. Carruades de Lafite

Pauillac, 1996
Bordeaux, $61.99

V: "Youthful Bordeaux. Flavors of vanilla from oak. To drink or to age." Suggests serving with steak.
PEW: The second wine of the four-star Lafite-Rothschild. Not rated separately. The '96 is a recommended vintage. Of Pauillac generally: "Very varied in style."

Sober Tasting

C.B. No legs.
P.J. (*who has a slight cold*) Nose is subtly bad.
C.B. Ugly nose. Chalky complexion. . . . You know this trick about wine tasting? If you're at a loss, describe someone who's in the room.
P.J. I'll have you know that this nose has been broken three times. Twice in fistfights.
C.B. Manly nose.
P.J. And once in a riding accident.
C.B. Okay, okay, I'm sorry.
P.J. Well, actually, it was the pony at the church carnival.
C.B. Let's have a drink. (*They do.*) Subtly good.
P.J. Tastes okay. Kind of stinks.

Drunk Tasting

P.J. Smells too sweet, tastes too bitter.
C.B. Cloying nose, mildly annoying taste. It's getting worse.
P.J. Awful.

C.B. Skouras?

P.J. Skouras.

Conclusion: As for serving it with steak—Philly cheese steak comes to mind.

5. Château Cheval Blanc

Saint-Emilion Grand Cru, 1989
Bordeaux, $299.99 (magnum)

V: "Made with the Cabernet Franc grape, as were the great nineteenth-century Bordeaux. An exceptional vintage year. Violets with cassis. Well-ripened, lots of structure. Leathery, woody, rich, length in palate."
PEW: Four stars (indicating "grand, prestigious, expensive"). "Intensely vigorous and perfumed. . . . For many the first choice in Bordeaux."

Sober Tasting

C.B. Has legs. Nose is (*smiles*) whew! Licorice, tar.

P.J. Tar?

C.B. Wow, is that complex! Don't quote me. Is it the Big Boy?

P.J. We'll have to drink several glasses to be sure.

C.B. P.F.G.

P.J. Is that a technical term?

C.B. Pretty f—ing good.

P.J. It's the Big Boy.

C.B. Definitely the Big Boy.

Drunk Tasting

None was left.

Conclusion: The English Huswife, published in 1648, says, "The wines that are made in Burdeaux are . . . the most full gadge and sound Wines." Mr. Buckley and Mr. O'Rourke think like the English Huswife and, by this stage, spell like her too.

6. Skouras

"Mediterranean Red" (no vintage)
Peloponnese, Greece, $5.99

V: "The American importer designed his own label. He drew a sketch of sailboats and sent it to Greece. The printed labels came back with pictures of kites on them."
PEW: Two to three stars, Mediterranean Red not rated separately. Of the Peloponnese generally: "Vines mostly used for currants."

Sober Tasting

C.B. Sudsy legs.
P.J. Smells too pleasant.
C.B. Tastes very fruity. Way fruity. Juicy Fruit.
P.J. Château Wrigley.
C.B. Inviting you home. Almost playful.
P.J. You're cut off.

Drunk Tasting

C.B. Sweet. Terrible.
P.J. Creepy.
C.B. Livingston Cellars.
P.J. Don't know, don't care.

Conclusion: Be especially wary of Greeks bearing gifts of wine.

7. Château Lynch-Moussas

Pauillac, 1996
Bordeaux, $29.99

V: "Good vintage, full-ripened. Deep, rich, passionate flavor."
PEW: Two stars; '96 recommended vintage. A fifth growth but "making serious wine."

Sober Tasting

P.J. (*drinking deeply*) Either real good . . . or not.

C.B. Thick, almost Bulgarian legs. Pug nose. (*He, too, drinks deeply.*) And yet, and yet . . . not the Big Boy, but a Lady-in-Waiting.

P.J. A little sharp, a little bitter.

C.B. A little pipsqueaky.

Drunk Tasting

C.B. Fine, dignified nose. I like it a lot. It's grown, blossomed, since last time.

P.J. (*at that stage when he suddenly thinks he can talk wine talk—and probably Chinese*) Perfumy. Big. Tannin. A game wine, but too young.

BOTH (*more or less in unison*) Definitely Carruades. Unless it's Lynch-Moussas.

Conclusion: Buy some.

8. Frog's Leap

Cabernet Sauvignon, 1996
Napa Valley, $29.99

V: "Rich, with structure and complexity, but not at top of California level. Not overly weighty."
PEW: Two to three stars; '96 a recommended vintage. "Small winery, charming as its name (and T-shirts)."

Sober Tasting

C.B. Extremely leggy. Ghastly nose. (*He drinks.*) Upchucky.

P.J. No flavor at all and yet it tastes bad.

C.B. Wine I'd serve to house guests I was trying to get rid of.

Drunk Tasting

P.J. Actually, I think it has a better nose than number 7. (*He stubs out his Monte Cristo in the pâté plate.*) But shrieks of raw youth.

C.B. Probably Lynch-Moussas.

Conclusion: The only bad wine that got markedly better as C.B. and P.J. got markedly stewed. Consider this when serving those house guests—who are probably wearing Frog's Leap T-shirts.

9. Meerlust Merlot

Stellenbosch, 1995
South Africa, $19.99

V: "Acidic in a good way."
PEW: Three stars. "South Africa is the seventh-largest wine producer in the world—but as a consumer remains a mainly beer-drinking nation."

Sober Tasting

C.B. Slimy legs.
P.J. A lot like number 8.
C.B. Forceful nose. Bad in a new way. Slatternly.
P.J. I disagree. Bad without dirty thrills or novelty.

Drunk Tasting

C.B. Awful. Dignified nose. Taste a nasty surprise.
P.J. Eeeeeuw. God! Harsh. South African?
C.B. Let's hope it's the Ariel.

Conclusion: Mainly a beer-drinking nation.

10. Manischewitz

Concord Grape (no vintage)
Naples, New York, $3.49

V: "No comment."
PEW: Not rated. Concord grape generally used for "mostly grape juice and jelly . . . strong 'foxy' flavour, off-putting to non-initiates."

Sober Tasting

C.B. (*recoils*)

P.J. Really, really awful. Explains why Jewish people don't drink much.

C.B. Hypoglycemic finish.

Drunk Tasting

C.B. Manischewitz.

P.J. Manischewitz. (*Bottle is poured down sink.*)

Conclusion: Possibly all right with peanut butter.

11. Ariel

Dealcoholized Cabernet Sauvignon, 1997
Napa Valley, 1997

V: (Didn't know what to say.)
PEW: Doesn't say anything.

Sober Tasting

C.B. Chocolate nose.

P.J. Chocolate-covered oak, with gym shoes.

C.B. A soupçon of gym shoe.

P.J. Odd flavor, completely different from, and even worse than, the "bouquet."

C.B. Sweet and sour doggy bed. Paint.

BOTH Livingston Cellars.

Drunk Tasting

P.J. Time to hose out the kennels.

C.B. Awful. Awful.

BOTH Ariel!

Conclusion: The theory that alcohol is what makes booze taste bad is hereby exploded.

12. Franzia "Mountain Burgundy"

(no vintage)

Ripon, California, $9.99 for 5-liter box. (Price per 750 cl is $1.50—cheaper than some water.)

V: (winced)

PEW: One star, "Mountain Burgundy" not rated separately. "Penny-saver wines."

Sober Tasting

C.B. I'm having trouble with this nose.

P.J. Mine's been broken three—

C.B. You said that.

P.J. Sorry.

C.B. Aggressively unpleasant.

P.J. I *said* I was sorry.

C.B. The wine.

P.J. Oh, come on. Tastes okay. Pretty good cheap-drunk material.

C.B. Sangria material.

Drunk Tasting

C.B. Smells bad.

P.J. Tastes worse.

BOTH Box wine.

P.J. (*peeking*) It's the most popular wine in America.

C.B. No.

P.J. Says so right on the box.

Conclusion: Avoid the sangria.

13. Rosemount Estate

Cabernet Sauvignon, 1997

Perth, Australia, $9.99

V: "User-friendly. Good price. A riper, sweeter style of Cab, more Californian or New World."

PEW: Two to three stars; no vintage information; Cab S not rated separately. "Australian ideas and names are on all wine-lovers' lips. . . . Even growers in the south of France listen carefully to Australian winemakers."

Sober Tasting

C.B. Good legs.
P.J. Oh, cut that out.
C.B. Ambiguous nose.
P.J. The kind of nose shared by both good and bad wines.
C.B. Uh, yes.
P.J. Kind of winey-smelling.
C.B. Lots of tannin.
P.J. Bitter.
C.B. Shanghai Tang.
P.J. Not very good, but let's drink some more of it.
C.B. Headachey finish.

Drunk Tasting

C.B. Promises more than it can deliver.
P.J. Sort of loud and upside down.
BOTH Australian.

Conclusion: Loud, upside down.

"When the *Business Fun* expense vouchers are audited," said my wife, "I hope the IRS shares your sense of humor."

It was lumped under *Research,* I said. Here's how I'm going to end the article:

It was Mr. Buckley and Mr. O'Rourke's fondest hope that, if they got drunk enough, wine would cease to be a qualitative matter and become a quantitative issue. They aspired to stifle wine snobbery and reduce all tiresome oenophilic queries to the basic question: "Is there more?" They failed. In fact, drinking seemed to sharpen their critical skills. The bad wines got mostly worse as the bacchanal wore on. And, more's the pity, so did the good ones. Messieurs Buckley and O'Rourke both felt just terrible the next day and were forced to admit to the wisdom of their friend V, who had disparaged the entire idea of the Blind (Drunk) Wine Tasting. "Wine," said V, "is to enhance food, enliven the mind, lubricate conversation, and enrich life. If you do all that, drunkenness will come naturally. And anyway, for getting drunk, vodka is better."

"A good thing," said my wife, "because we're out of gin."

About a week later, just when I was starting to feel better, the Political Nut who lives around here showed up. Do you realize, he said, that this is the second anniversary of Bill Clinton's impeachment?

"Seems like two years ago," said my wife.

On January 8, 1999, said the Political Nut, the United States Senate, in all its dignity, solemnly swore. . . . And talk about great TV! Especially when Trent Lott got tongue-bungled and said that the Chief Justice "will now administer the oaf." Anyway, the United States Senate, in all its dignity—if we don't count Senator Barbara Boxer, who was wearing a brown pants suit perfect for Breakfast Bingo at Wal-Mart. And what was with Rehnquist's robe? Adidas stripes on the sleeves, big old zipper down the front—it looked like a novelty beach wrap for vacationing gospel choirs. Nevertheless, on January 8, 1999, the United States Senate . . . got free souvenir Oath Book ballpoint pens with *United States* misprinted as *Untied States*. Senators Bunning and Mikulski tried to return theirs. They are good-government types, unwilling to receive the smallest perquisite at public expense. Either that or they can spell.

However, the Clinton impeachment was a thing of manifold splendors anyway, and it had no downside. If sixty-seven senators said so, we were rid of a half-cracked slab of sophomorocism, a moral midden heap, ethical slop jar, and backed-up policy toilet, a blabby, overreaching nooky-mooch and masher. The dirty, selfish pest would be removed from office.

If not, we were spared a busy, silly toad-eater puffed with all the bad ideas available at Harvard. That self-serious bootlick Al Gore would not be—as it turned out, would never be—chief executive.

And if the Republicans got spanked in the voting booth for prosecuting Bill, they'd get the hairbrush for the wrong offense, true, but they deserved the wallop on general principles—or, rather, lack thereof. What a feckless, timid, timeserving revolution that was in 1994, as if the sansculottes had stormed the Bastille to get themselves jobs as prison guards.

Alas, some people opposed the impeachment. They decried the expense of the special prosecutor's investigations. But when had the federal government spent millions in such an entertaining fashion? Certainly not by funding PBS. True, there was the shuttle launch when NASA shot an aging politician into space. But then NASA decided to bring John Glenn back.

Some critics of impeachment claimed that the office of president would be diminished to a mere custodial role. Yes! George W. Bush, report to 1600 Pennsylvania Avenue and sign for your mop and broom.

Other naysayers argued that America's most talented politicians would be scared away from careers in public service. But the private sector will no doubt be able to put America's most talented politicians to use—making unsolicited dinnertime telemarketing calls.

It was said that the press was being discredited. This was a blind item planted by Jerry Springer because Ted Koppel had been swiping the most depraved guests.

It was said that we were entering an era of sexual McCarthyism. Bring on the congressional hearings! "Sharon Stone, are you now, or have you ever been, showing your boobs for purposes without redeeming social importance?"

And some earnest souls went so far as to aver that impeachment distracted President Clinton from . . . from raising taxes, destroying health care, appointing 1960s bakeheads to high political office, soliciting felonious campaign contributions, hanging friends out to dry for Arkansas real estate frauds, giving missile secrets to the Chinese, taking credit for the benefits of a free market about which he knew little and cared less, using U.S. military forces as fig leaves for domestic scandals and au pairs for the UN, leading foreign policy back into the flea circus of Jimmy Carterism, having phone sex, groping patronage seekers, and snapping the elastic on the underpants of psychologically disturbed school-age White House interns entrusted with the task of delivering high-level government pizza.

Plus there were the other benefits we derived from this imbroglio. Feminism was revitalized as Mack Daddy Clinton forced the tired jades of *Ms. Magazine* to get back out on the media street corner in fishnet stocking and tube tops. The true agenda of the Movement Left was revealed, albeit thirty years late: They want to get entrée to the nation's highest political office—and play with themselves in it. And wild GOP private lives were revealed. The very thought of naked Republicans should go a long way to curing America's obsession with the lewd.

Practically everyone involved in the impeachment came up a winner. Paula Jones got a nose job. Monica Lewinsky got a Barbara Walters interview. And a number of sycophants and dupes on the White House staff won a chance to prove their fealty by paying huge legal bills. Susan McDougal had her jailhouse lipstick privileges restored. Lucianne Goldberg obtained copious PR, and her skills as a literary agent have attracted many important authors who saw Vince Foster beamed up by a UFO. Vernon Jordan also secured free advertising, and everything that slithers on its belly in Washington headed to his law office. Linda Tripp got a reason to stick to that diet. Saddam Hussein and Osama bin Laden received the air strikes from infidels that they needed to make their own pollsters happy. Newt Gingrich got some how-to tips on sex in the workplace. And Ken Starr's lecture fees have soared on the skinny-sideburn-and-big-belt-buckle conspiracy-buff circuit. Furthermore, think of the blessing to millions of future U.S. high school students trapped in the dreary confines of American History class. Finally, a chapter that boogies.

And who cares that Clinton won in the end? Let me put this in terms that a boy from Hope will understand. No matter what, Bill, your girlfriend's ugly, your wife's a bitch, and your dog can't hunt.

My daughter Muffin appeared in the doorway and said, "What's *bitch*?"

It's a grown-up word, honey. It means junior senator from New York. You should never say words like junior senator from New York.

"Mommy wants to know if the nut is still waving."

Raving, I corrected. Tell Mommy she can come back in the living room. The Political Nut promises to quit talking about the impeachment.

Even though now, in the bright morning light of a new Bush administration, the legacy of the Clinton impeachment scandal has finally become clear.

Republicans in Congress impeached Clinton for doing what a Republican would have loved to have done if the intern hadn't cracked the Republican across the face with a Coach bag full of cell phone batteries. Democrats defended a no-account, conniving jerk who used the wadded-up principles of liberalism to pad the bulge in his political jeans because congressional Democrats knew Democratic voters are so dumb they think they got their jobs at Burger King because Clinton was dating the cow. The First Lady, realizing her role in a Gore administration would be making balloon animals at birthday parties for Tipper's kids, embraced that paragon among husbands and fathers, Bill. The stud-puppy himself ran off to do things such as view tornado damage. That way, when he looked like a sorry sack of rubbish, he looked like he was sorry for someone other than himself. And the media took time off from prodding the corpse of Princess Diana, looking up Ellen DeGeneres's pants leg, and going through the garbage behind the JonBenet Ramsey home to wax sanctimonious about how intrusive, sex-mad, and trashy Washington had become. The legacy of the Clinton impeachment scandal is—a bequest of enormous hypocrisy to the nation.

It was about time. We needed some. If you look up *hypocrisy* in *Webster's Third New International Dictionary* (unabridged)—which we know Bill Clinton used because he said, "It depends on what your definition of the word *is* is," and the *to be* verb gets nine and a half column inches in there, plus the Clinton White House had three copies, due to Robert Rubin, Donna Shalala, and Madeleine Albright's all needing them to sit on to reach the table during cabinet meetings. Anyway, if you look up *hypocrisy,* you'll find it means "pretending to be what one is not or to have principles or beliefs that one does not have," from the Greek *hypokrisis,* "playing a part on the stage." Republicans, Democrats, Hillary, Bill, and the TV networks were acting—acting as if they knew right from wrong, good from bad, et cetera. This was great. It meant they had some notion of the difference. They didn't used to.

Before the advent of Monica Lewinsky, Republicans earnestly believed they were fulfilling their "Contract with America" by attending meetings of the Conservative Citizens Council while wearing bedsheets and playing dead during budget fights. Democrats were sincere and fervid in their battle against the woes of the Great Depression and didn't have a clue that the thing had been over for fifty-some years. Hillary was trying to rebuild the Berlin Wall brick by social-program brick, in pious obedience to the tenets of Wellesley-chick socialism. Bill truly felt he was beloved, even by Hillary. And the TV networks actually thought the hair farmers behind the anchor desks knew what they were talking about.

It's great to put that behind us. Furthermore, being a hypocrite looked good compared to being the one person who was absolutely plainspoken and forthright during the Lewinsky affair: Larry Flynt.

Hypocrisy, as a concept, required this boost. It's been the pariah among late-twentieth-century sins. The Seven Deadlies have all been fashionable. Envy and Covetousness in the Reagan administration. Anger whenever it's convenient to swat Saddam Hussein. And then there's Lust, Pride, Sloth, and Gluttony, or, as we call them these days, "getting in touch with your sexuality," "raising your self-esteem," "relaxation therapy," and "being a recovered bulimic." Accuse a person of breaking all Ten Commandments, and you've written the promo blurb for the dustcover of his tell-all memoir. Call somebody a sleaze and you've hired him as your lawyer. But everyone is ashamed of the hypocrite tag.

Perhaps this is part of the cult of authenticity to which we orthodontically corrected, surgically enhanced, pompadour implanted, and Prozac-ed moderns adhere. Or maybe informing significant others that they look like hell and need to diet is simply more fun than clothing the naked and feeding the hungry. Hypocrisy is "the vice of vices," declared Hannah Arendt, supposedly one of the most prominent moral philosophers of our time.

"Only the hypocrite is really rotten to the core." Arendt said that—and so did a whole bunch of teenage daughters dressed in black, with pierced eyebrows, stamping their platform shoes on the Ikea kilim in the open-plan kitchen and shrieking, "You and Mom did drugs! You and Mom screwed around! You are *such* hypocrites!"

This is why it's vital for Washington to show leadership in the hypocrisy field, because I'm afraid we might be raising one of those daughters. True, Muffin's only three. But in eleven brief years we will be faced with the awkward task of explaining to our child why she should behave like Gidget while I, at her age, was paging through *On the Road, Junkie,* and *120 Days of Sodom* with a highlighter pen, making a list of things to do before I shot my family.

Of course there are artifacts of popular culture such as *Pinocchio* to warn children what a world that punishes hypocrisy would be like—like a botched rhinoplasty. But rented videotapes do not have the same impact as the living example of an entire capital city full of the nation's highest elected officials and most prominent arbiters of opinion blowing smoke out their fundaments.

The American political establishment must be thanked for the time and effort it put into getting the impeachment right, with extra kudos to the women's movement for providing a model of the sophistry, casuistic self-justification, and talking out of both sides of the mouth so necessary in the crucial parenting years. I mean, I almost had to tell Muffin an outright lie. ("You shouldn't take drugs because when I was young I overdosed and died horribly, choking on my own vomit.") Or, worse, I almost had to tell Muffin the truth. ("Yes, I was a hippie, but looking back on it I wish I had joined the Marine Corps—because drugs were cheaper in Vietnam.") Now all I have to do is be full of it. And this, as a middle-aged dad, I already am.

To prove my thesis, let me note that when the cardinal virtues are named—Wisdom, Courage, Temperance, Justice, Faith, Hope, Charity—the list does not end with "and no B.S." If you put on a big show of being deep-thinking, brave, prudent, just, faithful, and optimistic, then that's pretty much what you are—or close enough for government work. And it's hard to fake charity if everybody saw you put that five-spot in the crippled beggar's cup. Unless you run back and snatch it out. But you'd better be quick; some of those crippled beggars can really move.

Then let us also consider what the impeachment process would have been like if all the participants had been brutally honest: Republicans screaming, "Don't you understand what a criminal this president is? He stole our issues! He swiped our illegal campaign donors! He nabbed the interns with the bonus bazoombas!" Democrats yelling, "If the opinion polls told us dogs had a seventy-five-percent approval rating, we'd be on *Larry King Live* licking our privates!" The press hollering, "We did that—*slurp-slurp*—right on national TV! And there was nothing you could do about it! Nobody elects us! Nobody impeaches us! We're the rottweilers on the porch! Now watch us pee on George W. Bush's leg!" And Chief Justice Rehnquist shouting from the bench, "I'm naked from the waist down under this robe!"

6

FEBRUARY 2001

Maybe George W. Bush will be a big hypocrite and then you'll be happy," said my wife. "For all we know he wasn't wearing a thing under his pants at the inauguration."

There was an expression on his face, I said, before he stepped up to the rostrum to speak—he certainly looked like he felt something cold on his balls.

"Honey, your language —"

"Daddy," said Muffin, "does the president have balls with Goofy and Mickey on them like I do?"

We'll have to wait and see, I said, and changed the subject. Here we are, two months into 2001, and the 1990s still don't have a name. Almost every decade of the twentieth century has a name: the Swinging Sixties, the Roaring Twenties, the Painfully Unhip Fifties, the War-Torn Forties, the Depression Era, the Decade of Greed, the Me Decade. But what distinguishes the nineties? Triangulation of the issues? The Third Way? Compassionate conservatism?

"How about the Me and Oh, Yeah, You Too Decade?" said my wife.

"It could be that you're too old for named decades," said my young assistant, Max. "I understand time passes more quickly as people age. Maybe, for you, naming the nineties would be like the rest of us naming the past month and a half."

That reminds me, Max, I've got a research project. I picked up a copy of *Them* magazine. See these people on the cover? Who the f—?

"Honey," said my wife.

Who the free-subscription-offer *are* these people? Is it just me or are there more celebrities nowadays than there are things to be celebrated? Everyone knows the last important LP was *Rubber Soul,* there's been nothing worth watching on TV since *Hawaii Five-O* was canceled, and they quit making really good movies after *Apocalypse Now*. Yet, fresh crops of allegedly famous actors, singers, and who-knows-whaters keep being foisted upon me.

In last year's "50 Most Kissed-Up To" issue of *Them,* the only name I knew was JFK, Jr. And I thought he was three. It turned out he was married and dead. No, there was one other person I'd heard of, that fellow that my godson's sister Ophelia dragged home in the middle of the night. And Nick, Sr., threw him off the porch. It turns out the kid gets $21 million per picture.

So, Max, what I want you to do is go out and buy the current issues of *Celebrity Excess, Yammer, Entertainment All Night, Puff,* and *Inanity Teen* and read them and report back. And, Max, if you happen to be too *old* yourself to know who some of these people are, you can consult my godson Nick, not to mention his sister.

I'm going to do a piece on famous folks I've never heard of for *Business Fun.* Because it's important for those of us in the peak of our productive years to keep up on these things. It helps us communicate with our children. Although that's a laugh. Nothing is more embarrassing to children than "hip" parents. Remember the poor fellow in high school whose mother wore miniskirts and whose father claimed to "dig" the Beatles?

"Actually," said my wife, "no. I was two."

However, staying current with popular culture does make it easier for us senior-management types to relate to the twenty-somethings who are so prominent in today's computer-driven web-intensive business world. Hmmm. Forget that. All those fresh-whelped dot.com billionaires are in Chapter 11. They've gone back to playing "Duke Nuke 'Em" in their parents' rec room where they belong.

No, the ugly fact of the matter is, this article will be for middle-aged men who want to know who modern celebrities are so we have something to talk about when we hit on our future ex-third-wives at Au Bar, the Viper Room, or wherever it is the honeys hang out these days.

"Ahem," said my wife.

I'm just talking journalistic concept here.

"In other words," said Max, "if you are a decent person, a responsible business executive, and a good family man, you won't have to read this article at all."

Max returned a week later, looking a bit glassy-eyed. "Let me pull up my 'Who the F—' file," he said.

And that, I said, is precisely what I'm going to call my article: "Who the F— Are These People?" Let's start with Leonardo DiCaprio.

"Oh, come on," said my wife. "Don't *try* to be square. You do too know who Leonardo DiCaprio is—the one you weren't looking at when Kate Winslet's clothes got wet, clingy, and diaphanous in *Titanic*."

I'm using Leonardo as a baseline, I said. He's the one celebrity that my *Business Fun* readers will have some inkling about. After that it's downhill into the abyss of stardom.

"I've arranged the information in categories," said Max, "WHY ANYONE CARES, INSIDE INFORMATION, TELLING DETAIL, and so forth, plus KNOWING COMMENTS for you old guys to make, so you won't sound pathetically out of it."

Here is Max's printout:

Leonardo DiCaprio

WHY ANYONE CARES

Enormous heartthrob among females who have issues with male secondary sexual characteristics.

Inside Information (The 411, as the Chronologically Unimpaired Say)

Before wretched excess of fame, had critically acclaimed roles in *This Boy's Life, What's Eating Gilbert Grape, Marvin's Room,* and other movies to which men get dragged by women. But latest, *The Beach,* bombed so—for all we know—Leo isn't famous anymore after all.

TELLING DETAIL

Once made an educational film called *How to Deal with a Parent Who Takes Drugs.*

KNOWING COMMENT

You say: "Some claim the Columbine killings were inspired by DiCaprio's performance in *The Basketball Diaries.* This falsely presupposes anyone could sit through that movie."

OPTIONAL WISECRACK

If wife, daughter, or other female insists on subjecting you to *Titanic* on video, wait an hour, then nudge your companion and say, "Honey, would you ring down for ice?"

REASSURING FACT

In June 2000, Howard Kurtz of *The Washington Post* wrote that George W. Bush had "acknowledged" he didn't even know "who Leonardo DiCaprio was."

Matt Damon

WHY ANYONE CARES

Starred in *The Talented Mr. Ripley* as a charming sociopath who misplaced his charm somewhere and in *Good Will Hunting* as brilliant ignoramous minus the brilliance.

INSIDE INFORMATION

With pal Ben Affleck, co-wrote *Good Will Hunting*—story of a troubled slum kid working as a janitor at a Harvard-like school who turns out to be as smart as Al Gore. This won an Oscar for best screenplay.

TELLING DETAIL

Father was an investment banker. Mother was a lefty activist. Went to Harvard.

NOT TO BE CONFUSED WITH

Pal Ben Affleck, who starred in *Reindeer Games* as a charming sociopath, is taller, didn't go to Harvard, and has bedded Gwyneth Paltrow.

TELLING DETAIL ABOUT BEN AFFLECK

Once directed a short film titled *I Murdered My Lesbian Wife, Hung Her on a Meat Hook, and Now I've Got a Three-Picture Deal with Disney*.

LIKELIHOOD OF ENCOUNTERING MATT DAMON IN THE RACQUET CLUB BAR, ON THE MAIDSTONE FIRST TEE, OR AT YOUR DAUGHTER'S DEBUTANTE PARTY

Well, Matt *did* go to Harvard, but so did such characters as Al Gore.

Hilary Swank

WHY ANYONE CARES

Played a girl playing a boy in order to get girls in *Boys Don't Cry*.

INSIDE INFORMATION

She is a girl.

WHAT ALL THIS MEANS

Let's not ask.

TELLING DETAIL

When she starred in *The Next Karate Kid* (who's a girl), *The Washington Post* said, "What is the sound of one hand clapping? The audience giving it up for *The Next Karate Kid*."

ITEM OF HOLLYWOOD GOSSIP THAT TELLS US LITTLE ABOUT HILARY SWANK BUT EVERYTHING ABOUT HOW THE ENTERTAINMENT INDUSTRY VIEWS HISTORY

According to *Variety*, Swank is up for the lead in a movie called *The Affair of the Necklace* in which she'd play "an aristocratic beauty who, while searching for her heritage, manages to overthrow the French regime."

Angelina Jolie

WHY ANYONE CARES

Best Supporting Actress Oscar for rubber-ranch chick flick, *Girl, Interrupted.* Daughter of actor Jon Voight.

WHY ANYONE REALLY CARES

At her first wedding, wore black rubber pants and a shirt with the groom's name written in blood on the back. Had a steamy make-out scene with her brother at Academy Awards ceremony. Broke up own marriage and several others. Became Billy Bob Thornton's fifth wife in a quickie Las Vegas ceremony. Now they talk about their sex life constantly in interviews. All this before age twenty-six.

WHO THE F— IS BILLY BOB THORNTON?

Actor/auteur/jerk. His *Sling Blade* was latest in long series of hillbillies-in-hell movies that aren't as good as *Deliverance.* Was seen at a gym wearing his wife's underwear. Said of Jolie, "I was looking at her in her sleep, and I had to restrain myself from literally squeezing her to death." To which Angelina responded, "I was nearly killed last night, and it was the nicest thing anyone ever said to me."

TELLING DETAILS ABOUT BILLY BOB

Born in Hot Springs, Arkansas. Mother was a psychic. Fourth wife accused him of abuse. How did we escape having him as president of the United States?

TELLING DETAIL ABOUT ANGELINA

As a child, aspired to be a funeral director.

KNOWING COMMENT

"In the nineteenth century it was about having big hips. In the twentieth century it was about having big breasts. In the twenty-first century it's about having a big mouth."

Will Smith

WHY ANYONE CARES

Rap singer, star of long-running TV sitcom *The Fresh Prince of Bel-Air,* and Tommy Lee Jones's partner in best guy pic of the 1990s, *Men in Black* (although it was no *Apocalypse Now).*

KNOWING COMMENT

"Every American generation has its obligatory nonthreatening person of color. And now that Denzel Washington is getting scary . . ."

OPTIONAL KNOWING COMMENT IF YOU HAPPEN TO BE A PERSON OF COLOR YOURSELF

"It's enough to make Bill Cosby join the Fruit of Islam."

INSIDE INFORMATION TO GO WITH KNOWING COMMENTS ABOVE

Some homeboy Will is—his father's an engineer and his mother works for the school board.

JUST BETWEEN MAX AND P.J.

Smith is talented, has a sense of humor, and you would, in fact, even like his music. Do not let this get out or it will ruin his career.

Sean "Puffy" Combs, aka "Puff Daddy"

WHY ANYONE CARES

Rap impresario, rap being a form of music created by one performer shouting obscenities in a singsong voice while other performers torture a cat and throw garbage cans down a flight of stairs.

INSIDE INFORMATION

Puffy has been involved in a feud with West Coast rappers that has resulted in several shooting deaths. But, so far, the killing has not been extensive enough to bring melody back to the popular song. Has dated actress Jennifer Lopez, even though she's supposed to be a nice girl from the Bronx.

TELLING DETAILS

Got his start in 1991 by organizing a charity basketball game at New York's City College, which was such a success that nine people were trampled to death by the crowd. Was arrested last year on weapons charge after a disco dust-up that left three people wounded. Jennifer Lopez was arrested too.

KNOWING COMMENT

"Some say his career is over, but *no one* says Puffy 'can't get arrested.'"

Jennifer Lopez

WHY ANYONE CARES

Nice girl from the Bronx. Great butt. Starred in *Selena* as a nice girl from Texas with a great butt. Gave the snake something worth squeezing in *Anaconda*. Ditto George Clooney in the Elmore Leonard (now *there's* a celebrity) movie *Out of Sight*.

INSIDE INFORMATION

Got her start on *In Living Color*, which was a *Saturday Night Live* for non-nonthreatening people of color. But still a nice girl from the Bronx even if she has dated Puffy Combs.

TELLING DETAIL

Being a nice girl from the Bronx, when arrested she cried because her cell was not provided with (this was in *Rolling Stone*) cuticle cream.

WHAT YOU'D THINK ABOUT JENNIFER LOPEZ IF YOU THOUGHT ABOUT JENNIFER LOPEZ AT ALL

Great butt.

Beck

WHY ANYONE CARES

Dweeby fellow who "combines folk, blues, and hip-hop in a new sonic collage." Pass the Tylenol.

INSIDE INFORMATION

Most noted for the slacker-generation anthem "Loser."

PRIVATE THOUGHT

Slacker generation? Isn't that all those kids with the damn Harvard MBAs who caused the dot.com mess?

TELLING DETAILS

Beck dropped out of school after junior high so we can't blame the dot.com mess on him personally. But we can blame things on his mother, who was a denizen of Andy Warhol's Factory and knew that poor Edie Sedgwick girl who came from such a good family.

Moby

WHY ANYONE CARES

Moby, who looks like something the guinea pig just gave birth to, is a Beck for the next, even worse, generation. He blends "archival blues and gospel vocals with modern-day techno"—techno being a form of music that sounds like a combination of a skipping record, the chime from the car door being left open, the microwave telling you it's finished with defrosting, and the spin cycle on your washing machine.

INSIDE INFORMATION

Moby is very antiestablishment, which is so mainstream these days that every track from his recording *Play* has been sold for use in a feature film, TV show, or commercial.

MORE INSIDE INFORMATION THAN YOU NEEDED

Moby is also a vegan. Vegans eschew not only meat but any food that "exploits animals." This is why, when you had your godson Nick and his sister with the nose ring over for steak and you offered Ophelia a toasted cheese sandwich instead, she got all huffy and went out and grazed in the yard.

KNOWING COMMENT

Unnecessary. Just realizing he's not a novel by Herman Melville puts you ahead of the game.

A MESSAGE FROM MOBY'S WEB SITE

"I define basic rights . . . as the framers of the Constitution put it, the ability to have 'life, liberty, and the pursuit of happiness.'"

PRIVATE THOUGHT

That would be the Declaration of Independence, hay-breath.

Jakob Dylan

WHY ANYONE CARES

Remember when you were temporarily smitten with the beatnik girl in San Francisco during the first Nixon administration? And you went to her "pad" and she put on a record by that fellow named Bob who had a very bad adenoid problem? This is his son. (And, come to think of it, you yourself may have a kid about this age, traipsing around Mendocino in Birkenstocks, unbeknownst to you. But that's another matter.)

INSIDE INFORMATION

Got his start playing the Kibitz Room of Canter's Deli in Los Angeles. *Oy vay.*

KNOWING COMMENT

"Because Jakob can carry a tune and write songs that make sense, critics feel he lacks his father's talent."

Limp Bizkit

WHY ANYONE CARES

A band that combines heavy metal with rap. Oh, joy.

INSIDE INFORMATION

Even *Rolling Stone* describes Bizkit fans as "backward-cap-wearing beefheads."

TELLING DETAIL

Band name was coined when friend of founder and tattooed idiot Fred Durst mentioned having "a brain like a limp biscuit."

KNOWING COMMENT

"In the matter of proposing pop-band names, let me suggest A Noise."

Boy Bands

'N Sync, Backstreet Boys, et cetera, but don't bother to learn the band names because there's another one every fifteen minutes.

WHY ANYONE CARES

Prepubescent girls care intensely. Let us hope that the *Business Fun* readers have no Nabokovian interest in that fact. More to the point: Prepubescent girls are in command of such large amounts of discretionary spending that the introduction of a popular new boy band can cause the Fed to raise rates in an attempt to curb demand-side inflation.

INSIDE INFORMATION

Boy bands are manufactured in Orlando by an evil Geppetto named Lou Pearlman. The Orkin man has taken care of Jiminy Cricket.

KNOWING COMMENT

"The whale would gag on Lou Pearlman."

INSIDE INFORMATION, PART II

All boy bands consist of the "cute" one, the "moody" one, the "rebellious" one, the "ethnic" one," and the "dork." It worked for NATO.

FURTHER KNOWING COMMENT

"Orlando is the center of modern musical culture, and modern musical culture deserves no better."

Eminem

WHY ANYONE CARES

A beyond-Faulknerian specimen of double-Y-chromosome white trash who mimics all that's loathsome and stupid in ghetto-thug culture—resulting in a toilet-mouth recording, *The Slim Shady LP,* that made a lot more money last year than your NASDAQ investments.

INSIDE INFORMATION

His debut single was called "Just Don't Give a F—."

KNOWING COMMENT

"Really, what else *would* one call it?"

TELLING DETAIL

His mother has sued him for slander.

MORE TELLING DETAILS

Last year, Eminem was arrested for assault and carrying a concealed weapon. His estranged wife attempted suicide. They fought over custody of their child, then got back together. The CEO of Eminem's record company is married to noted child-care expert and author of *The Girlfriends' Guide to Pregnancy,* Viki Ivone, who is also a former Playboy Playmate. Where is the Christian Right when we need them?

WISECRACK (IN THIS CASE NOT OPTIONAL)

"How did God, with all his tornadoes, miss this particular trailer park?"

Britney (sic) Spears

WHY ANYONE CARES

Young, really young, pop star—younger than your readers' dinner jackets if they've kept fit or their Bordeaux if they haven't—who sings songs that would make Billie Holiday blush and wears clothes that would cause Cher to scream in embarrassment and wrap herself in a bedspread.

INSIDE INFORMATION

Former cast member of a postmodern *Mickey Mouse Club* apparently broadcast from a different planet than the one occupied by Annette Funicello.

TELLING DETAIL

According to the "Mr. Showbiz" web site, Britney "went to regular high school for a year."

NOT TO BE CONFUSED WITH

Fellow Mousketeer and bitter rival Christina Aguilera, who is the dirty version of Britney Spears if such a thing can be imagined.

COMMENT TO KEEP TO YOURSELF ABOUT CHRISTINA AGUILERA UNLESS YOU WANT TO BE THOUGHT OF AS A STODGY OLD DRIP TRYING TO BE CUTE

"Makes Madonna look like a virgin."

PRIVATE THOUGHT

Britney, Beck, Buffy, Puff, Snoop Dogg: a whole generation of celebrities seems to be named after our pointers and retrievers. Are there, even now, show business people calling themselves Rover, Spot, Fido, and Shep?

"I've also," said Max, "included a section called SHOW-OFF BOX. It's for bonus points when you're talking to people with lip jewelry."

Rage Against the Machine

Metal group that fancies itself so politically radical that its web site provides a Marxist book list, including *Kwame Nkrumah: The Conakry Years, His Life and Letters,* for fans who want a good read.

Blink 182

Say, "Too commercial. I prefer the classics, like Green Day."

Carson Daly

To be mentioned disparagingly. MTV veejay so thoroughly dumb and ordinary as to have won the hearts of every dumb and ordinary adolescent girl in America, probably including the one your readers are hitting on.

Lil' Kim

What the drag queens will lip-sync in 2025. She went to the opening of the Urban World Film Festival wearing string bikini, giant cross, fur coat, and cha-cha heels.

Russell Crowe

Gladiator guy, therefore not hip, but it's hip to know he has a rock band named 30 Odd Foot of Grunts.

Sisqó

Shrimpy peroxided rapper with hit song about women's behinds. Rappers Juvenile and Mystikal have hit songs on same subject. So there may be something to be said for this musical genre, if not for its practitioners' ability to spell.

Insane Clown Posse

White rap duo from Detroit. To name them is to know them—mentally ill gang types who dress in circus clothes.

"Plus," said Max, "there's what I call the PASSÉ PADDOCK."

You Didn't Used to Know Who They Were and Now You'll Never Have to:

Marilyn Manson
Smashing Pumpkins
Ricky Martin
Hanson
Phish
Brad Pitt
M. C. Hammer

"And *Daddy!*" said Muffin, who saw me one Sunday morning on the NRA political commentary show *Friendly Fire* and since then has been convinced that I'm something of a celebrity.

"Your godson will be here any minute," said my wife.

Always a pleasure to see Nick, I replied. Did he get thrown out of school? Remember the time he and his friends made a Polo-Playing-Deaths Memorial Quilt and spread it on the South Quad during Aids Awareness Month?

"He gets a week off for Presidents' Day," said my wife. "And when he helped Max with that F-word article of yours, you said, *Nick, if there's anything I can do for you* . . . There is. You're going to teach him to drive."

He's come to the right man, of course. But where'd his father go?

"Nick's father tried to teach Nick's sister Ophelia how to drive."

Yes. That made the Metro Section of *The New York Times.*

"I believe she would have killed him, except she's a vegan."

And fashionably dyslexic, causing her to mix up the D and the R on the shift lever.

"Well, be careful."

Nick isn't a thing like his sister.

"I was thinking about the driveway. *Somebody* is having trouble borrowing a snowblower this year."

* * *

The great thing, Nick, about driving a car in the winter is it's so convenient. Compare what it's like, being inside a car in February, to what it was like a hundred years ago, being inside a horse. This was much less comfortable and couldn't have been good for the animal. Another convenient thing about winter driving: If you have an attached garage, you can start your car, leave the garage door down, and kill yourself and your entire family. That is, you can achieve the same results using your automobile as you'd get from a gigantic flaming wreck on the highway without the bother of leaving home.

"P.J.!" said my wife.

"Don't worry, Mrs. O," said Nick. "We don't have an attached garage."

But, Nick, the most convenient thing about driving a car in the winter is you often can't. This is a perfect excuse for staying home, and what could be more convenient than that? If you have to drive during the winter months, it's important to own the right car. Jeeps, Suburbans, and Range Rovers won't do. When your brand of automobile is shown delivering Sherpa food to Sir Edmund Hillary during every Super Bowl time-out, it isn't convincing to tell your headmaster you can't get out of the driveway. Buy something with no clearance, like a Corvette. Probably the best I-can't-get-there winter driving car ever was the old Austin-Healy with the original exhaust system in place. You could get hung up driving one of those across a putting green, and I once did. But that was before you were born.

Be sure to get a car that has no traction either—something big, with rear-wheel drive and all the weight in the front. Don't get front-wheel drive. A car that has good traction will go fast on ice-covered roads. It's obviously dangerous to go fast on roads like that. Also, if you have poor traction, you might go off the road and wind up in a soft snowbank, but if you have good traction you might make it to school and wind up translating Horace. Winnebago motor homes are huge and have all the weight in the front. Get one of those, and when you get stuck in a snowbank, you'll have a bathroom and a kitchen and it will be almost like staying home in the first place.

But if you really have to get somewhere in the winter, make sure your vehicle is properly prepared. You have to decide whether to use your regular tires, which have hardly any tread, or your snow tires, which have hardly any tread because you were driving around on them all summer. A lot of people choose all-weather tires because you can let those get bald without feeling guilty for not changing them every spring and fall.

Of course, the best choice would be studded snow tires, but the tow truck and ambulance lobbies have made them illegal in most states. The next best thing to studded snow tires is tire chains, except it's impossible to attach tire chains unless you are physically able to lift your car and have prehensile toes to put the chains on while you're holding the car aloft. The only other way to attach tire chains is to drive your car up on a stump so that all four wheels are off the ground. Then wait for a glacier to come along and knock the car off. If you can't get the chains on and are forbidden by law to have studded snow tires, you can use four cement blocks to improve winter driving. Put your car up on the blocks and fly someplace where the weather is warm. You can rent another car when you get there.

Preparation, of course, is only part of the winter automobile problem. Getting a car started when it's ten below can be even more difficult than getting it off the stump after you've put the chains on. Some people leave a light on all night in the garage on the theory that it will generate just enough heat to keep the crankcase oil from congealing. This does not work. During a bad cold snap last winter, I left my headlights on all night in the garage and the car wouldn't start at all the next morning. It is true, however, that congealed crankcase oil makes a car hard to start. Use a lighter weight oil in the winter. Johnson's Baby Oil, for instance. Rub this all over somebody cute, stay home, and forget about starting the car.

Turning the engine over frequently works, too. When the weather gets extremely cold, you should get up in the middle of the night and start your car. Keep it running long enough to get to the airport, and fly someplace where the weather is warm.

Proper use of antifreeze can also help. Alcohol is effective as an antifreeze. Gin has alcohol in it. So does vermouth. Mix eight parts gin to one part vermouth, call your headmaster, and say you can't get out of the driveway.

You really shouldn't go out of the driveway, either. Once out of the driveway, winter driving requires all sorts of complex special techniques. One of these is the foghorn technique such as ships use in bad weather. When visibility is poor, drive very slowly straight ahead and beep your horn every ten seconds. This worked for the *Andrea Doria.* Actually, come to think of it, it didn't.

Anyway, the first rule is to go slow. Get up late, have a big breakfast, take a nap, have a second breakfast, call your headmaster, and tell him you can't get out of the driveway after all.

The second rule is steer into a skid. This is a difficult rule for a lot of people to understand, and I'm one of them. What's that mean, "Steer into a skid"? Is it a command? Are you supposed to go someplace and find a skid? Is it a general observation? Does it mean if you steer then you'll skid? And who are they fooling anyway? If you're able to steer where you want—like "into a skid"—then you're not skidding. Forget this rule.

You don't actually need my help, Nick. You can teach yourself many of the techniques of winter driving. Just cut the brake lines on your dad's car, remove the tie rods, put ice down the front of your pants, and accelerate full speed into a crowded shopping-center parking lot. This will exactly simulate driving in the middle of winter on icy roads in heavy traffic. What it will teach you is not to do any such thing.

You may call this a painful lesson, but that shows your youthful lack of consideration for others. Think how amused the rest of us will be when we read the newspaper story about how you cut the brake lines, removed the tie rods, and drove full speed into a shopping center with a Fudgesicle in your boxers.

Many other winter driving situations can be practiced beforehand. Practice trying to operate the accelerator, brake, and clutch pedals in a great big pair of boots by playing the piano in oven mitts. Practice starting cars with dead batteries by taking a Sears Diehard to the grocery store, leaning over into the meat freezer, and thawing a butterball turkey by running a twelve-volt current through it with jumper cables.

One type of practice for winter driving doesn't even require any physical activity. It's strictly a matter of mental preparation. After all, driving on icy roads has a lot to do with how you think about them. Conceive of a metaphor for icy roads so you'll know how to behave.

Think of icy roads as politicians, for instance—crooked, slippery, and treacherous. If you hit a politician on the nose (equivalent to hitting the brake pedal on an icy road), you'll go to jail. If you kick a politician in the butt (equivalent to putting your foot onto the accelerator), you'll go to jail also. (Going to jail is the equivalent of getting stuck in a snowbank.) Using the politician metaphor, wintertime is one long election day. Do what any sensible person does on election day and stay home.

The rest of winter driving techniques don't have anything to do with driving because you're stuck in that snowbank. When stuck in a snowbank, use the "cradle" method of rocking the car back and forth: Rock back and forth, back and forth, then stick your thumb in your mouth and cry.

Remain inside your car when you are stuck in a snowbank. This will make your body easier to find later. But, if you have your cell phone with you, maybe you should call the AAA. Anybody who does any winter driving should belong to the AAA. Non-AAA towing services are expensive and often don't come. AAA towing services don't come for free. Actually, that's not true. The AAA is a very good organization, and they'll come get you as soon as they can in the spring. But, as good as the AAA is, what's really needed is an organization that, instead of helping you get home in bad weather, would help you stay home in bad weather by bringing some drinks over to your house or by calling your headmaster and saying your driveway is a snow emergency area and the Red Cross has flown you someplace where the weather is warm.

Meanwhile, as long as you're stuck in a snowbank, this is a great opportunity to jacklight deer. Build a fire in your car so the game warden will believe you when you say you thought you were going to have to stay there all winter. Jacklighting deer, of course, is only one of the many outdoor winter activities that can be enjoyed with an automobile. Ice fishing is another. Drive car right out onto the ice. It will fall through. Oil and gasoline will seep out into the pond, and in the spring, all the fish will be lying there dead right on top of the water, and you can scoop them up with your hands and not have to fuss with expensive poles and lures. Cars are great for skiing, too. The point of skiing is to pick up girls, and you can pick up a lot more girls if you tell them your car is a Corvette.

"Or a BMW Z8," suggested Nick, helpfully.

Anyway it's all covered with sleet and ice and probably stuck in a snowbank so they can't tell. But the very best automotive winter sport is just going for a ride in the country. Make that country Australia. It's summer down there now. And your headmaster will never find you in Sydney.

"Nick, maybe you should get Mrs. O to teach you to drive," said my young assistant, Max, whose next assignment is going to be researching where the driveway is with a snow shovel. "She can parallel-park in one move. P.J. has to drive around until he finds a handicapped spot and then limp when he gets out of the car. Besides," said Max, "the automobile is just an appliance."

Max, you webhead, I protested, the automobile is not just an appliance. The automobile bears a symbolic weight that the espresso maker and the Cuisinart never can. The automobile is an icon of modern existence—more so than the electric dynamo, the skyscraper, the atomic bomb, or the damn cell phone. Will you and Nick please turn your stupid ringers off? The automobile *means* something.

The automobile means mastery over technology. It means power, speed, control. It means freedom, autonomy. It means we don't have to walk home.

Oh, sure, we could rely on other means of transportation—mule, sled dogs, our own two feet. But a walk-up movie wouldn't be much fun—standing outside in the evening damp with that big metal speaker box hooked to our belts. If we had a wrecked donkey on cement blocks in our front yard, it would smell. And a wintertime shopping-mall parking lot full of yelping, snarling, biting Alaskan malamutes would be an inconvenience, especially when we emerged from the supermarket with a bag of steaks. Then there's the train, but it won't fit in the garage. And can you picture the president of the United States scooting along a parade route with one knee in an armored Radio Flyer?

So can I. Therefore we should all be grateful to the automobile. But me in particular. I'd be a shoeless pumpkin-knocker rolling down his overalls to count to eleven if it weren't for cars. My grandfather Jake O'Rourke was born in an unpainted shack on a tenant farm in Lime City,

Ohio. There were nine other children, and great-granddad was a drunk. How much formal education my grandfather had I don't know. He may have finished sixth grade. His spelling was approximate. And his acquaintance with higher mathematics and the classical languages was nil. But then the car was invented. Jake went to work for the Atwood Motor Company of Toledo, Ohio. He started as a mechanic, became a salesman, sold the first Willys Overland in Toledo, and went on to become the nation's top Willys salesman, averaging 110 cars per year.

By the 1940s, Grandpa O'Rourke had converted to Buicks. He and his eldest son, my Uncle Arch, owned a dealership on Main Street in East Toledo. My father was the sales manager. Uncle Jack was the ace glad-hander. Uncle Joe ran the used-car lot. Cousin Ide was in charge of the parts department. Various aunts kept the books. And my Great-aunt Helen cooked midday dinner for them all in Granddad's house across the alley.

Everybody in the family worked for O'Rourke Buick, if work was what you'd call it. The spoiled, soft citizens of the twenty-first century define everything as work. Making pie graphs on the laptop is "work." Recreational sport is a "workout." Lollygagging on a couch in a psychotherapist's office is "working on personal issues." But the O'Rourkes came from a time and a social class where work meant lifting things. And we didn't lift anything. O'Rourkes spent the day loafing beneath the stuffed sailfish and mounted deer heads in the Buick showroom, smoking cigarettes and shooting the breeze with prospective car buyers. And this was what my relatives would have been doing whether they had jobs doing it or not. It left them with plenty of energy at the end of the day for smoking cigarettes and shooting the breeze with prospective car buyers beneath the stuffed sailfish and mounted deer heads of various bars, pool halls, and bowling alleys.

Cars made the O'Rourkes happy and prosperous. And it was as a happy and prosperous little O'Rourke that I was born in 1947. My first memory is of a car, a 1948 Roadmaster convertible in electric blue with rolled and pleated red leather upholstery. It was a thing of astonishing beauty. Automotive engineering and design have not been bettered since, in my opinion. All right, aerodynamics. I'll give you that. But there never was a quieter transmission than the Dynaflow, especially during the thirty to forty minutes required to reach 60 mph under full acceleration. And talk about safety features, the '48 Roadmaster weighed 4,300 pounds, rode on 16-inch wheels, and—consider the size of that bumper, the heft of those teeth in the grille—could mash a Volvo flat.

My moral and emotional life was immersed in cars. I first experienced responsibility dangling from my father's knees steering his 1952 Special Coupe in erratic wiggles down the highway while he worked the pedals. My idea of loyalty was measured by the Buick trademark. I fought the kid across the street whose parents had gone so far as to buy a De Soto. And when my father died suddenly in the fall of 1956, my grandfather could think of no way to console me except to bring over a 1957 Century hardtop a week before the introduction date and drive me around for hours.

Not to sound callous, but I think those 1950s new car introductions affected my outlook more than my father's death. The annual all-American excitement over the latest models shaped my philosophy and politics. I have faith in democracy and free markets. I believe in human progress. I know in my heart that, given the vision, the commitment, and the will, all mankind can achieve attractively updated chrome trim. Indeed, automobiles have taught me most of life's lessons. The existence of evil, for instance, was revealed in the person of a bullying lumpen stepfather who also sold cars. And I found that evil did not go unpunished. The stepfather arrived at the beginning of the 1958 model year, and soon after marrying my mother he landed a job as manager of an Edsel dealership.

My own first employment was, of course, at O'Rourke Buick. I worked on the used-car lot, cleaning and waxing clunkers with Shorty and Rubin, who had a number of teachings. "Always leave some lint in the corner of the windshield," said Shorty. "That way they know you washed it."

From my first car I learned how, if you remove the hubcaps, reverse the tires so the whitewalls don't show, ventilate the muffler with an ice pick, replace the giant oil bath air cleaner with something cool in chrome, and pound aluminum spacers into the coil springs to jack up the front end . . . you'll still look like a dick in a 1956 four-door Ford Customline sedan your grandmother gave you. The more so if it's salmon pink.

And there was my first wreck. I was driving my stepfather's appalling 1959 flathead-six Plymouth. (He'd quit the Edsel dealership and bought a Dairy Queen on the road to Detroit, but the expressway opened in 1960 and it had been four years since anybody'd stopped for an ice-cream cone.) I made an unsignaled left turn from the far right lane on a four-lane street and ran door-to-door into a passing Impala. This taught me that Satchel Paige was exactly wrong when he said, "Don't look back. Something may be gaining on you." My stepfather decided to teach me a lesson, too. He sold my Ford, emptied my save-up-for-an-MGA bank account, and declared I'd never drive another of the household vehicles as long as he lived. Which wasn't long. He got cancer in 1965, and I remember the words I used to comfort my mother the night he passed away. "Mom," I said, "can I borrow the car?"

Naturally there came a time when I rebelled against the automobile. For a while I was infatuated with motorcycles. But I kept falling off them. I had a nasty little X6 Suzuki that I put over the high side of a windy road through my college campus. I went sailing on my back across the dew-lubricated lawn, looking up and thinking what a beautiful night it was with the sky full of stars. And I saw all the more of them when my head hit the tree.

The bike was unhurt except the front brake cable was snapped and the rear brake pedal was jammed against the frame and useless. I rode home gingerly, parked the Suzuki behind my apartment building, and that night some idiot stole it. The police called a week later and said they had my motorcycle. I went to get it. It was a pile of rubble. Apparently the idiot cranked the Suzuki through all six gears and then came to a curve. "We found it *way* at the bottom of a ravine," said the police.

I owned some other motorcycles too, but I fell off them and (possibly due to head injuries) became a hippie. Cars no longer meant anything to me, except as a means to an end. That is, it's very rare to be given a lift by a pedestrian while hitchhiking to Big Sur. I was above thinking about cars. I was concerned with political liberation, world peace, spiritual enlightenment, and convincing Moonbeam Feinholt that the ecosphere was in imminent danger from man's rampant waste of fossil fuels and that she and I had better double up in the shower to save earth's precious resources. I could care less about cars. Although I do remember sticking an enormous doobie out a vent window and attempting to use a Volkswagen microbus as a room-sized bong. I was so fully recovered from my boyish enthusiasm for automobiles that I made appreciative noises about an old bread truck somebody had painted with a five-inch brush in ten colors of Dutch Boy semigloss interior vinyl. Cars were for squares. Or so I said. But while leading a life of outward conformity with its drug binges, orgies, and rioting in the streets, I also maintained a fantasy existence. I'd get a haircut and a job and a Ferrari California Spider, an Aston Martin shooting brake, a Lotus Elan, a Morgan Plus 8, a Pegaso Z-102, an E-type Jag, a 289 AC Cobra, and, for practicality's sake, in case I daydreamed up a wife and kids, a Facel Vega.

There was another hippie with kindred secrets, Alan R (now a respectable commercial artist). How we found each other out, I don't know. Perhaps we were so stoned that right in the middle of a discussion of astral projection, one or the other of us blurted something about Weber carburetors or de Dion axles. Anyway, we would closet ourselves in the furthest reaches of the crash pad and jabber for hours about the relative merits of Bertone, Zagato, and Pinifarina.

Alan R and I did eventually get jobs and haircuts, if not Ferraris. And in 1975 I noticed I hadn't renewed my driver's license since the late sixties. After all, the world had been going to end in atomic holocaust and a revolution had been about to happen and I'd meant to move to Kathmandu. But I found these arguments unpersuasive with the Highway Patrol.

To get a new driver's license I had to take driver's education as if I were a sixteen-year-old instead of just someone who'd been acting as if he had a sixteen-year-old's brain. Thus I wound up in night courses at a Manhattan high school. My class consisted of half a dozen Asians who spoke no English, half a dozen Eastern European women in babushkas who wouldn't speak at all, ten jiving teens clustered at the back of the room, and me. The instructor wore liberal clothes, a medley of corduroy in dirt colors. His pedagogical method was simple. "The function of the steering wheel is to control the direction of the car," he'd say. And then he'd ask, "Can anyone tell me what function the steering wheel performs?" The Asians stared politely into space. The babushkas looked at the floor. The teens continued to exchange high fives, dis each other, and rhyme things. "Can anyone tell me what function the steering wheel performs?" the instructor repeated. I lifted a mitt. "Yes, third row," said the instructor.

"The steering wheel controls the direction of the car," I said.

"Good," he said, and continued his lecture. "The function of the accelerator is to control the speed of the car. Can anyone tell me what function the accelerator performs?" No response. He repeated the question. Again, nothing. The instructor had the look of resigned insignificance that comes from years of inner-city teaching. I could see he was prepared to keep asking this question for the next fifty minutes or until I went nuts and strangled him. I raised my hand. "Yes, third row."

"The accelerator controls the speed of the car," I said. And so it went every Monday, Wednesday, and Friday for six weeks, with the liberal in corduroy saying, "Yes, third row," each time as if he'd never seen me before. And to this day, if you want to know what function the steering wheel performs, I'm the guy to ask.

The written part of the driver's license exam was given in the horrible Department of Motor Vehicles building downtown, in a number of languages, fortunately including English. "The function of the accelerator is to control the speed of the car. T or F" was one question. We were given forty minutes to complete the test. It took five. I handed my exam paper to a large irritable woman at the front of the room who laid a template over the pencil-checked answers and said, "Ditchyoo cheat?"

"Did I what?"

"Nobody got all them right before," she said. Which tells us everything we need to know about New York drivers. And apparently I'd become one because I flunked the driving test. I'd borrowed my boss's Chrysler. After an Age of Aquarius spent illegally driving paisley bread trucks and Volkswagen microbuses full of marijuana smoke, I was unused to automatic transmissions, much less power brakes. Attempting to back into my parallel-parking space, I belatedly realized I'd put the Chrysler in drive instead of reverse.

"My sister did something like that," said Nick.

I gave a good hearty Volkswagen microbus stab to the brake pedal and spring-launched the driving examiner—who was not, by the way, wearing his seat belt. His clipboard hit the dash, he hit the clipboard, and the clipboard clip left a big red ankh mark in the middle of his forehead. He drew an X through my paperwork.

I think it was that precise moment—seeing the ancient Egyptian symbol for eternal life impressed on my driving examiner's face—when my love of automobiles returned in full force. About this time I also quit smoking pot and began to drink again. And the next thing I knew I was waking up with a terrible hangover realizing I'd bought a 1965 Alfa Romeo GTC convertible from Alan R's brother.

This is how I happen to write for car magazines. A few days later I was in Gillhooey's on Thirty-fourth Street in New York, which was my neighborhood tavern and also a hangout for the employees of *Down-Shift* magazine. I was standing at the bar next to Jim Williams, then *Down-Shift*'s sport editor. He said, "I heard you bought an old Alfa. It so happens I've got an old Alfa repair kit."

"You do?" I said.

"Yeah. A truck full of money to follow you everywhere you go."

When the editor-in-chief of *Down-Shift*, David E. Davis, Jr., learned that there was someone stupid enough to own an old Alfa and silly enough to be obsessed with Buicks, he gave me an assignment to take a silly old Buick on a stupid trip across the country. The '56 two-door Special broke down every day. I remember being somewhere in New Mexico, reduced to tears, beating on the fuel pump with the fat end of a screwdriver and howling words of Anglo-Saxon etymology.

That was when you were in diapers, Max. I remain absorbed in the culture of the automobile. David E. Davis has sent me on numerous stupid trips since. And, although the GTC was sold and the Buick fixation eased somewhat, a succession of silly vehicles has accrued to me anyway, including—whoops—another Alfa; a pickup truck made from the front half of a Jimmy that had been in a head-on and the back half of a Chevy Fleetside that had been rear-ended; a Rabbit convertible for which I took cruel "chick car" ribbing from your father, Nick; a Subaru wagon so well built and reliable that I traded it in out of boredom; a BMW 325 convertible with more miles on it than the Jupiter probe; a 911 used mostly for urban commuting; and a Jeep that I've just, unaccountably, had restored even though it's a 1984 and as rare as eating disorders in the fashion industry.

To this day I can be found out in the garage reduced to tears, beating on a fuel pump with the fat end of a screwdriver, howling words of Anglo-Saxon etymology, and causing my wife to say, "I thought you knew something about cars."

Perhaps this is the moment to confess that I do not. I mean, "The steering wheel controls the . . ." But I don't know much else. And I suspect none of the O'Rourkes ever has—at least since Grandpa quit being a mechanic about the time the acetylene headlamp was invented. As a kid I would be given a couple of simple tools and sent to amuse myself on the wrecked cars behind the O'Rourke dealership. This is how I learned to hammer on things with the fat end of a screwdriver. The rest of my knowledge of automotive construction and repair I gleaned from building plastic scale-model kits. Whenever my car makes a funny noise I first make sure the engine is still glued in and then check whether my sister has knocked the continental kit loose by sitting Barbie on the trunk lid during a doll homecoming.

To tell the truth, I'm not much of a driver either. That is, I'm okay—in theory. I went to race-car driving school and did very well in the classroom work. I remember the instructor telling me so, just as the large, irritable woman at the Department of Motor Vehicles had done. Though the race-car instructor didn't accuse me of cheating since, on the track, I was the absolute slowest of the ten people in my course. In fact, I believe the instructor's exact words to me were, "You've got a goldbrick mouth and a tin-slug gas-pedal foot."

Never mind. To me, automobiles are not mere physical objects. My love of motor vehicles transcends the material plane. The flivver, the jalopy, the crate—these are things of the spirit. The place taken by religion, philosophy, or art in other men's lives is occupied by cars in mine. Spend an hour in a church and where are you? Spend an hour in a car and you're at the beach. Three thousand years of Western philosophy has not been able to answer the question "What is the meaning of life?" But when you're driving a car, the meaning of life is to find a parking place. And as for art, take the most beautiful and sublime sculpture by a Renaissance master—it brakes, corners, and accelerates like a large chunk of marble.

7

MARCH 2001

You should write a book," said my godson Nick, who was back at our house, having slipped chicken sushi onto the hors d'oeuvres platter at his school's alumni lunch.

I stared balefully at Nick. [It so happens that I'm the author of a number of books, including *The Agoraphobe at Large* and *New Truths About Eternal Verities* and *One-Man Honeymoon* (travel); *A Dog's Breakfast* (poetry); and *Woolly (Thanks to Rogaine) Bully,* recounting a month on the road with the Sam the Sham and the Pharaohs reunion tour. This was briefly on the best-seller list in, I believe, the Netherlands. Plus there's the forthcoming *How the Financial Collapse of 2001 Happened, Unless It Didn't*. Not to mention a series of "Rape Mysteries" written under the pseudonym Scarlet O'Bronte: *Rape Be Not Proud; Rape Comes for the Archbishop; Night of the Living Raped; Rape Takes a Holiday,* etc.]

"I mean a real book," said Nick. "You know, a memoir."

Yes, Nick, that's the modern idea. After years of effort in the author trade, I discover an ideal topic, an inexhaustible subject of discourse, a literary inspiration—me. I'll write a memoir. I don't know why I didn't think of this ages ago. It will be liberating to sit down at the typewriter and just be myself, as opposed to being you, Nick, which I don't have the clothes for.

Even though my memoir is still in the idea stage, I'm full of enthusiasm. I'll give the secret of my success—the success I plan to have as a memoir writer. As far as I can tell, the secret is thinking about myself all the time. No doubt my memoir will be inspirational, inspiring others to think about themselves all the time. They'll see the meaning in their lives—they've been meaning to write a memoir, too.

So what if it's a crowded field? My memoir will stand out. It will show readers a side of life they little guessed at, the side with the writer sitting in his boxer shorts surrounded by six empty coffee cups and three full ashtrays playing Go Fish with the dog.

Maybe readers *had* guessed at that. But I'm going to recount my personal struggles, such as having to come up with things to write about all the time. I've spent decades looking for stories that would interest other people. I've surmounted enormous obstacles—thinking about other people, just for instance.

But enough about them. This isn't going to be a mere self-help book. This is the story of how one young man grew up to be . . . a lot older. That is probably the most serious issue I need to work through in my memoir. The issue being that I haven't really done much. But I don't feel this should stand in my way. O. J. Simpson wrote a memoir, and the jury said he didn't do anything at all.

There's also a lot of anger I need to deal with. I'm angry at my parents. For memoir purposes, they weren't nearly poor enough. They weren't rich either. And they failed miserably at leading colorful lives. My mother did belong to Kappa Kappa Gamma, which is a secret society, I guess. And my father was a veteran of the Pacific war, but the only casualty in his battalion was one fellow crushed by a palm tree. Furthermore, we lived in Toledo, Ohio. I suppose I could write a comic memoir. But in today's society there are some things you just don't make fun of, and chief among these is yourself.

My parents also neglected to abuse me. They're gone now, alas. (Downside: no publicity-building estrangement when memoir is published, to be followed by tearful reconciliation on *Oprah*. Upside: I'm an Adult Child of the Deceased.) I've thought about asking my wife's parents to abuse me, but it seems too little, too late. I did have a stepfather who bowled.

Perhaps I'll keep the section on my childhood brief, just emphasize that I'm a survivor. That's what's unique about me, and there are six billion people in the world who know how unique I feel. This should guarantee excellent sales. And—here comes that literary inspiration again—memoirs do sell. Readers want to know what real people really did and really felt. What a shame that the writing geniuses of the nineteenth century wasted their time making things up. We could have had Jane Austen Reality Prose: *Got up. Wrote. Went out. Came back. Wrote some more. Vicarage still drafty*.

Modern book buyers have become too sophisticated for imaginary romance and drama. They want facts: Roswell, New Mexico; the missile that shot down TWA flight 800; the Republican majority in the Florida popular vote. Unfortunately, I don't have many facts like that, but I do have some terrific celebrity gossip. I've read all their memoirs.

I also know about some awful things my friends have done. I've noticed, while memoir reading, that one of the main points of the genre is ratting on your pals. I was going to gather that material together and commit it to paper. Then I realized that other memoir writers, as a class, seem to have very few friends who weigh 200 pounds and own shotguns.

Probably confession is a safer route. I've done all kinds of loathsome deeds myself and am perfectly willing to admit them, if it sells books. But thumbing through my memoir collection, I noticed another thing. Good memoir writers only confess to certain of the more glamorous sins—drastic sexual escapades, head-to-toe drug abuse, bold felonies after the statutes of limitation have run out. Nobody confesses to things that just make him look like a jerk-o. Nobody admits he got up at 4 A.M. with a throbbing head after five hours of listening to the kid's pets squeaking in the exercise wheel and drowned the gerbils in the toilet. Most of my transgressions fall into this category and will need to be excised. I don't want to get caught writing one of those "unauthorized autobiographies."

This brings me to the other little problem I'm having with the story of my life, which is remembering it. There were the 1960s. I recall they started out well. Then there were the 1970s. I recall they ended badly. In between, frankly, I am missing a few candles on the cake. Also there were the 1950s, when nothing memorable happened, and the 1980s, when everything memorable was happening to somebody else. And the 1990s went by in a blur. But, no worries, I've been keeping a diary: *Got up. Wrote. Went out. Came back. Wrote some more. Drowned the gerbils.*

Maybe I can make up for my lack of reminiscences by inserting various vivid fantasies I've had. But this is cheating on the memoir form, since I'm admitting that those things—the *New York Review of Books* swimsuit issue, for example—never happened.

Or perhaps I should go back to all those challenges I've faced. I've had to endure enormous prejudice. True, since I'm a middle-aged white male Republican, the enormous prejudice came from me. But I still had to endure it. This is one reason that learning to love myself was another huge challenge. But I've overcome that too. Although, now that I'm completely self-infatuated, I keep waiting for me to give myself a raise. It's been a bitter disappointment.

Thank goodness. Bitter disappointments are crucial to memoirs. Thinking of something to write in this memoir has been a bitter disappointment so far. That means I can write about not being able to write. Should be good for a chapter, if I can make it sound bitter enough.

Wait. I'm forgetting spiritual transformation. I've been touched by an angel—and a big one, too, all covered in glitter. It got me right in the forehead three months ago, when the dog knocked over the Christmas tree.

And I have a good title: *My Excuse for Living*. That should count for something.

Anyway, I'm not daunted. The memoir is the great literature of the current era. All that we ask of art, the memoir provides. Beauty is truth, truth beauty, and if we can get a beauty to tell the truth, then Kathryn Harrison's *The Kiss* is all ye need to know. Art justifies God's ways to man like *The Art of the Comeback* does. God is going to fry Donald Trump in hell, and He is perfectly justified. As with all art, the memoir holds a mirror up to life, and if there are some lines of cocaine on that mirror, so much the better. Out of chaos the memoir brings order—a huge order from a major bookstore chain, it is to be hoped. The memoir is nature's handmaiden and also nature's butt boy, bagman, and patsy if *Behind the Oval Office* by Dick Morris is anything to go by. The memoir exists on its own terms, art for art's sake, if you happen to be named Arthur—vide *Risk and Redemption: Surviving the Network News Wars* by Arthur Kent. The memoir speaks to us; indeed, it won't shut up. *Vita brevis est, memoir longa.*

And mine is going to be really long. Nick, thanks to you, I've got a major book happening here. After a whole ten minutes spent wrestling with my muse, I've made a vital creative breakthrough. I now know how to give my memoir the moral, intellectual, and aesthetic impact that the works of Shakespeare, Goethe, Dostoyevsky had on previous generations. As with all insights of true originality, it's very simple. It's called lying.

"Speaking of books," said Nick, "I've got to read one. And write a report as makeup work in my Touch and Feel World History class."

Which part, I asked, of world history are you studying?

"The part that's happening right now," said Nick. "Our teacher believes that the best way to learn history is to start at the present and move forward. He says this allows us to rid historicality of Western-hegemonized false narratives in male gender perspectives."

What?

"Beats me," said Nick. "Anyway, I'm supposed to read *The Third Way* by Anthony Giddens."

The director of the London School of Economics?

"I guess so."

Let me take a crack at that. Max went to the London School of Economics. I'll get the inside skinny on Giddens from Max.

"Uncle Peej, the last time you wrote a book report for me I got an F. Or I would have gotten an F if my school gave Fs. I got an Inappropriate Socialization and a Has Issues and had to lead the football team sensitivity sessions for a month."

Nick, I said, would you rather read *The Third Way* or practice backing the car out of the driveway?

Book Report: *The Third Way*

Not to be dense about this, but I had no idea there was an actual political theory behind the whoreson activities of modern left-wing politicians. Of course I recognized a pattern of behavior common to Britain's New Labor, America's New Democrats, Europe's New Social Democrats, and—for all I know—Rwanda's New Hutus. But I thought this was an example of the universal applicability of the political strategy, "Fake right, run left." And I was aware that Anthony Giddens had written a book. But so had Dennis Rodman and former president Bill Clinton's former pet cat. I assumed that *The Third Way* was merely a repackaging of socialism in order to sell it to a public that wasn't having any. In the 1950s there was a breakfast cereal called Sugar Pops. During the earthy, all-natural 1970s the name was changed to Honey Pops. Now, in the health-conscious new millennium, the label reads Corn Pops.

But then I was forced to read *The Third Way*. And, to my surprise, I was impressed by Anthony Giddens—not impressed enough to finish all 155 pages of his dreary book, but impressed. Giddens explains the difference between the Third Way and the traditional left. Tony Blair, Hillary Clinton, and Gerhard Schröder (and Anthony Giddens!) confess to a belief in the marketplace. Granted, as a Road to Damascus experience, this is like being blinded by the realization that you're headed in the Damascus direction. Not believing in the marketplace is akin to not believing in gravity. No amount of Marxist theory or utopian social experiment will change the fact of the marketplace, just as no amount of theoretical physics or laboratory experiment will get me to finish reading *The Third Way*. A physicist may have all sorts of ideas about antigravity, and he may even demonstrate his ideas in a particle accelerator. But if he drops a cement block on his foot—ouch.

Old-line Marxists must be feeling a pain in their toes. Disbelief in the marketplace was the very heart of traditional leftism. Yet Blair, Clinton, and Schröder *are* traditional leftists. They want politics to interfere in every possible aspect of life. But they are leftists who have abandoned the central tenet of leftism. If the leftists don't believe in leftism, what—as it were—is left?

This is where *The Third Way* comes in. On page 66 is a boxed précis titled THIRD WAY VALUES. A number of these little boxes appear in the Giddens book. It's an almost endearing touch—obviously meant to lighten the workload of the young assistants who actually do the reading for Blair, Clinton, et al.

Here are the values, six of them:

- "Equality." A nice nostalgic touch, equality being the essential false vow of socialism since at least Wat Tyler's Rebellion in 1381. Of course, nowadays you'd reach Wat at peasantsrevolt.com, where he'd be promising the masses e-rebellion home delivery.
- "Protection of the vulnerable." And the vulnerable are—as you realize if you've been watching daytime television and reading modern therapeutic literature—all of us, all the time. Unfortunately, what we seem to be most vulnerable to is Tony Blair, Hillary Clinton, and so forth.
- "Freedom as autonomy." As opposed to freedom as an old unmatched sock. Although either definition of freedom is incompatible with the previous two values, since you can't put one sock on the feet of everybody, and we're all vulnerable to cold feet.
- "No rights without responsibilities." Moderate voters read this as meaning "Throw the bums off welfare." The bums, more accurately, understand it as "If you want an old unmatched sock, it is your responsibility to vote for Hillary Clinton."
- "Cosmopolitan pluralism." Hard to say what this means, but seeing when the book was published, it could have been a plea to

mayor Rudolph Giuliani to let various colorful New York characters out of jail in time to vote for Hillary Clinton.

- "Philosophic conservatism." In the accompanying muddled text, Giddens claims to be referring to an emerging political consensus about loving nature or some such. But consider how the word *philosophical* is used today: "He's philosophical about his wife leaving him." "He's philosophical about losing his job." The meaning of *philosophical* is "doesn't give a damn."

So here is the broad—philosophical, if you will—outline of the Third Way, a sort of clarion call to whatever. But the Third Way also focuses on specific issues, hundreds and hundreds of them. Some of these issues are heartfelt (or perhaps, due to the cement block, toe-felt) by the traditional left. But other issues seem to be raised just to show that, when the Third Way is at work, everything is an issue. Interesting how they sound when they're grouped together: women's rights, gay rights, animal rights. Try matching these rights with Anthony Giddens's just-cited fourth value, "No rights without responsibilities." I invite Democratic congressional candidates to go on the hustings in 2002 and hold forth on women's responsibilities, gay responsibilities, and the responsibilities of animals.

The Third Way, however, advocates special rights for special groups, not because these rights make sense but because they don't. Special rights for special groups is an idea that's dangerous to a peaceful society—as has been well proven in the Balkans, Lebanon, Ireland, India, the United States, and practically every other place in the world. And that's the point. A peaceful society doesn't need as much political machinery as a society where everybody hates everybody's guts.

Increasing the amount of—and the need for—political machinery is the unifying theme behind all Third Way thinking. I quote Giddens, brazenly saying in his book, "The state should expand the role of the public sphere." Ecology is a splendid way to do so. What could be more complicated—and hence more needful of political mediation—than making sure the whole of nature keeps working, that the entire universe continues to operate? In the past an omnipotent God was required to do this. Gosh knows how many Parliamentary white papers and regulatory bureaucracies it will take now. (And forget what the striking coal miners of yore would think of a Labor Party that cares most about the pit ponies.)

Bribing the minorities, healing the earth, preventing the privatization of social insurance, making educational systems as academically bad and as freighted with inappropriate social responsibilities as possible, providing universal medical care, universal day care, universal home care for the disabled, the partially disabled, and those of us who are okay in the morning but tend to be a bit unsteady after lunch—these are no-brainer methods of expanding the political machinery. Not that the Third Way isn't brainy also. For example, the British Labor/U.S. Democrat handling of the illegal drug issue is masterful in its cunning. Our Third Way men are social liberals—with all the hanky-panky that implies. What we do in our private lives is private. We can take all the drugs we like as long as we don't admit to it publicly. But *publicly,* Labor and Democratic politicians are careful to denounce drugs as bad and a danger. This allows them to promote extensive political programs educating us about the dangerous badness of drugs. So, now we're empowered to take drugs by the social liberals plus we're informed by the social liberals that drug-taking is a naughty thrill; therefore we take drugs. And oh, how the political machinery gets busy. The Third Way has to arrange for all of us to have our sentences suspended and go to drug-treatment facilities and get some of that home care for the disabled, too, because—as any social liberal will tell you—addiction is a disease.

Chairman Mao pulled something similar with his "let a hundred flowers bloom" speech, except Mao just killed the victims of his phony permissiveness tactic. He didn't make them fill out National Health Service paperwork while going through detox.

Sometimes Third Way policy positions are too deep for the uninitiated to plumb. Conservatives were flummoxed by Bill Clinton's interventions in Haiti, Bosnia, Kosovo, and elsewhere. But Clinton had found a way to conduct "peace by other means." He was purposely using military force solely as an instrument of pointless moralizing, on missions that neither defended American security nor extended American geopolitical power. Clinton thereby was able to harness warmongering's increase in political power and prestige without losing the support of smug lefty pacifists. He was Franklin Delano Gandhi. (Plus this kind of military conflict doesn't create any Republican war-hero generals to run against your party in future elections.)

But why is the Third Way so intent on this expansion of political machinery? If they know socialism is imaginary, what are they pursuing in its stead? What do they want to accomplish? Well, Anthony Giddens has another little boxed précis on page 70 of his book, THE THIRD WAY PROGRAMME:

- "The radical center." Let's compromise and kill *half* the Kulaks.
- "The new democratic state (the state without enemies)." Hmm, there's me.
- "Active civil society." No more sleeping in church.
- "The democratic family." Dad and the canary vs. Mom and Junior. Rover has the tie vote. Looks like we stay home and do yard work instead of going to the Hamptons.
- "The new mixed economy." Easy on the vermouth.
- "Positive welfare." Would you like a large entitlement check? Are you *positive?*
- "The social investment state." We'll use my high school diploma to make a down payment on a beach house, and we'll buy a Range Rover with an inner-city literacy program.
- "The cosmopolitan nation." Goat cheese in Cedar Rapids!
- "Cosmopolitan democracy." Nope, just smelled like goat cheese; actually it's the 2002 Democratic congressional campaign.

Does that clarify everything? No? Then you should do what I do whenever I become truly confused by political ideas. Pretend the entire world is our school and all the prominent people are students in my class. What's everybody up to? The popular kids are out having fun. The smart kids are reading Adam Smith. The ambitious kids are working nights and weekends. The talented kids are playing sports and rehearsing for the school play. I'm drinking beer behind the Dairy Queen. And the insufferable twits? They're running for student government.

* * *

"Gee, thanks, Uncle Peej," said Nick, "but I'm not sure if that's exactly what Mr. Sturbridge had in—"

Any other makeup work to do? I asked.

"A composition for my Creativity class."

On?

"Creativity."

Started it yet?

"No," said Nick. "I was thinking I'd write about how the Bible could have been more creative. You know, in the 'begats' sections, for instance. There's a bunch of begats in First Chronicles, chapter six, and it's way dull, especially if you consider what a begat involves. The chronicler could have done a lot with this material.

"Eleazar begat Phineas doggy-style. Phineas begat Abishua standing up behind a tent. And Abishua begat Bukki totally by mistake, after a party. Bukki begat Uzzi on the back saddle of a camel when he was taking Uzzi's mom, who was sixteen, home after she'd been baby-sitting for Bukki's kids. Uzzi begat Zerahiah and there was a huge custody fight, except this time both parents told King Solomon to go for it, and his majesty split Zerahiah like a melon. That was when Zerahiah was fifteen and by that time he'd already begotten Meraioth.

"But Zerahiah's mother claimed Meraioth was Bukki's kid and everybody believed it, because Bukki was such an old goat. Meraioth begat Amariah, which surprised all twelve tribes of Israel, who were sure Meraioth was gay. Amariah begat Ahitub, who was called Ahitub because his mother hooked up with Amariah in the ritual bath. Ahitub begat Zadok, or that's what Ahitub's wife said, even though Ahitub had been away on a caravan for eleven months before Zadok was born. And so on," said Nick. "But then I was thinking that was maybe a little—"

Too creative.

"Yes," said Nick.

So do what I do when I'm stuck, I said. Consult *Bartlett's*, pick a random quotation on the subject, and trash it. Let's have a look. C . . . R . . . E . . . nope, Muffin has torn that page out of the index. We'll try "art," that'll do. Here's "canons of a." Sounds interesting. Page 697, number 15. Hmmm, I'd hoped *Bartlett's* was misspelling *canons*. But it's an Alfred North Whitehead quotation, and he's always a sack of crap.

> The canons of art are merely the expression, in specialized forms, of the requirements for depth of experience.

"That sounds like something we'd hear in Creativity class," said Nick.

Two indisputable canons of art, I said, are that all movies need a car chase and all plays need a sword fight. Shakespeare was generally mindful of this and Hal Needham always was. Other stage and screen auteurs, however, have shown themselves to be aesthetically ignorant or maybe just lazy. Why don't you write some sword fights and car chases? You can insert them into various plays and movies that lack a certain—well, sword fight or car chase.

There's one of those artsy video-rental places downtown—all sorts of theater performances on tape and talky-weepy subtitle movies. Then you can practice parallel parking outside while I visit the Pig and Whistle next door.

FIDDLER ON THE ROOF

By Joseph Stein (based on the stories of Shalom Aleichem)

From ACT I, SCENE 10

As the wedding dance reaches a wild climax, the CONSTABLE *and his* MEN *enter, carrying clubs. The dancers see them and slowly stop.*

CONSTABLE: I see we came at a bad time, Tevye. I'm sorry, but the orders are for tonight. For the whole village. All right, men.

The RUSSIANS *begin their destruction, turning over tables, smashing dishes and windows.*

TEVYE: As the good book says, Oh, no, you don't!

PERCHICK: Specifically, the good book *Das Kapital*. The Masses will resolutely struggle against imperialist hooliganism and exploitation!

PERCHICK *pulls rusty old Cossack swords, pitchforks, ancient muskets, and other weapons from under a bed and distributes them to the villagers. The* RUSSIANS *retreat.*

CONSTABLE: (*over his shoulder*): Boy, are you going to be sorry when you find out how Stalin feels about Jews!

TEVYE (*sings*):

If things weren't such a bitch, man,
Daidle deedle daidle
Digguh deedle daidle dum,
All day long I'd biddy biddy bun,
If workers controlled the means of production!

WAITING FOR GODOT
By Samuel Beckett

From the beginning of ACT I

VLADIMIR: What do we do now?

ESTRAGON: Wait.

VLADIMIR: Yet, but while waiting?

ESTRAGON: What about hanging ourselves? (*Audience fidgets hopefully.*)

VLADIMIR: From a bough. *They go toward the tree.* I wouldn't trust it.

ESTRAGON: We can always try.

VLADIMIR: Go ahead.

ESTRAGON: After you.

VLADIMIR: No, no, you first.

ESTRAGON: Why me?

VLADIMIR: I don't understand.

ESTRAGON: Is this more amusing in French or what?

VLADIMIR: I don't know. *Je ne sais pas,* as the French say it.

ESTRAGON (*searching behind tree*): Look, here is a pair of swords. *He picks swords up and hands one to* VLADIMIR.

VLADIMIR: We'll have a sword fight.

ESTRAGON: Exactly.

VLADIMIR: A coup droit!

ESTRAGON: A parry de quatre!

VLADIMIR: A parry de sixte!

ESTRAGON: A riposte!

VLADIMIR: A flying cut-over!
ESTRAGON: This is no use. These are metaphorical swords.
VLADIMIR: You're right.
ESTRAGON: Let's hang ourselves after all. *They do. Audience applauds.*

DEATH OF A SALESMAN
By Arthur Miller

LINDA (*calling*): Willy, you coming up?
WILLY (*uttering a gasp of fear, whirling about as if to quiet her*): Sh! *Sounds, faces, voices seem to be swarming in upon him, and he flicks at them, crying*: Sh! Sh! *Suddenly music, faint and high, stops him. It rises in intensity. He rushes around the house.* Shhh!
LINDA: Willy?

There is no answer. LINDA *waits.* BIFF *gets up off his bed and stands listening. He is still in his clothes.*

LINDA (*with real fear*): Willy, answer me! Willy!

There is the sound of a car starting up.

LINDA: No!
BIFF (*rushing down the stairs*): Pop!

BIFF *jumps in the car beside* WILLY. *Images of moving scenery are projected on the scrim.*

WILLY: Get out of here, Biff! I'm going to drive off the road and kill myself so you can have the insurance money.
BIFF: No, Pop! No! BIFF *reaches beneath the seat and pulls out two fencing foils.* I bought these at Mr. Oliver's sporting goods store . . . all right, okay, I stole them. Anyway, I know you always wanted me to be a football star, but fencing is what I really like. Let's stop somewhere and I'll kill you in a sword fight.
WILLY: Too late, boy, we're already being chased by a cop.

KRAMER VS. KRAMER
Directed by Robert Benton

Int: Courtroom
TED *takes* BILLY *by the arm and pulls him into the aisle.*

TED: Fuck! I mean, fooey on . . . this, Billy. We're getting out of here.

CUT TO:

Ext: Street, Day
TED, *still holding* BILLY *by the arm, hails a taxi.*

CUT TO:

Int: Taxi, Ted's POV
TED (*to taxi driver*): Drive like the dickens, cabbie. We're feeling the conventions of American parenthood!
CABBIE: You bet!
BILLY: Mom's weepy all the time, like Meryl Streep or somethin'.

CUT TO:

Ext: Courthouse steps
JOANNA *waves frantically for a cab. Her* LAWYER *stands beside her.*

JOANNA: Help! I'm losing emotional contact with my child!

CUT TO:

Ext: Day, *a winding cliffside road, an interstate, a multistory parking garage, the face of Mt. Baldy, under the L tracks on Queens Boulevard, a dusty road on the West Texas plains.* TED *and* BILLY'S *taxicab drives the wrong way against traffic, is chased by airplanes, plows through a storefront, corners on two wheels, beats a speeding freight train to a railroad crossing, makes screechy sounds, goes underwater, loses hubcaps, fenders, roof.* JOANNA *and* LAWYER *follow in second taxi. Both cabs leap the Grand Canyon.*

CUT TO:

Close-up: Open taxi door
BILLY'S *lifeless form spills to the ground.*

LAWYER: Well, there goes the custody case.
JOANNA: Let's sue for neglect.

THE BATTLESHIP POTEMKIN
Directed by Sergei Eisenstein

Sailors grimace . . .
Sailors shake fists . . .
Empty bread dishes . . .

Title Card
EMPTY BREAD DISHES

Sailors run around decks . . .
Sailors shout defiance . . .
Brooding shot of the sea . . .
Sailors gesticulate . . .
Sailors exhort one another . . .
Officers jump into automobiles and head for the stern . . .

Title Card
COMRADES! ARE AUTOMOBILES INVENTED AS YET?

Title Card
PERHAPS NO. BUT SOON THEY WILL BE WHEN WE ACHIEVE VICTORIOUS SOCIALIST BROTHERHOOD.

Sailors jump into other automobiles and chase officers around the decks . . .

Title Card
COMRADES! IF ONLY WE CAN MAKE THE AUDIENCE STAY UNTIL THE CZARIST TROOPS MASSACRE EVERYONE ON THE ODESSA STEPS, WE WILL NOT NEED THIS FOOLISH AUTO PURSUIT.

DAY FOR NIGHT
Directed by François Truffaut

There actually *is* a car chase in *Day for Night*. It's part of the movie-within-the-movie called "Meet Pamela." The chase scene lasts only about three seconds; a Triumph Herald goes over a cliff. It isn't much, but it does prove that when it came to the canons of art François Truffaut was cool.

Brilliant! I said.

"And in *When Harry Met Sally,*" said Nick, "Harry can just jump on Sally's bones in the orgasm scene. I mean, depending on your definition of sword fight. The lady at the next table can still say, 'I'll have what she's having.' But I've got a problem with *Thelma and Louise*. There has to be a way to keep the happy ending without wrecking the T-Bird."

"Hi, Nick," said my young assistant, Max, bringing in the day's mail. "You on spring break?"

"I wish," said Nick. "I'm grounded until I'm thirty. My dad says I have to spend spring break doing community service—reseeding the lawn."

"Too bad," said Max. "When I was at school, spring break was—"

Max, I said, you went to the London School of Economics. What did you guys do for spring break? Go to Brussels, cozy up to the EU demand curve, and cop a feel?

Ah, spring break—the very words send me into a sort of reverie.

"A little Madness in the spring/Is wholesome," said the poet Emily Dickinson, who had no idea what she was talking about. Spring break was not a feature at her alma mater, Mount Holyoke Female Seminary. Emily lived with her dad her whole life, never bumped monkeys, and went outdoors about once, in 1851. Still, students everywhere take her point. The vernal equinox is crossed. Day lengthens, or at least the part of the day spent in Comparative Lit class seems to. Secondary sexual characteristics peek from unzipped folds of Polar Fleece in the student union. The hibernating animals of Business Administration 102 begin to stir. Watery fluid containing nutrients rises, bringing plants to bud and messes to bedsheets. Lush verdure bursts forth from ATM machines. The call of the open road is heard: FINES DOUBLED IN WORK ZONES, SEAT BELTS ARE MANDATORY IN NORTH CAROLINA. It is time for spring break.

It's time to go on campus leg bail, get grade-point parole. Time to take a powder—and, what the heck, some pills. Time to yank the pull tabs on the six-pack of life. Screech to the beach. Helio hallelujah, wave worship, ab and pec genuflection. *Zing* go the string bikinis of the heart. It's time to drop laptop and give lap dance a chance. Turn the love thermostat up to *Ouch*. Chill down the micro-brew breakfast in the motel toilet tank. Bend over and show the world your vertical smile. It's time to freak. It's time to frolic. It's time to . . .

It's time to remove the snow tires, fertilize the grass, and make sure the camcorder batteries are charged for the Montessori Easter pageant. Muffin plays a purple egg.

That last part was spoken to you, Nick and Max, from across the abyss of the Great Midlife Fun Divide, on the other side of which I firmly stand or, rather, sit. There comes a time in every life when the definition of pleasure makes a sudden and cataclysmic shift. One morning you awake thinking, Puking in my buddy's Timberlands, drinking flaming Bacardi jiggers, striking out with Mt. Holyoke poetry majors, getting up at 4 P.M. and eating a Taco Supreme that somebody sat on last night, falling off hotel balconies, going through the roof of the Tiki Bar, being hauled away in an ambulance—when did *that* stop being fun? Then you attempt to figure out why. Was it the first hemorrhoid operation? The second wife? The fifteenth glass of warm domestic champagne at nephew Arnie's wedding reception? But one thing you do know, nothing will put you back into a spring break frame of mind.

Of course I could try to create an adult version of a South Padre Island blowout—Concorde to Paris, suite at the Ritz, dinner at Le Grand Rôti de Cheval, and shopping with the Mrs. on the Champs-Élysées. What this will get me is spring broke.

Or I could endeavor to relive the past. I suppose I might, with a great deal of wheedling and child-care juggling, get sixteen or eighteen of my buddies to share a Daytona Beach Ramada room. We'd be up all night just like we used to be, except this time it would be because of sciatica and poor lumbar support in lumpy hotel mattresses. And what kind of sexual encounters would we be able to generate? ("Show us your dentures!") Then there'd be the spectacle of venerable and well-seasoned alcoholics attempting to get actually drunk on beer without making their prostate-impaired bladders explode. Plus the endless chirps and beeps of cell phones and pagers as management problems arise, homework meltdowns occur, and spousal ire reaches critical mass. Our drug of choice would be Pepcid AC. And the only thing that would get us climbing over balcony railings would be if the Dow Jones dropped a thousand points.

The ideal Easter vacation for old guys is eight hours of sleep, a boss with the flu, and, in our wildest fantasy, a perky, buff, and willing young person who would . . . reseed the lawn for less than $20 an hour.

But youth is not the only requirement for a true spring break. Also needed are the problems of youth. These are temporary and therefore you can temporize about them. It may hearten you two to know that time, gravity—and divorce—will cure your romantic perplexities. Max has already discovered that leaving school solves school difficulties. And years of work in pointless and unrewarding jobs, like the one he's got now, will end all worries about finding a career. On the other hand, middle-age problems—kids, indigestion, baldness—stop only in the Alzheimer's care facility or the cardiac ward. You can't *get* away from things that won't *go* away.

"Such as," said Max, "the fact that you've signed contracts with your publisher for three different books, and you haven't started any of them, and you've spent the advances."

Good example, I said. Although *Kid Pro Quo: The Management Secrets of Mothers with Toddlers* is practically finished—in my mind. But my publisher is an old friend. He understands the artistic temperament and the sensitivities to which writers are prey.

"He sure does," said Max, "to judge by the letter you got from him today."

Dear P.J.,

I need a quick introduction for a book, *The Manly Life*. You're about the worst person I can imagine to write this, but, on the other hand, you owe me a ton of money. Give my love to the family. I'll be over for dinner on Friday.

Yours,
Morgan Entrekin
Publisher, Grove/Atlantic Inc.
P.S. Manuscript enclosed.

THE MANLY LIFE
Introduction by P. J. O'Rourke

This book is too much for me. The "Ice Climbing" chapter, for example. I've been ice climbing for years, and there's no overestimating the skill and courage required to get the car up my driveway when I've forgotten to put on the snow tires. But here is someone ice climbing on slopes even steeper than those of the Mt. Pleasant neighborhood where I live in Washington, D.C., and doing it without the benefit of driveway salt, or even a driveway, and instead of being inside a car he's dangling from a rope. I am amazed. Also perplexed. What is a "crampon"? Has anyone thought to register it as a trademark? It's an excellent name for a feminine hygiene product to provide relief during the difficult time of the month, which, it occurs to me, the target audience for this book never has. Nor do I. I'm past menopause. Plus I'm a guy.

Being a postmenopausal guy, this book isn't targeted at me either. Men my age are not much for wielding ice axes unless the automatic cube dispenser on the Frigidaire jams. And we aren't interested in kayaking Niagara Falls, magma boarding in active volcano cones, taking unicycle tours of the Andes, or butt-skiing the Great Pyramid of Khufu. Not that we're averse to facing danger in the outdoors. Just last year a friend of mine dropped dead of a heart attack while mowing the lawn. But what's the point of my risking life and limb when both will be useless soon? It's more fun to risk money. Preferably other people's. You, the reader of this book, want to fly an airplane. I, the writer of this introduction, want to raise venture capital for a start-up pharmaceutical company—principal asset, the Crampon trademark—and buy a Gulfstream jet.

That G-5 I'm getting is another reason this book is too much for me. Look at the chapter "How to Survive a Small Plane Crash." The information is sound, the advice is intelligent, but none of it applies in my case. Once a fellow is into the colorectal-cancer-exam years, the way to deal with plane crashes is by making a list: back taxes owed, alimony due, yard chores outstanding, amount of school tuition to be paid next year, net loss when Crampon Inc. went into Chapter 11, date of next scheduled colonoscopy, etc. Then, if the plane gets into trouble, I pull out this piece of paper and die smiling. What's with this Adventure Travel anyway? You want excitement and risk on your vacation? Go anywhere with a beach or pool and tell your wife she looks fat in her bathing suit.

Huh? I'm getting a little deaf in this ear. Old draft-dodging injury. What's that? Ah, it's the Voice of Youth saying, if I'm not mistaken, *Shut up*. Yes. Good point. Who wants to hear one more ex-spliff-sucker in pinstripes choke on his Gelusil over what's the matter with kids today? I shall mock no more the generation of

Cubicle workspace, calf tattoos,
Itty-bitty phones, and great big shoes.

Especially since you with the ore freighters on your feet are supposed to purchase this book—thereby making ex-spliff-suckers a bunch of money. Which reminds me of another business opportunity idea. (My publisher claims that book buyers in your age cohort often have a billion dollars from founding web sites. Can you keep that much as personal property when you file for bankruptcy? Anyway, perhaps you are looking to diversify your investment portfolio.) It's a national franchise chain of mall-based cosmetic surgeons specializing in laser tat removal and invisible closure of body piercing holes. The retired bookkeeper who runs the bake sale at my church has a tongue stud and a four-inch-wide American Indian thingy permanently inked around her bicep, so the hip phase of this trend is over.

But where was I? I think I was saying that this book contains too much stuff about achieving physical fitness and improving sexual performance and not enough about raising money to fight Alzheimer's.

I envision a dramatic national campaign. Slogan: ALZHEIMER'S—FERGEDABOUDIT!

Come to think of it, I wasn't saying anything about Alzheimer's. Of course a fund-raising campaign would accomplish tremendous good. Although a little late for me. Actually, I was saying that I have to stop making fun of your generation for fear of hurting book sales, getting my own book contracts canceled, and so on. But it's not just that. Consider what *The Manly Life* would be if it were, indeed, written for my generation instead of yours. Imagine the chapter headings:

PLAID SHORTS, PLAID SHIRTS, BLACK SOCKS, AND WING TIPS
Not just for Dress-down Fridays anymore?

HOW TO OPEN THOSE PESKY CD CASES
When the Grand Funk Railroad LP is hopelessly scratched

THREE-DAY SOLO SURVIVAL COURSE
Finding food, clothing, and the TV remote while your wife visits her sister in Atlanta

I BET I DIE
Everything that's ever been printed or said about life insurance

Plus the artwork would be color photographs of Christie Todd Whitman in her underwear and other age-appropriate illustrations.

No, this is a better book, even if it is full of advice on sit-ups instead of excuses to sit down. You have no business sitting down anyhow. You're not tired yet. Plus a workout will add zipper noises to your private life because you can still get bulges in your clothing that interest women—other than the bulge in the right hip pocket.

The bulge that pops the top two buttons on my cardigan sweater doesn't seem as effective, although the vagaries of fashion may bring pudge into style. Perhaps one day I'll be walking down the street and major babes will holler, "Yo, Budweiser Balcony, you're looking . . ." Looking, no doubt, like this book makes me feel—superannuated, out of shape, and green with envy.

Not that I haven't enjoyed every page of *The Manly Life*. And envy is the key. I hate you for being young and fit, of course. But don't mind me. Read everything in here and take it to heart. I'll be home beside the lava lamp, listening to Grand Funk Railroad and smiling with the secret knowledge that—if your generation actually goes on every adventure listed in this book, plays each of the sports, does the whole program of exercises, and practices all the recommended sexual techniques—you're going to kill yourselves.

8

APRIL 2001

Waaaaah!" cried Muffin. "I want Mommy!" [Advice to parents whose children love the story of the dinosaurs: Don't give away the surprise ending.]

"I'll put her to bed," said my wife. "You go downstairs and be nice to the neighbors—please."

Refresh my memory, I said. Why?

"Because," said my wife, "the neighbors' daughter, the single mom, has moved back home, and the single mom has a girl who's fifteen, and fifteen-year-old girls *baby-sit*."

Okay, I said, I get it. Leave everything to me. What I'll do is start a conversation going on a subject that the neighbors are really interested in.

A couple of aging liberals like you, I said, are probably worried about how Social Security is becoming a political issue. The danger with political issues, for liberals, is that you might try to understand them. This would bum you out. Big government, that you're so fond of, is as complicated as airline fares. You'd go nuts if you really tried to fathom all of Washington's programs, regulations, restrictions, discounts for seniors, and frequent campaign-donor upgrades. So you do with the U.S. what you do with US Airways: you hand over the money and let yourselves be sent to hell by way of Pittsburgh with nothing but peanuts on the trip. Economists call this "rational ignorance," meaning that you *could* go to hell for $20 less (and get two bags of peanuts), but the time and effort wouldn't be worth it.

Now, even though I'm a conservative, I don't believe that this exploitation of your rational ignorance is a conspiracy. Well, with the airlines it is. They know what they're doing when they throw you into their briar patch of ticket prices. But politicians—especially liberal politicians—are as confused by the abstruse underbrush of government as you are. They just say, the way you do, "Gimme those peanuts!"

Speaking of which, average Social Security benefits are now about $745 a month. This will pay for your blowout at the Cheers-theme airport bar during your layover in Pittsburgh. Social Security is an example of rational ignorance at its most ignorant—and most rational. We're all getting what we want from Social Security without understanding it at all. You old folks get something to carp about—$745. Your unmarried daughter gets to tell you to shove off. That $745 will be a fortune in Sun City. She needs your bedroom for a home yoga studio. A huge number of government bureaucrats get a huge government bureaucracy to run. And politicians get an issue that everybody's for and nobody's against. Plus, every couple of election cycles there's a "crisis" with this issue—a crisis politicians don't have to do much about, but that allows politicians to make thoughtful, caring, and statesmanlike noises.

At the moment, the crisis with Social Security is that the Social Security Trust Fund will run out of money in 2032. This is right around the corner—if you're a sequoia. Whatever the politicians propose, these politicians will be safely on the way to their eternal reward (via Pittsburgh) before their proposals wreck the nation. Meanwhile, in the name of "shoring up the Social Security Trust Fund," the politicians have an excuse to spend surplus tax dollars. I remember, in 1999, when President Clinton—claiming he'd saved the Social Security system—told the public, "We could give it all back to you and hope you spend it right. . . . But . . . if you don't spend it right—" So, on top of everything else, Social Security saved you from foolishly buying a snowmobile just when you thought an Al Gore administration with all its global warming was about to occur.

If you begin to investigate Social Security, you could blow the whole thing. You should not, for example, peek into that Social Security Trust "lockbox." There's nothing inside. Since 1939, the Social Security payroll tax on employers and employees has been used simply to pay Social Security benefits.

In 1916 an Italian immigrant named Charles Ponzi created an investment fund that paid large dividends without making any investments. Money from new investors was transferred to old investors while the new investors received money from newer investors yet. The system had flexibility and boldness and worked as long as an ever-expanding pool of suckers could be found.

Charles Ponzi made a profit on this, and so does the U.S. government. Social Security payroll tax receipts have always been greater than Social Security benefit payments and will continue to be until about 2013, when the baby-boom sucker pool retires. The federal government has taken this surplus revenue, spent it, and given the Social Security Trust Fund IOUs in return. That is, the government spent the money and then promised to spend it again later.

Debts owed to the government by the government are absurd in the first place. Furthermore, these IOUs have the same force of law as, oh, the statutes against perjury and obstruction of justice do in an impeachment case against the president of the United States involving sex. Our Social Security taxes don't have to be spent on Social Security. In 1937 the Supreme Court ruled that Social Security taxes "are to be paid into the Treasury like any other internal revenue generally and are not earmarked in any way." This despite President Roosevelt's pledge that—you guys are probably old enough to remember him making it—"Those premiums are collected in the form of taxes . . . held by the government solely for the benefit of the worker in his old age."

Roosevelt also said, "We put those payroll contributions there so as to give the contributors a legal, moral, and political right to collect their pensions." But in the 1950s a deported communist filed a capitalist suit to reclaim his Social Security premiums. The Supreme Court said, "To engraft upon the Social Security system a concept of 'accrued property rights' would deprive it of the flexibility and boldness in adjustment to ever-changing conditions which it demands."

Charles Ponzi—unlike FDR—never had the opportunity to appoint Supreme Court justices. He went to jail.

Having a Social Security Trust Fund is exactly like not having a Social Security Trust Fund. Social Security will go into the red no matter what. Without a Trust Fund, the government will have to pay off the Social Security deficit by raising taxes and cutting benefits. *With* a Trust Fund, the government will have to pay off the Social Security deficit by raising taxes and cutting benefits.

Unfortunate people who scrutinize the Social Security Trust Fund discover two facts: It's not there. It's not theirs. But for the rest of you who are rationally ignoring such things, the real question is how are you doing with this retirement fund that doesn't exist and that you don't own? You're doing surprisingly well. You're getting an average of over 16.5 percent return on your employer/employee payroll contributions—if you're eighty-one years old. I guess you're not. Hard to tell what age you are in those dumpy hand-knit sweaters. Let's say—being kind—that you're sixty-seven. Then you're getting about one quarter of one percent return—a financial coup you could have managed on your own, without the help of the federal government, by selling your collection of Peter, Paul and Mary albums on eBay. For the rest of us, ages twenty-four to sixty-two, we can expect a return of between minus .34 percent and minus 1.7 percent and might be better off leaving the money in our blazer pockets and going through the closet when we retire.

Here again you see the genius of Charles Ponzi. Initial payments into Social Security were very small. From 1937 to 1949 the combined employer/employee payroll tax rate was 2 percent, and this tax was levied only on the first $3,000 of annual income. The generation that made these payments then went on to surprise demographers, shock heirs, and delight Winnebago dealers by taking a really long time to die. The first Social Security recipient, Ida M. Fuller of Vermont, retired in 1940 after paying Social Security taxes for three years. She and her employer had put a total of $44 into the system. Ms. Fuller lived to be a hundred and collected $20,933.52 in benefits. Mr. Ponzi could have done as well, and been honored for his business savvy, if only he'd had the legal and legislative muscle to create a Ponzi scheme that preyed upon the most gullible of all suckers—people who hadn't been born yet.

But although the Social Security system does a good job of stealing prospective candy from future babies, this won't work for long. There are too many of you old people. In 1950, America had 16 workers for every retiree. Now there are 3.3—the 0.3 being down in corporate communications eating hash brownies and putting the company web site together. By 2025, each George Bush or Bob Dole will be supported by only two George W.'s or Libbys. We're going to need a really aggressive assisted-suicide program: "Sure, Mom, it feels like indigestion, but it's probably pancreatic cancer. I'll help you tie the plastic bag over your head."

And that is the great conundrum of Social Security, the thing that makes you liberals stay as ignorant as you can about it: Every political move to fix Social Security makes it worse.

Politicians could, for example, forget the whole concept of Social Security as a government-run pension and insurance system and just pay the benefits out of general tax revenue. This would be more honest, which is why it's such a bad idea. Your delicate fabric of rational ignorance would be destroyed. Voters would see where retirement money was coming from—from voting for any candidate who'd raise Social Security payments to $100,000 a month. You old people vote like the dickens. And tapping general revenues does nothing about the fundamental ratio problem of one geriatric duffer getting AARP sky-diving rebates to two of me trapped in an office cubicle.

Or politicians could stick to the present system, which, as mentioned, would mean raising taxes, cutting benefits, and increasing the retirement age so much that Reagan would still be president.

Politicians could also stick with the present system while trying to put some real money into the Social Security Trust Fund. Over the next fifteen years we're supposed to get trillions in federal budget surpluses. Let's save it all to pay for Social Security. Except this can't be done. The federal government does not have the same relationship to money as a human does. The federal government issued that money.

When the money comes back to the federal government it must go away again or it gets unissued, in effect destroyed. Yanking trillions in currency out of the economy would cause howling recession. When the government reissued that currency, dumping trillions into the economy would cause screaming inflation. And such money-supply shenanigans would give Alan Greenspan a heart attack. Where would we be then?

When a budget surplus happens, politicians can (per Clinton's 1999 suggestion) give it back. This is nice because then there's more money and we can all have some. Or politicians can pay down the national debt. This is nice too, because then there's more money to lend and we can all borrow some. Or politicians can do what they usually do, which is fund public television, welfare, Medicare prescription-drug plans, the military, and so on. And this is also nice because then we get more Clifford the Big Red Dog, surplus cheese, Prozac, and maybe (if the draft is reinstated) free trips to former Yugoslavia.

What politicians can't do is save that money in the Social Security Trust Fund. The only way to deposit money in there, as opposed to IOUs, is for politicians to have the government buy something real—say, Microsoft stock. This would put the government in an interesting position with its antitrust suit against that company. Just kidding, Bill.

Having a government that owned economic assets is what made the U.S.S.R. the success it is today. Maybe bolshevism could be avoided, but conflict of interest couldn't. Businesses would all want a slice of the federal investment pizza and so would labor unions, special interests, pressure groups, and every ad hoc group of jacklegs, scallywags, and hard graspers you can imagine. Not to mention that the government itself might be tempted by all the mushrooms, pepperoni, and extra cheese sitting around uneaten.

The track record of trust funds run by individual states is not encouraging. California and Illinois raided their funds to balance state budgets. Pennsylvania put $70 million into a Volkswagen plant now worth half that. Kansas wasted between $138 and $236 million because Kansas legislators insisted on investing in Kansas. Minnesota tried to be moral and lost $2 million selling off tobacco stock. Connecticut tried to be amoral and lost $25 million bailing out Colt Industries. And the

Missouri State Employees' Retirement System venture capital fund was shut down because of low yields and lawsuits.

The only real solution to Social Security is to buy it—to privatize the whole system of national social insurance and get rid of the politicians. This would still leave the country with enormous unfunded liabilities owed to people like you who are too old to go private. But we'll have those anyway. And privatization would work. There is no twenty-year period in American history when stocks lost money. And even from 1930 to 1939 a conservative portfolio—half stocks, half bonds—would have made 2.27 percent a year. That's not a spectacular return, but it beats waiting until I'm sixty-five to rummage through the Brooks Brothers for change to buy screw-top wine.

However, thanks to people like you who love politics and politicians so much, privatization will never happen. Thirty-eight percent of the federal budget is spent on Social Security and other social insurance. By 2020 that share will be between 59 and 68 percent. Two-thirds of a politician's throw weight will come from controlling social insurance dollars. Money is power. What use is it for a politician to endure political indignities—such as voters like you—if a politician can't obtain mastery over people's lives? Politicians would rather give away their spouses than give away two-thirds of their power. Some politicians would much, much rather.

Besides, if privatization did happen you'd have to take responsibility for yourselves and maybe even for your unmarried daughter and her kid. You'd need to pay attention, learn things, make difficult decisions. It's far more pleasant to slide along in blissful (and rational!) ignorance and hope that before you lose the rest of your teeth (and your shirt) something will come up. It did for Charles Ponzi. After he got out of jail he went back to Italy and became a top economic advisor to Benito Mussolini.

Saw the neighbors leaving, said the Political Nut who lives around here. Where were they going in such a huff?

"Home to destroy our best hope of affordable child care," said my wife, who went back upstairs in something of a huff herself.

Did you read *The New York Times* obits today? asked the Political Nut. Another beloved old black-listed screenwriter has died. "Francis X. Bugbaum was highly respected in Hollywood for his significant screenplay work as well as his refusal to testify before the House Un-American Activities Committee," said the *Times*. "In the 1940s and early 1950s Bugbaum wrote scripts for hit movies including *Abbott and Costello Meet the Scottsboro Boys, Dead End Kids on Strike,* and *Uncle Joe Goes to Heaven*. He was fired from MGM because of his communist affiliation and for the next twenty-one years was forced to write under the pseudonym I. M. Apykno. Not until the mid-1970s was Bugbaum finally given a screen credit, for his contribution to Disney's *That Darned Military Industrial Complex*."

How come, asked the Political Nut, we never see any obits of beloved old Nazis? "Kurt Waldheim was highly respected in Washington for his significant UN work as well as his refusal to testify before denazification authorities in occupied Austria after World War II." By golly, Kurt stuck to his guns—or poison gas canisters, as the case may be. He felt his personal politics were nobody's business. Why didn't the *Times* give Kurt a big wet kiss when he kicked? You know, the important thing is to teach our kids idealism. It's not so much what you believe in, it's that you believe in *something*—and that you're *loyal*. Jim Jones never named names. Neither did Charles Manson, Idi Amin, Papa Doc Duvalier. . . . Ever think how good Hitler would have been on *Oprah?* He was in touch with his feelings. His faith was tested. He loved animals. He was a vegetarian—

"Shut up and go to bed!" shouted my wife from the top of the stairs.

Anything in the mail, Max?

"*American Spree* magazine sent some extra copies of the issue with your story about how illegal drugs taught a generation of Americans the metric system. Plus they forwarded a letter from an irate reader. She says that illegal drugs are no laughing matter, and she encloses a copy of the Office of National Drug Control Policy's 1999 report to Congress—extensively underlined."

I'm afraid that irate reader is right. I'm ashamed of myself. Although 1999 is a bit out-of-date. Perhaps the irate reader drinks. I've noticed, I said, mixing myself an eye-opener, that serious drinkers often get irate at illegal drug use—and confused about what year it is.

"I'm a little confused myself," said Max, who is still of an age where logic makes sense to him. "How *do* you feel about legalizing drugs?"

Max, I said, I am in favor of legalizing drugs because I am a staunch libertarian who believes that a human being has the right to exercise individual freedoms including the freedom to snort mounds of blow, the freedom to get fired, the freedom to be kicked out of his condominium, and the freedom to end up sleeping on my sofa for months except he doesn't sleep, he sits up all night dribbling snot and drool on the slip covers and yammering about the great times we had back when we were both majoring in street pharmacology at Bong State, blah, blah, blah, until I'm ready to shoot him, and—being a staunch libertarian and thus an opponent of gun control—I will.

But don't tell Mrs. O I'm a libertarian. She thinks I'm an old loadie. In her opinion this produces less sofa wear and tear than libertarianism: one husband-sized butt print facing the TV versus an entire old college buddy with saliva pools, coke boogers, bullet damage, bloodstains, et cetera.

However, calling me an old loadie is unfair. I don't do drugs anymore. They interfere with the lithium, Viagra, and painkillers. Anyway, if drugs were legal I wouldn't abuse them. I would take drugs with the same discipline and moderation that I exercise in my consumption of alcohol unless I've had a hard day or lunch with an editor or the Orioles have been losing. And I wouldn't even touch the hard stuff. You have to be nuts to fool with tootski. Nuts or really tired. Because sometimes it's nice to have a little bump to get you through the evening. It's like coffee. And if you buy your coffee at Starbucks, cocaine's probably cheaper. It's like coffee that you can't stop drinking even though you're swollen to the width of a wheelchair-access toilet stall and spurting used java out of every body orifice. Still you keep chugalugging, the hotter the better. Get up on the counter, wiggle on your back, slide your head right onto the Mr. Coffee hot plate. Smell those neck hairs burn. Suck that filter paper. Feel your tongue split and pop like a ball park frank. Who needs tongues? Tongues just get in the way of drinking more coffee, of getting more awake, more alert, more. . . . Speaking of alert, have you noticed that Starbucks shops aren't built? They just appear. You're crossing the street, there's a dry cleaners over there, you look up to check the walk light, look back, and it's a Starbucks. I'm calling *X Files*. Ouch, who boiled my gums? And why's this toilet stall ankle deep in latte? I'd better take some heroin to calm down.

As I was saying, I am against legalizing drugs because I am a stoner dirtbag who believes that a human being—given half a chance—will get shit-witted and do stuff that sucks.

Retired general Barry R. McCaffrey, Clinton's director of the Office of National Drug Control Policy, who was otherwise known as the Drug Czar, which is easily the coolest government job title ever—sort of like hip young Anastasia got Nicholas II and the Czarina to ditch Rasputin and go to a Phish concert . . . It really makes you think how the Russian revolution could have been mellower. I mean, it does if you've had a couple of tokes. But I digress. The Drug Czar, in his report to Congress, used arguments against drugs that could be used against anything. Notice how these quotes—with slight modifications that I've penciled in—make an effective plea for banning the penis: "[Penis] abuse impairs rational thinking and the potential for a full, productive life. . . . [Penises] drain the physical, intellectual, spiritual, and moral strength of America [and its bladder]. . . . Crime, violence, workplace accidents, family misery, [penis]-exposed children, and addiction are only part of the price imposed on society [by penises]." The worst thing about these arguments is that the Drug Czar was right—about drugs *and* penises.

On the other hand, the Drug Czar's report also contained some powerful reasoning in *favor* of drug legalization, although I don't think it meant to, unless Jerry Garcia isn't really dead but assumed a disguise and went undercover as a mole in the Office of National Drug Control Policy. Funny how you never saw all ten of General McCaffrey's fingers. The federal drug control budget went from an average of $11.25 billion a year during the elder Bush administration to $17.9 billion in 1999. But the Drug Czar's report said that half a million more Americans used drugs in 1997 than in 1991. Over the same period the number of marijuana smokers increased by 700,000, which is the population of a medium-sized city (a city with record Mallomar sales). And adolescent dope-takers went from 1.4 million to 2.6 million, which explains Eminem, Tommy Hilfiger clothes, and why the kid behind the McDonald's counter gets lost on his way to the french fries. Meanwhile, between 1991 and 1998, the price of a gram of cocaine declined from $68.08 to $44.30, and the price of a gram of heroin fell by $549.28. These are figures obtained by the DEA. God knows how cheap smack is if you don't show your badge when buying it. Jerry was doing a great job at the ONDCP.

The people fighting drugs may be a fifth column. But the people fighting drug prohibition are working for the other side, too. There is, for example, the legalizers' argument that banning drugs is ridiculous when it's the perfectly legal substances, alcohol and tobacco, that cause most of America's health problems. Like, after we're through with the hooch and the Luckies, let's go stand out in a thunderstorm with car aerials in our hands.

Then there's the argument that, if drugs were legal, the free market would somehow keep people from taking them. Steven Duke and Albert Gross, authors of *America's Longest War: Rethinking Our Tragic Crusade Against Drugs*, claim that the number of drug bums wouldn't increase after legalization because "the use of heroin and cocaine in a free market system would adversely affect the quality of the lives of the users." Am I missing something about the current non–free market system? Is there a special Joy Popper VISA card that gives me frequent overdose discounts?

Legalizing drugs will lower their price, the more so if price is measured not only in dollars but also in time spent with dangerous maniacs in dark parking lots, not to mention time spent in jail. If drugs turn out to be a case study showing that price has no connection with demand, every economics textbook will have to be rewritten. This will be an enormous bother if all the economists are stoned.

Maybe there's some other way to avoid more drug-taking. The pro-legalization Netherlands Drug Policy Foundation has a pamphlet containing the following sentence: "Young people who want to experiment with drugs will be stimulated to learn to do so in a controlled way." Our boy Hans is doing so well in history and mathematics, but he's flunking LSD.

A certain weird—not to say high and spacey—optimism can come over people when they discuss opening the floodgates on the Grand Coulee dam of drug legislation and letting America's river of junk bunnies, blow fiends, hop hounds, pipe hogs, mezz rollers, hypo smeckers, and yen-shee babies find their own level. Milton Friedman believes the crack epidemic was the result of cocaine being against the law. He says crack "was invented because the high cost of illegal drugs made it profitable to provide a cheaper version." Milton Friedman is a brilliant man, a courageous defender of liberty. I respect Milton Friedman. I revere Milton Friedman. But from drugs Milton Friedman doesn't know. Crack is less expensive than powdered cocaine—for ten seconds. It was the marketing guys who thought up crack, not the people in accounting.

I've read a lot of stuff by Ethan Nadelmann, who has a PhD from Harvard and an MA from your alma mater, Max, the London School of Economics. Nadelmann is the director of the Lindesmith Center, a drug policy research institute funded by George Soros. Nadelmann is no vulgar legalizer but a champion of the medically pragmatic and the politically possible. He is one of the most sophisticated advocates of drug law reform. And even he can get fuzzy: "Perhaps the most reassuring reason," Nadelmann writes, "for believing that repeal of the drug prohibition laws will not lead to tremendous increases in drug-abuse levels is the fact that we have learned something from our past experiences with alcohol and tobacco abuse." Ethan, what I have learned from my past experiences with alcohol and tobacco abuse is that I am a pig dog—a pig dog with a bad cough and a liver that looks like Chechnya.

The problem with illicit drugs is that nobody knows anything about them—except for those of us who found out too much, and we have memory problems. There are precedents for this. Tobacco smoking among educated people began in the sixteenth century, and it took those educated people until 1964 to figure out that tobacco killed them. Beer has been around since Neolithic times. That means wives have had ten thousand years of experience handling husbands who've been ice fishing. And my wife still can't reason with me when I'm blotto. So how is society supposed to cope with XTC, which dates back only to the second Reagan administration? We may be talking A.D. 20,001 before anybody knows what to do about a complete stranger who hugs you on the dance floor and says she's in love with the purple aura that's shining out your nose and ears.

Drug research doesn't add much to the debate. Eighty-five percent of the world's research on the health aspects of drug abuse and addiction is funded by the U.S. government's National Institute on Drug Abuse. The scientists studying drugs are getting their money from the politicians who made drugs illegal. Do you think the scientists want to get more money? What kind of conclusions do you think the scientists will reach? Compare and contrast these conclusions with the conclusions reached by scientists funded by the Medellín cartel.

Even assuming that the scientists aren't crooked, imagine the problems involved in studying something that's illegal, secret, shameful, sometimes heavily armed, and always stupid. And imagine doing this when you're pretty stupid yourself, as the Department of Health and Human Services famously is. The DOH's National Household Survey on Drug Abuse is cited all over the place whenever drug policy is discussed. The Household Survey is America's main source of information on everything from sniffing paint (14.2 percent of white non-Hispanics aged eighteen to twenty-five have used inhalants) to dipping snuff (0.1 percent of blacks aged twelve to seventeen are current users of smokeless tobacco). And do you know how the survey takers get the—to use a dated but apposite slang expression—inside dope? They go door-to-door and ask people. They really do.

"Hi, I'm from the government. Do you use illegal drugs?"

To which everyone responds, "Yes siree Bob. Come on in, we're just cooking up a batch of meth."

Then the survey takers "adjust for nonresponse through imputation," which is called, in layman's terms, making things up.

It's hard to exaggerate official ignorance about drugs. In the aftermath of Clinton/Lewinsky et al., America's governing class will confess to most things, but what you can't get a political figure to admit is that he doesn't know what he's talking about. An admirable exception is William von Raab, who was customs commissioner under President Reagan. Commissioner von Raab instituted the Zero Tolerance policy, which meant if you sailed into Miami with so much as one soggy roach in the scuppers of your bazillion-dollar yacht, you lost the whole bikini barge. Drug law reformers did not like von Raab, but I did. Zero Tolerance gave me hours of pleasure just thinking about planting blunts on the floating gin palaces of Donald Trump, Ted Turner, and their ilk.

Anyway, von Raab came up with Zero Tolerance because, as he says, "You can be for legalization or against legalization, and no one knows what you mean." The commissioner decided to find out what we mean when we say it's illegal to import drugs into the United States. He found out we didn't mean it. I had drinks with von Raab the other night. "Zero Tolerance," he told me, smiling with satisfaction, "was something of a public relations disaster."

When von Raab was appointed customs commissioner, Secretary of the Treasury Nicholas Brady asked him a straightforward question: "How does the cocaine business work?" The secretary wanted to know what it costs to grow coca and refine it, who the farmers and middlemen are, what kind of profits they make, how the distribution network is organized, who provides venture capital—all the things a good Republican normally wants to find out about a company he plans to squash like a bug. Commissioner von Raab didn't know. He called a meeting of the various federal law enforcement agencies. They didn't know. Upper ranks asked middle ranks. Middle ranks asked lower ranks. "Finally," says von Raab, "someone found an article in *High Times*."

U.S. drug policy was being guided by the incoherent scribblings of some half-starved freelancer who . . . wait a minute, *I* was a half-starved freelancer back then. That article could be by me. I may have been in control of U.S. drug policy. I wish I'd known. "Cocaine comes from—um, Mars," I would have written, "and enters the United States only on yachts owned by Donald Trump and Ted Turner."

Maybe, when we're arguing about drugs, we should stick to what we *do* know, Max. And we do know a few things. Drugs have bad effects. Even chamomile does—to judge by the morons who drink herb tea. And let's not kid ourselves with the likes of medical marijuana initiatives. Incidentally, I've got a good idea for a bumper sticker: MEDICAL MARIJUANA MAKES ME SICK!

But the bad effects of drugs themselves—as opposed to the bad effects of drug laws, drug gangs, drug money, or, for that matter, drug legalization—are bad effects mostly on us drug users. And we're bad already. There are worse things than overdosing that John Belushi could have done. He could have lived to make infomercials. We don't deserve sympathy. And we don't deserve help. What we deserve is to have drugs legalized. No, subsidized. No, given to us free until we're put to bed with a shovel and are out of everybody's way. You may think that draconian drug laws are hard-hearted, that mandatory minimum sentences are horrible. And, indeed, sending federal agents to troll the Lilith Fair parking lot so that nineteen-year-olds can spend ten years in the pen for selling grocery-store 'shrooms is not warm and caring. But legalization is cold too. Smoking crack is a way for people who couldn't afford college to study the works of Charles Darwin.

Drugs have bad effects; likewise the war against drugs. In the first place, the paradigm stinks. War excuses everything. You can drop an A-bomb on the Japanese. No sacrifice is too great, no expense is too high to win a war. This is why politicians love the war thing. War is steroids and free weights for government. Budgets, bureaucracies, and the whole scope of legal and regulatory authority get pumped and buff. This is why we have the War on Poverty and the War on Cancer. But you don't cure lymphoma by dropping an A-bomb. Rather the reverse. If poverty surrenders, do we put the poor on trial like the Nazis at Nuremberg? And whom do you draft in a war against drugs? Certainly not eighteen-year-old boys. They're the enemy. Some people, including a number of fricasseed residents of Nagasaki, think that "the War on _____" isn't a good idea, even during a war.

Furthermore, it is very expensive to mistake Robert Downey, Jr.'s impulse-control problems for an attack on Pearl Harbor. There's the federal government's aforementioned $17.9 billion antidrug budget, plus an almost equal amount of state and local spending, plus the more than $8.6 billion it costs to keep war-on-drugs POWs incarcerated. That's about $44 billion dollars a year to stop the use of narcotics. And even so, government gets outspent. The Drug Czar's office itself estimated that Americans spend $57 billion a year getting beamed up by Scotty.

The drug war has also taken a toll on an institution that's even more noble and venerated than our wallet. Drug control zealotry has led to what constitutional scholar Roger Pilon calls "the drug exception to the Bill of Rights."

I. *Freedom of religion*—except for religions involving peyote.
II. *Right to keep and bear arms*—except when you point one at ninja-dressed members of a SWAT team that breaks through the wrong door at 3 A.M.
III. *Quartering soldiers in our houses*—to be fair I haven't noticed any soldiers actually in the house, but some National Guard helicopters have been hovering over my backyard marijuana patch.
IV. *No unreasonable searches and seizures*—except mandatory random piss tests.
V. *No self-incrimination*—except that urine in the bottle.
VI. *Right to counsel*—except if the government suspects your lawyer is being paid with drug money.
VII. *Right to trial by jury*—except in the case of RICO property forfeitures
VIII. *No cruel or unusual punishments*—except to those caught selling 'shrooms at rock concerts.
IX. *The enumeration of certain rights shall not be construed to deny others*—except when it looks like you might have drugs in your car.
X. *The powers not delegated to the United States by the Constitution*—are reserved to the DEA.

So let's protest and sing folk songs—"The answer, my friend, is blowin' up your nose"—and stuff flowers into . . . mmm . . . the jaws of drug-sniffing dogs at airports. Peace now!

But, Max, how shall we make our peace with drugs? All societies regulate the consumption of intoxicants either by law or by custom or by waiting until you pass out and rubbing Limburger cheese under your nose and putting a live frog in your BVDs. The most libertarian of governments would have some regulations, at least to protect the frog.

One easy and uncontroversial reform would be to get rid of insane penalties. Even McCaffrey favored something called "equitable sentencing policies," which would have eliminated one or two federal mandatory minimums for simple possession. I personally think that people caught with drugs should be made to go door-to-door with the National Household Survey on Drug Abuse questionnaire.

As for legalization, each drug ought to be considered individually and judged upon its own merits. What fun to be on the jury. First, take the case of marijuana. Pot has become America's alternative brewski. Weed is not going away, especially since weed is, in fact, a weed and grows like one. Besides, how much can you really say against a drug that makes teenage boys drive slow?

Nonetheless I'm reluctant to see marijuana legalized. No drug will be permitted by law in the United States without being licensed, regulated, taxed, and hemmed about with legalization like alcohol is. No advocate of legalization is asking for anything else. Ethan Nadlemann says marijuana should be "decriminalized, taxed, and regulated." Governor of New Mexico Gary Johnson favors moving the drug economy "from illegal to legal, where it's taxed and regulated." And Milton Friedman bases his arguments for repeal of drug prohibition on the assumption that drugs would be "handled exactly the same way alcohol is now handled."

So, instead of the National Guard hovering over my marijuana patch, I'll have the Food and Drug Administration, the Department of Agriculture, ATF&D (Alcohol, Tobacco, Firearms and Doobies), the Internal Revenue Service, and the EPA. Instead of going to jail for growing pot, I'll go to jail for violation of the federal wetlands protection act. And marijuana will have legal standing so the next time some adolescent puffs a goofbutt and walks through a glass patio slider, me and every other old hippie selling nickel bags will be a defendant in a gigantic class action lawsuit—same as the gun and cigarette companies. Since only the richest corporations in the world will be able to stand the expense and bother of selling marijuana, we'll end up trying to get a virtual high off a digital joint delivered via Internet from AOL/Time-Warner.

All that is nothing compared to the cow-having that would be involved in legalizing anything other than marijuana. In fact, legalizing hard drugs won't happen. Americans are remarkably puritanical—when they aren't high as kites. And to understand this aspect of our national character, it helps to have a bad hangover. What probably *will* happen, rather than legalization, is therapy. America will go from the punishment mode to the treatment mode with hard-drug users. We do it already when we catch our own kids using hard drugs—if we have the lawyers, doctors, and money. What was a crime will be a disease. Junkies will get an Rx for heroin. Addiction will be covered by the Americans with Disabilities Act. "You can't fire my client, he's stoned."

This, of course, will do nothing to stop murder, theft, corruption, or the black market in drugs. Since when was going to the doctor or the lawyer cheaper than hanging out on the corner? We'll end up building thousands of "treatment facilities" and sending dopers there instead of prison. The countryside will be festooned with Betty Ford Centers, except bigger, with barbed wire around them, and with no cute actors, rich kids, or politicians' wives inside. At least in prison you get out when your sentence is up. In treatment you don't get out until you're "cured." Who gets to decide? I hope it's not my wife.

NO LEGALIZATION WITHOUT NO TREATMENT is my motto. And maybe no legalization even then. Suppose that we do manage to obtain an unregulated free market for all drugs. And suppose that this somehow doesn't cause a horrendous head-on collision between "Pursuit of happiness" and "Where's the party?" Suppose we legalize and it works. It won't work anyway.

Give Americans a legal right and they'll think they've got a federal entitlement. As I said before, we drug users deserve free drugs. Sounds like a vote-getter to me. Pretty soon Democrats in Congress will be lambasting Republicans for cutting school-lunch morphine portions. And if you think Social Security is expensive now, wait until Medicare covers Granny's freebase.

Nor should we imagine that drug legalization will get us our $44 billion back. The Drug Czar won't get fired or end up sleeping on my sofa. He'll just shift the focus of his efforts from jailing Woody Harrelson and annoying the peasants of Peru to educating America's youth: "It may be lawful, but ain't it awful." Maybe the Drug Czar will spend the $44 billion on more of those very trippy antidrug TV ads. Have you seen the one with the cute chick busting up the kitchen? "This is what your family goes through!" she yells as she whacks the dinner china with a skillet. Who hasn't wanted to do that to the 'rents?

What's the sensible answer to America's drug policy conundrum? It's the same as the sensible answer to the National Household Survey of Drug Abuse. Just lie, Max. I don't do drugs anymore. You don't do drugs anymore. End of discussion. New topic. And everyone who's involved in America's drug policy debate: Calm down and have a drink.

Speaking of which, I said, I think I'll have another. I've got to take Muffin to an Easter egg hunt that some Martha Stewarted parents from her play group are giving. The kids will be searching for colorfully dyed caviar.

9

MAY 2001

Fortunately," mused my wife, "it turns out not to matter what the neighbors think of you—as far as baby-sitting is concerned."

The teenage baby-sitter from next door breezed into our kitchen. "My grandparents," said the baby-sitter, "are patronizing bores. Last night they told me they were proud of the way Eminem handled himself at the Grammy awards, which were three months ago. And nobody ever says that about Yo Yo Ma. Sorry I'm late, Mrs. O, but my mom got stuck in a power yoga position. I had to pour canola oil on her legs to get her untangled. She sent a treat for Muffin. They're called 'vegesicles.' You make them by putting vegetable soup in Popsicle molds. They're awful."

Muffin took an experimental lick.

"Mr. O," said the baby-sitter, "didn't you used to be more important? When you were on TV? I was thinking about this while I was watching my Sunrise Semester macroeconomics course. And I was wondering, how did *you* get on television?"

Keep wondering, I said. And check your answering machine. You may be next, young lady. Have any broadcast experience? Familiar with TV production? Are you a nationally recognized expert in a particular field? Me neither. But *60 Minutes* made me a commentator—briefly. And brief is what a commentator must be. The comments aren't supposed to last too long. Ditto, I guess, for the career.

Molly Ivins, Stanley Crouch, and I were hired to debate Important Issues. Molly is a seasoned journalist with a thoroughgoing knowledge of America's political nuts and bolts—especially, since she's a liberal, the nuts. Stanley is acclaimed as a critic and an essayist. I understand why *60 Minutes* wanted to bring their arguments into America's homes, but I just make fun of things. Everybody's got a person like that around the house already: wisecracking spouse, young assistant who thinks he's a hoot, smart-aleck teenage baby-sitter.

Anyway, the *60 Minutes* disputations were to be about gun control, abortion, Medicare funding, that sort of thing. And we were supposed to bring a light touch to these subjects. *You* try bringing a light touch to Medicare funding. But don't try it on my father-in-law. He's pretty handy with that cane. Thanks to Medicare funding.

Molly, Stanley, and I were given helpful instructions—someone called and told us not to wear plaid. And we received a hearty welcome from the program's senior humor commentator of long standing, who shall go nameless. He had many valuable suggestions for us, such as conducting the debates in mime or doing our segment with our backs to the camera or walking around in traffic until we were run over by a bus.

Then we went into the studio, although not together. Molly lives in Austin, Texas. Stanley's a New Yorker. And I was off searching for things to make fun of, in a bar somewhere. We didn't even go to different studios at the same time. Each segment was taped separately. The only debater I could see or hear was me, on the studio monitor. Getting in an argument with yourself on national TV is not a résumé builder.

At a videotaping you sit alone on a hard chair in the middle of a room staring at bright lights for an hour while behind you a dozen people experience technical difficulties. Meanwhile there is a single thought in your head: "Put a digit in a nostril and I'm on somebody's blooper tape forever." The script appears in bottom-of-the-eye-chart letters on the TelePrompTer, which is located slightly above the camera lens. Thus when you're reading from a TelePrompTer, you're not quite making eye contact with the viewers, and your pupils are moving back and forth, plus you're squinting. The result is a shifty, unblinking thousand-yard stare usually seen in the segregation units of maximum-security federal prisons. An earpiece the size of an escargot is jammed in your aural canal. From this emanates much static and hissing and, occasionally, an instruction from the segment producer, such as "Take your finger out of your nose."

Bad as a taping is, it gets worse when it's over because then you have to watch the tape. This is when I discovered the one thing that sets real television professionals apart from the rest of us—other than enormous amounts of money. They can sit still. I cannot. My first try on *60 Minutes* should have been titled "Watch Mr. Fidget." I squirm in my seat as if I need to be wormed. I wave my hands around like a Sicilian greengrocer. The way my head swivels you'd think I was watching a Ping-Pong match. A cable TV aerobics class has less on-camera movement than me bringing a light touch to Medicare funding.

Real television professionals deserve those enormous amounts of money. They can sit there like bumps on a log for hours on end—as you may have noticed if you watched the 2000 election night coverage. I can't even get my clothes to hold still. My collar points pop out. My lapels flap. My tie gets loose and starts doing a hula. And just when I think I'm getting things under control, one of the technical-difficulties people will yell "Makeup!" because I'm starting to look, on camera, the way I look in real life.

Makeup is the toughest thing of all about being a television commentator. Not tough for me, of course. I just sit there with a bib around my neck. But it's darn tough for the person trying to get me to look like a decent citizen not in need of ninety days at Rancho Mirage. It's one of life's depressing moments when you first sit down in front of that mirror with all the lightbulbs around it and hear the makeup artist sigh and say, "This is going to take time."

So there I am in the studio, sitting on my hands, wearing so much foundation and powder that I *can't* move my head anymore. Little pieces of gaffer's tape are scattered all over my body, holding my wearing apparel in place. The technical difficulties are over. I'm learning to live with the TelePrompTer and the earpiece. The tape is rolling. Everyone's quiet on the set. And . . .

This is when I realize I'm talking to 270 million people—minus a few poor souls tuned to *America's Funniest Home Videos*. And I don't have anything to say. What do I know that 270 million people don't? What insight or information could I possess that's so important it needs to be loudly announced to the entire nation? I've thought about this quite a bit. "Never eat a taco that's larger than your head." That's the best I can do.

So I'm off the air now. I'm not exactly sure why *60 Minutes* ended my commentator stint. My theory is that somebody at *60 Minutes* watched the show. Anyway, I'm glad I did it. I learned a lot, and I acquired new respect for television professionals. It's amazing the way they sit still and keep their fingers out of their noses. Unlike most viewers, I've been behind the scenes. I understand what it takes to be a television commentator. When you see a person doing commentary on TV, young lady, you probably just think something like *What a big idiot*.

Not me. Not anymore. I think, *Come on. Give me another shot. I can be a bigger idiot than that*.

What in the heck, I asked the teenage baby-sitter, were you and Muffin doing in the backyard?

"It's a game my mom invented when she was teaching Montessori School," said the baby-sitter. "It's called Tug of Peace. Each side takes hold of one end of a rope and tries to *help* the other side across a line. As you can see, it doesn't work at all. My mom is a total flake."

"Now, now," said my wife.

"Mrs. O," said the baby-sitter, "I can't work tomorrow. I've got to go with my mom to her court date."

Court date? I said.

"She got arrested last month at Earth Day, for chaining herself."

To—? I asked.

"The earth."

I remember the first Earth Day, I said. Thirty-one years ago, all across America, a couple million of my sandal-strap-entangled, natural-food-burping, hair-ball pals and I led the March to Ecological Consciousness. We found Ecological Consciousness, as I recall, behind the bandstand in Central Park, wrapped in aluminum foil. A guy named Groovy was selling it for $5.

"Honey!" said my wife.

"Don't worry, Mrs. O," said the baby-sitter, "I don't use drugs. It's impossible to study differential calculus on drugs."

Earth Day wasn't really a march, I continued. Marches were the kind of thing that serious, intelligent, well-organized civil rights activists did. If Martin Luther King, Jr. had been the leader of a bunch of gooey globe-smoochers, his famous 1963 march would have been called the Wander into Washington. When MLK gave the "I have a dream" speech, half his audience would have been going, "Man, I'm seeing things too," and the other half would have mistakenly assembled in Washington State.

Anyway, there we were on April 22, 1970, vowing to loiter for the sake of the planet, to get everybody to love trees as much as trees loved them, and to keep staring into space and mouth-breathing until Richard Nixon quit putting DDT into bird nests. I remember my cousin, who was a hippie-dip even worse than myself, coming back to our pad with a small bottle in his hands. "A dude laid this on me," he said, in sacerdotal tones. "It's water—from the Hudson River." We lived two blocks from the Hudson River.

To normal people, Earth Day must have looked like a lot of—to use a word then in vogue—pollution: the fetid stench of patchouli oil, the ugly sprawl of tie-dyed fabrics, the awful din of Tibetan finger cymbals and Peruvian nose flutes. Here was environmental blight indeed. Also, when your nation's college-educated young people suddenly discover the ground they're standing on, that's not a good sign. The Youth Goof phenomenon was not just a reaction to the pill and the war in Vietnam; rather, it was the result of an entire baby boom full of cretins.

It's a wonder the squares didn't round us up then and there and feed us to the nearest endangered species—which, in the drug-plagued New York of 1970, would have been anyone carrying a wallet after dark.

Twelve days later the squares did, in fact, cull our herd at Kent State. But then something odd happened. The normal people turned green.

Shortly after the first Earth Day regular folks—folks who, when you say "Gaia," they think "Karmen"—began to spout all sorts of eco-blather and enviro-twaddle. Now my aunt's canasta partner says, "This is the only planet we have," even though the lunatic daughter from whom she heard the phrase would be perfectly at home on Mars. The guy at Slick Lube tells us that our used oil will be recycled—probably by being drained through a gunnysack and sold to someone else as new. And so on. The general public caught this from my generation, like head lice. Thus, long after most features of the Age of Aquarius have succumbed to common sense (or A-200 Pyrinate shampoo), Earth Day lives on.

But is the earth better for it? No one seems to argue that the ecological situation has improved greatly in the past three decades. And if some progress has been made, can the credit go to those of us with a terrible crush on nature? Are atmospheric chlorofluorocarbon releases down because I want to go steady with the sky? Has putting the make on terra firma prevented any environmental damage at all? Or does carrying a torch for Mother E just make things worse?

Not inside my head it doesn't. Maybe the rain forest is toast, but that doesn't mean the ecology movement isn't hugely successful at protecting and nurturing my self-esteem. There's nothing like telling the world I'm wearing u-trou made of hemp to give me a nice sense of false accomplishment (and a rash).

Consider the environmental condition of the earth to be a kitten up a tree. Do we get a ladder? Do we seek trained professional help from the fire department? Or do we sit at a folding table in the mall getting signatures on a PETA petition against using domestic animals in metaphors about the environmental condition of the earth?

The danger of a fondness for false accomplishment is that it gives aid and comfort to people whose accomplishments are even more false than ours—the cretin baby boomers who ran for president last year, for instance. Any mass action is inherently political, even a mass action as sweet and feckless as Earth Day, which—according to a newspaper clipping I have here—listed, among various global activities:

- In the Philippines, a huge environmental concert for youth was broadcast live all across Asia. Actually, if you've ever heard a Philippine rock band, this could be construed as fairly serious eco-terrorism.
- In Mexico, 30,000 high school students planted trees in the capital. After which 30,000 college students doubtless ripped them up and used them to build strike barricades.
- In Ghana, a three-day workshop taught women and youth skills in natural resource conservation: starving as a good way to conserve food, for example.

When we gather in a big public crowd, we want the political system to do something. If we wanted to do something ourselves, we'd be at work. If we wanted to learn something, we'd be at school. And if we were really interested in natural resource conservation, we'd conserve some resources by staying home. Politicians don't fix scientific and economic problems. The last time political types were totally in charge of scientific research and economic planning they built the Chernobyl nuclear plant.

Shall government be the steward of our priceless natural heritage? Suppose a ruthless corporation owned Bikini atoll in the South Pacific. Crass and materialistic pursuit of profit might lead that corporation to destroy bird and animal habitat, degrade air and water quality, and sell sunblock with an SPF of less than 40. But would the corporation test an H-bomb on its luxury leisure development?

The answer, of course, is yes—for the right price. But the price would be high. If somebody came to me and said, "We'd like to detonate a thermonuclear device on that lakefront lot you own in Maine," I'd want more than assessed value. But we're talking about a real estate sales prospect here, for which price is no object. And what customer cares nothing about price? The steward of our priceless natural heritage, the government, that's who.

We can't go to the polls and vote our way into a better environment—unless the environment we really like is grubby little curtained booths with chads on the floor. And a better environment won't come as an answer to our prayers just because we've made ecology our church and Earth

Day our Easter. (Earth Day baskets have chocolate bunnies, marshmallow chicks, *and* gigantic California condors made of tofu.)

We worship our children too, you know. But not literally. We want Muffin to be clean, healthy, and not on the endangered species list. We do not, however, sit her on a corner shelf, surround her with candles, and jam a stick of incense in her ear.

Neither church nor state will breed the rhino or return the polar ice caps to the freezer or make the Detroit River a taste treat. In fact, checking the history of the past millennium from, say, the First Crusade to the Second World War, we see that what church and state do best is send mankind back to the Stone Age.

"Deep ecologists" might think this is a good idea, but even prehistoric man had a problematic relationship with the environment. After all, mammoths are extinct because of Paleolithic atmospheric emissions—the air was full of spear points. Also, billions of poor people around the world are just now emerging from Stone Age living conditions. If we overfed Earth Day fans decide to gag on our wallets and make everybody go back to living with Fred and Wilma in Bedrock, poor people will be peeved and they'll kill us.

Death is a handy reminder of how many environmental problems aren't simply problems, they're costs. Population pressure, for example, is the cost we pay for not being dead. Harvard population expert Nicholas Eberstadt has pointed out that the twentieth century's population explosion was "entirely the result of health improvements and the expansion of life expectancy." Imagine the kind of regulatory actions needed to curtail this ecological threat. Hitler and Stalin already did. Global warming, too, is a cost we pay for certain things we want, such as staying warm. How do we manage these costs? Many of us have done extensive experimental work bouncing checks and juggling credit card balances in an attempt to answer the question of cost management. Unfortunately, the solution to paying our bills never turns out to be going to a jolly gathering of like-minded individuals and hugging them. We need money.

Money buys research. Money buys technology. Money buys rain forests, wetlands, coral reefs, and even—as you may have noticed if you followed the campaign fund-raising scandals—Al Gore. Most of all, money buys the kind of comfortable, prosperous life where we can get time off from hunting mammoths to extinction and trying to make greenhouse gas–producing fuels stay lit in damp caves and celebrate Earth Day instead. Not that I did. There was no Planet Picnic for me. Even though April 22 fell on a weekend this year, I worked. I wrote a piece poking fun at Earth Day and made some money.

"I can't baby-sit today either," said the teenage baby-sitter. "My mom got arrested again. She was protesting George W. Bush's missile defense plan and she chained herself."

To a missile? I asked.

"She couldn't actually find a missile so she chained herself to the stack of cannonballs in front of the Arlington County courthouse."

Did the police take her to jail?

"No, the police decided to just leave her chained to the cannonballs. I've got to take her some sprouts on the Metro."

I've been thinking about making some sort of missile-defense protest myself, I said, after the baby-sitter had left.

"You could go into your office and chain yourself to making a living," suggested my wife. "*Moral Majoritarian* magazine only paid you seventy-five dollars for the Earth Day article."

I need a forum that's more public than working in the den, I said. I'd like to do something that would make the entire nation sick with fear at the prospect of an attack on America using missiles armed with nuclear warheads. Unfortunately I don't know how to perform this stunt. The missile attack part is easy enough. There are scientists, generals, and irrational zealots all over the world who know how to do it. But the sick-with-fear aspect of the feat is daunting.

If I write something that says Washington, D.C., is the target, readers say it's about time. The way our politicos have been acting, something had to be done. A mushroom cloud consumes Manhattan? Considering recent NASDAQ performance, it's probably just an e-commerce stock crashing—another "dot.bomb." When Palm Beach County, Florida, gets nuked, the dimwit residents will think the flash of light comes from more television cameras outside. If they do figure out what's going on, they'll be dialing 991 or 119 or P*A*T*B*U*C*H*A*N*A*N.

There we are in a pile of rubble, bleeding profusely. Everything we have is gone. You and Muffin scream in agony. If we don't die, we'll die anyway—from hideous radiation sickness. How did this get to be a joke?

Well, it's remarkable what a small group of dedicated activists like the baby-sitter's single mom can achieve. For forty-some years the ban-the-bomb bums, unilateral-disarmament goonies, nuclear-freeze sleaze, peace creeps, and no-nukes kooks bragged about the horrors of atomic war. There was no end to their end of the world. They painstakingly detailed Armageddon, polished the Apocalypse, rubbed and loved a radioactive holocaust that made the Jonathan Edwards sermon "Sinners in the Hands of an Angry God" sound like a vacation postcard from Cozumel. "Better red than dead!" they shrieked. They could have gone to Stalin's Russia, Mao's China, or Pol Pot's Cambodia and been both.

This PR for extinction had a dramatic effect on popular culture. There were books, movies, plays, even Top 40 songs about how we were all going to die, plus at least half a dozen *Twilight Zone* episodes where people emerged from their fallout shelters to find the world ruled by three-headed mutants in a bad mood. It scared the dickens out of us. But so did being late for work for the third time in a week and that ominous clunk in the car's transmission and the kid having a temperature of 103 degrees. Extremely bad things might happen, maybe, in the future. But fairly bad things will happen, definitely, right now. We could expend only so much of our adrenaline being panicked "on the come." Frankly, we got pooped with the horrors of atomic war. And then one day in 1989 the Berlin Wall fell and it was over. No more *On the Beach,* no more *Dawn of Destruction,* no more nuclear winter that would be a hundred times worse than global warming—plus colder.

Except it isn't over. It's just begun. And the fact that the whole world will not be blown up doesn't mean our house won't. There are "rogue states" to be considered, and in the long haul of history it turns out that all states are rogue states sooner or later. We certainly were, from the point of view of the Cherokee. Bland, unassuming Belgium ravished the

Congo basin. The boring do-gooders of Scandinavia, when they had their longboats, terrorized everyone from Moscow to Goose Bay, Labrador.

Knowledge of how to trigger fission and make ICBMs won't disappear like the lost works of Euripides. Too many laptops have been in and out of the Los Alamos Laboratory for that. How will rogue states—or rogue organizations or just plain rogues—acquire this expertise? Here's a dark side to the free-market sunshine in which mankind has been basking: They'll buy it. Too costly? The poorest of bad governments seems able to fund large armies, large espionage operations, and very large corps of secret police. Is one missile with the H-bomb option more expensive than snitching on everyone in Iraq? Then there's logic. The U.S.S.R. had some. Commies wanted to destroy America in order to dominate the planet. But if the planet were destroyed in the process, planetary domination lost much of its value. Ergo, Commies used Cubans, Vietnamese, and *The New York Times* rather than nuclear weapons. However, what if destroying America is an end rather than a means? Or what if the rogues are theosophists who, due to transmigration of souls, are going to be reborn as those cockroaches that will be the only things to survive? The result, as far as we're concerned, will be the same as the Cuban missile crisis—if Khrushchev had been drinking more and Jack had doubled up on the back pain medication.

So give a high five—high seven, if you've mutated—to atomic war twenty-first-century style. It doesn't happen only in places like Vladivostok and Chicago anymore. It happens anywhere anyone is mad at anybody, which is everywhere. There's no one pounding his shoe on a desk at the UN by way of warning. The bombs explode one by one instead of simultaneously. And this continues for . . . for as long as we happen to live or can bear to go on doing so.

But that's not the scary thing. The scary thing is the Americans who don't want to prevent this atomic war such as our neighbors and their single mom of a daughter. They're not a majority, perhaps, but if newspaper editorials and television commentaries are any measure, they're a minority of gruesomely influential proportions. These Americans say a missile defense would be expensive. Cleaning up the hole where San Francisco used to be is so cheap. They say the technology is imperfect. "Only twelve seconds in the air? Let's give it up, Orville, and go back to running the bike shop in Dayton." They say Russia and China will feel more comfortable, psychologically, with the ability to lob a missile our way. They say missile defense upsets the peacemaking efforts of our European allies—allies who, in 1914, 1939, and lately in the Balkans, have proven themselves so adept at making peace. And chief among the Americans who want nuclear weapons to be an option in contemporary international conflicts are the moldy old antinuclear protesters of yore. They have risen from their tombs of policy irrelevance and are marching on our homes in a grisly pack. The shock-wave ghouls, the test-ban zombies, the strontium-90 goblins are at least as good undead as red. They are ready to rip our flesh and roast our bones so that the hell they cherished all through the Cold War may yet prevail on earth.

"Really?" said my wife. "I don't think the neighbors are as mad at you as all that."

"I just got in a terrific argument with your assistant, Max," said the teenage baby-sitter, "about getting free music on the Internet with MP3 file-swapping technology. He says using MP3 helps protect First Amendment rights, while I say it helps expand market freedoms."

[Kids today may be wizards with virtual reality, yet they seem a little foggy about what makes reality virtu*ous*. I hate to lecture, but . . .] Young lady, I said, computers are helpful with many tasks, stealing, for instance. If you are adept with a computer, you can filch a Defense Department atomic bomb secret, some Limp Bizkit tunes, and a book report on *Moby Dick* without leaving your room. This takes less nerve and physical exertion than stashing a six-pack of beer under your coat and being chased down the street by an angry ball-bat-wielding package-store owner. Even if you get caught for the computer crime, the FBI agents assigned to cybertheft cases are polite. They come to you; you don't have to go to them. And they rarely use armed force, especially if you turn out to be a fifteen-year-old girl who weighs about a hundred pounds.

The age of information technology is upon us, and everything of value (other than, maybe, the six-pack) can be digitalized. Fortunes used to be made by means of such things as the Firestone Tire Company—an aggregation of factories, machinery, and products that blow up and roll Mrs. O's SUV into a ditch. Now fortunes are made by means of such things as Oracle Corp. Oracle is not an aggregation of factories and machinery, it's a bunch of 0's and 1's. Something else that's a bunch of 0's and 1's is the whole world's banking system, also all the financial markets on earth. Money itself is merely information—0's and 1's in a database such as a bank account—and I have checked mine and there aren't even any 1's in there, just 0's.

But when information travels into the global electronic network, the information is, in effect, a rich tourist wandering through the wrong part of town. The computer becomes the handgun of modern mugging. And it's hard to keep all this bankroll-flashing, Fodor's-consulting, Bermuda-shorts-wearing information safe from the locals. Encryption experts do their best. But the number of encryption experts is finite, while the number of young people who spend much too much time fiddling around on computers is infinite, if you and Max and my godson Nick are anything to go by.

All digitalized information is vulnerable, in some way, to being swiped. Most of you "hackers" don't have the skills to manipulate NASDAQ or empty the International Monetary Fund into your bank card accounts. But you can shoplift CDs and read magazines without buying them. If your printers hold out, you can get five-fingered discounts on books. Advances in technology will soon let you sneak into first-run movie houses, jump the Sony PlayStation 2 toy-store lines, and tell the cable TV people exactly where their next rate increase should go.

As more and more of you do this kind of thing, the likelihood lessens that any one of you will be caught or, if caught, prosecuted or, if prosecuted, punished. Thus is spawned a multitudinous generation of white-collar criminals who can't even be bothered with the collar. You are the sweatpants criminals slouching at your monitors, eating Skittles, drinking Jolt cola, and sacking and pillaging the earth.

This raises two questions: the question of right and wrong and the question *Who cares?* Let's leave the question of right and wrong to be settled between you and your conscience. Or, since I'm a political conservative and therefore regard the world as a thoroughly wicked place, let's just assume you're a bad person and don't have a conscience. Let's leave the question of right and wrong to be settled between you and the bodyguards of Sean "Puffy" Combs after Puffy discovers you've been using MP3 to rip him off for royalties.

The more interesting question is *Who cares?* Possibly, you. If information is free for the taking, available to the masses without cost or risk, then information becomes public property. "All information is public property" has a plummy utopian sound. But how would the fact of information being public affect the quality of that public information? Let me speak two words of caution: *Public toilet.* And, if all information is to be public, by what means will the public manage its information? Who'll be in charge? Will a completely open web promote idealistic anarchism? That is, will the plots of novels and casting for movies be decided by riots in Seattle? Or will representative democracy obtain? Will information be the responsibility of elected officials? I offer, for your imagination, the hip-hop stylings of the future group Bone Thugs 'N House of Representatives.

You may resist the idea of property rights on the Internet because, when you think of property rights, you think of the crabby neighbors—your grandparents—with the KEEP OFF THE GRASS sign, who come out on their porch and scream at kids when they ride bikes across their front yard. Property rights, however, mean more than unviolated herbaceous borders. Although not to your grandparents, who were—Max discovered, through information available on the Internet—the people who placed the anonymous phone call to the truant officer when they saw the boy across the street riding his bike during weekday school hours.

But forget about your grandparents. There is no human liberty without property rights. The most important property right is your own inviolable right to self-possession. You own you.

When other people get mixed up about the notion that you are your personal property, when they start thinking *they* own you, the consequences are horrendous: slave trade, the draft, my first marriage.

You also have property rights in your actions. You own your efforts. Otherwise labor unions would be good for nothing but softball leagues.

You own what you do. And there's the rub in the age of information technology. You don't do anything. Well, that's not true. You baby-sit. But eventually, when you grow up and get a career, you won't do anything. I know I don't. Hardly any of us adults have jobs where we actually make stuff. Most of us don't even provide a service in the traditional sense. Information technology means that what we do is think. And what we think is the information that the information technology runs on. Do we own our thoughts? Do we have property rights in the information that is available on everyone's computer? If we don't, it's back to screaming at the neighborhood brats for doing wheelies on our lawn. And if we do have property rights in the information, then we're sneaking up behind ourselves and stealing our own wallets.

"Gee, Mr. O, you might be right," said the baby-sitter. "I'll have to run some numbers on my computer and see if what you say makes sense from an econometric standpoint."

My God, read this! I said, waving a page of *The New York Times* at my wife. I promised myself I'd read the *Times* every day, no matter how mad it made me. And now I'm glad.

"That newspaper is a year old," said my wife.

I'm a little behind. But this article is still wonderful. It seems the San Francisco Board of Supervisors voted 11 to 0 to ban discrimination against fat people. The District of Columbia already has such a law—no Ted Kennedy jokes, please!—and so does the state of Michigan, as well it should. I was in Michigan not long ago, and at least two-thirds of the inhabitants beep when they back up. But San Francisco is a famously thin and wispy place. There's hardly a dirigible gut to be found within its city limits. Obviously the Board of Supervisors is acting from simple trendiness. Bless them. The trend comes just in time for me.

I'm not a complete dessert scow. Yet. But I'm looking a bit like Brazil where I used to resemble Argentina. Well, I say it's a poor man who can't build a shed over his tool. Prejudice against us wide-loads should, by all means, be made illegal—especially the very strong prejudice that cute young women seem to have when we ask them "Do you come here often?" or "What's your sign?" I'm happily married myself, so of course this type of insensitivity to People of Pudge does not affect me directly.

But I'm thinking of my fellow middle-aged slobs and how their rights are being violated in Hooters franchises every night, nationwide. Also, I presume that these new rotund rights apply to cute young wives, and that henceforth it will be a hate crime for a certain particular cute young wife to laugh out loud when I emerge in a Herman Melville–inspiring manner from the hot tub.

Government protection of pie wagons is law-giving at its most noble, legislation worthy of a Solon—assuming that he was a porker too. But the San Francisco Board of Supervisors does not go far enough in its concern for oppressed minorities. Or majorities, as the case may be, since current National Institutes of Health statistics indicate that everybody in America except Calista Flockhart is overweight. Yes, fatsos need the help of elected officials. For instance, any elected official who wants to come over to my house in the mornings and help me reach my shoelaces would be a plus. But the help of elected officials is also needed by boneheads. Of course, many elected officials *are* boneheads, but there is hardly room in Congress, state legislatures, the San Francisco Board of Supervisors, and so on, for all the country's nitwits. Meanwhile, numskulls lag woefully in college admissions, employment opportunities, career advancement, and remembering to open the garage door before backing the car out. (Don't those garage-door repairmen charge like the dickens?) How long can America bear the shame of its bigotry toward the dim? When—at long last—will we make bias against stupidity punishable by law?

Think of all the things our nation owes to birdbrains. The very voyage to America in the *Mayflower* itself was a pretty dumb idea, not to mention the settlement of the West with its log hovels, Indian scalpings, and San Francisco Board of Supervisors. What would be the state of professional athletics in the United States without hockey-score IQs among players, fans, team owners, and businesses willing to pay for Super Bowl television advertising time? Indeed, our entire entertainment industry depends upon a monumental unintelligence, the likes of which is . . . wearing a tone-on-tone shirt-tie-suit combo and asking people with hockey-score IQs monumentally unintelligent questions on a quiz show. The stock market depends on it too. And without mental retards, Internet chat rooms would be empty and instant messaging would go unused. Then there's politics. Just imagine politics with its dumbbell element subtracted. There would be no Republican candidates. There would be no Democratic voters. The whole system would collapse.

The fat and stupid are a vital part of America. We need forceful legislation and wide-ranging government programs to ensure that America's fattest and stupidest people receive the rights and opportunities, the benefits, and the hopes for a brighter future that every citizen of this republic deserves, plus a chance to run the mutual fund that our IRA is in. Although that has already happened.

And, speaking of NASDAQ, there still remains one more pressing issue of equality that must be addressed by the San Francisco Board of Supervisors and all the other governmental bodies in the land. There lingers in our society a bitter, narrow-minded residue of intolerance for bad people. If our laws are there to protect all Americans, why do we allow these laws to be used to harass certain Americans just because I took a trip to Disney World with my wife and daughter and tried to write it off on my taxes as a business expense? This is not what America is about. We need to search our hearts about this issue, and we also need to get a triple-patty burger from Wendy's with Biggie fries and watch *Who Wants to Be a Millionaire?* Meanwhile, if anyone's going to San Francisco—be sure to wear some flowers on your big fat head.

"My mom," said the teenage baby-sitter, "read that thing you wrote about fat people, on the web site for political nuts. She thinks you're a right-wing lunatic but really hilarious. 'Sometimes he's even hilarious on purpose,' she said. Anyway, she wanted me to bring you this book. She said it will yank your chain."

The book, I said to my wife, is *Guidelines for Bias-Free Writing* by Marilyn Schwartz and the Task Force on Bias-Free Language of the Association of American University Presses, published by Indiana University—*your* alma mater, I believe. And our baby-sitter's single mom has thoughtfully included an I.U. press release stating that, I quote,

Anyone who spends even a few minutes with the book will be a better writer. Well, I spent a few minutes with the book, and I feel a spate of better writing coming on.

The pharisaical, malefic, and incogitant *Guidelines for Bias-Free Writing* is a product of the pointy-headed wowsers at the Association of American University Presses who established a Task Force on Bias-Free Language filled with cranks, pokenoses, blowhards, four-flushers, and pettifogs. This foolish and contemptible product of years wasted in mining the shafts of indignation has been published by the cow-besieged, basketball-sotted sleep-away camp for hick bourgeois offspring, Indiana University, under the aegis of its University Press, a traditional dumping ground for academic deadwood so bereft of talent, intelligence, and endeavor as to be useless even in the dull precincts of midwestern state college classrooms.

But perhaps I'm biased. What, after all, is wrong with a project of this ilk? Academic language is supposed to be exact and neutral, a sort of mathematics of ideas, with information recorded in a complete and explicit manner, the record formulated into theories, and attempts made to prove those formulae valid or not. The preface to *Guidelines* says, "Our aim is simply to encourage sensitivity to usages that may be imprecise, misleading, and needlessly offensive." And few scholars would care to have their usages so viewed, myself excluded.

The principal author of the text, Ms. Schwartz—(I apologize. In the first chapter of *Guidelines,* titled "Gender," it says, in Section 1.41, lines 4–5: "Scholars normally refer to individuals solely by their full or their last names, omitting courtesy titles.")

The principal author of the text, Schwartz—(No, I'm afraid that won't do. Vide Section 1.41, lines 23–25: "Because African American women have had to struggle for the use of traditional titles, some prefer *Mrs.* and *Miss,*" and it would be biased to assume that Schwartz is a white name.)

Mrs. or Miss Marilyn Schwartz—(Gee, I'm sorry. Section 1.41, lines 1–2: "Most guidelines for nonsexist usage urge writers to avoid gratuitous references to the marital status of women.")

Anyway, as I was saying, Ms. Schwartz—(Excuse me. Lines 7–9: "*Ms.* may seem anachronistic or ironic if used for a woman who lived prior to the second U.S. feminist movement of the 1960s," and the head of the Task Force on Bias-Free Language may be, for all I know, old as the hills.)

So, Marilyn—(Oops. Section 1.42, lines 1–3: "Careful writers normally avoid referring to a woman by her first name alone because of the trivializing or condescending effect.")

And *that's* what's wrong with a project of this ilk.

Nonetheless, the principal author—What's-her-face—has crafted a smooth, good-tempered, even ingratiating tract. The more ridiculous neologisms and euphemistic expressions are shunned. Thieves are not "differently ethiced," *women* isn't spelled with any Y's, and men aren't "ovum-deprived reproductory aids—optional equipment only."

A tone of mollifying suggestion is used: "The following recommendations are not intended as prescriptive—" (Though in a project this bossy it is impossible for the imperative mood to completely disappear: "Writers must resort to gender-neutral alternatives where the common gender form has become strongly marked as masculine." Therefore, if the fire department's standards of strength and fitness are changed to allow sexual parity in hiring, I shall be careful to say that the person who was too weak and small to carry me down the ladder was a *firefighter*, not a *fireman*.)

And pains are taken to extend linguistic sensitivity beyond the realms of the fashionably oppressed to Christians ("Terms may be pejorative rather than descriptive in some contexts—*born again, cult, evangelical, fundamentalist, sect*"), teenagers and adolescents ("these terms may carry unwanted connotations because of their frequent occurrence in phrases referring to social and behavioral problems"), and even Republicans ("some married women . . . deplore *Ms.* because of its feminist connotations").

Levity is attempted. Once. This unattributed example of textbook prose is given to show just how funny a lack of feminism can be: "Man, like other mammals, breast-feeds his young."

A mea culpa turn is performed at the end of the preface: "Finally, we realize—lest there be any misunderstanding about this—that there is no such thing as truly bias-free language and that our advice is inevitably shaped by our own point of view—that of white, North American (specifically U.S.), feminist publishing professionals."

And there is even an endearing little lapse on page 36: "A judicious use of ellipses or bracketed interpolations may enable the author to *skirt the problem*" [italics, let this interpolation note, are my own].

Why then do the laudable goals claimed and the reasonable tone taken in *Guidelines for Bias-Free Writing* provoke an as laudable fury and a completely reasonable loathing in this reader? First there is the overweening vanity of twenty-one obscure and unrenowned members of the Task Force on Bias-Free Language presuming to tell whole universities full of learned people what is and what is not an "unwarranted bias." No doubt the task force went on to use feminist theory to map the genes in human DNA.

Then there is petitio principii, begging the question, the logical fallacy of assuming as true that which is to be proven. This book, a purported device to assist in truth finding, instead announces what truths are to be found: "Sensitive writers seek to avoid terms and statements implying or assuming that heterosexuality is the norm for sexual attraction." Which is why the earth is populated by only a few dozen people, all wearing Mardi Gras costumes.

Fallacious disregard for the truth is habitual in *Guidelines*. We are told that "sexist characterizations of animal traits and behaviors are inappropriate" (thereby depriving high school biology students of a classroom giggle over the praying mantis eating her mate after coitus). We are warned against considering animals in "gender-stereotyped human terms" and are given, as an admonitory example, the sentence "A stallion guards his brood of mares," although the stallion will do it no matter how many task forces are appointed by the Association of American University Presses. We hear that it is permitted to use "traditional technical terms, such as *feminine rhyme*" but are told to "avoid introducing gender stereotypes—e.g., 'weak' rhymes." But a feminine rhyme, with its extra unaccented syllable, is, in fact, feeble. Note the effect on this children's classic by Clement Clarke Moore:

'Twas the night before Christmas, when all through the housing
Not a creature was stirring—not even a mousing.
The stockings were hung by the chimney with caring,
In hopes that St. Nicholas soon would be thereing.

We are scolded for using "illegal alien" when "undocumented resident or undocumented worker is generally preferred as less pejorative." What, they *aren't* illegal? Try hiring one if you've been nominated as Secretary of Labor. And *Guidelines* goes so far as to urge utter dishonesty upon translators, saying they should make up their own sanctimonious minds about "Whether gender-biased characteristics of the original warrant replication in English."

When the book is not lying or creating reasons to do so, it is engaging in the most tiresome sort of feminist scholasticism. Thirteen pages are devoted to wrestling with alternatives to the generic "he." A central thesis of *Guidelines* is thereby nearly disproven. If they require thirteen pages to discuss a pronoun, maybe women *are* inferior. (Even Bill Clinton—beloved of feminists—didn't need that much space to parse "is.")

Why doesn't the task force just combine "she" and "it" and pronounce the thing accordingly. This would be no worse than the rest of the violence the book does to the language. Use of the obnoxious singular "they" is extolled. Shakespeare is cited by way of justification, and let me cite *Taming of the Shrew* as grounds for my critique. Dwarfism is described as a medical condition "resulting in severe short stature." Gosh, that was a strict midget. And the word "man," meaning humanity, is to be discarded, replaced by "people" or "person." *What a piece of work is person!*

No, not even the members of the Task Force on Bias-Free Language are this tin-eared. They admit "these terms cannot always substitute for generic *man*" and suggest that "other revisions may be preferable." For instance, the sentence can be recast so that the first person plural is used: *What a piece of work we are!*

Much of *Guidelines* is simply mealymouthed, touting the Mrs. Grundyisms (she lived before the second U.S. feminist movement) that pompous nonentities have always favored: "*congenital disability* . . . is preferable to *birth defect*" and "manifestations of epilepsy are termed *seizures*, not *fits*." But on some pages pretension progresses to delusion: for example, "terms such as *mentally deranged, mentally unbalanced, mentally diseased, insane, deviant, demented,* and *crazy* are not appropriate." Which statement is—how else to put it?—mentally deranged, mentally unbalanced, mentally diseased, insane, deviant, demented, and crazy.

The members of the Task Force on Bias-Free Language should be exiled to former Yugoslavia and made to teach bias-free Serbo-Croatian to Serbs and Croats for the rest of their natural lives—that is to say, until their pupils tear them limb from limb. But this is just for the book's minor sins. Bad as *Guidelines* is so far, it gets worse.

The text assaults free will: "Most people do not consider their sexuality a matter of choice." Oh-oh. Left my zipper down and there goes Mr. Happy. Who knows what he'll do? Better lock up your daughters. Also, of course, your sons. And since "Writers are enjoined to avoid gratuitous references to age," better lock up Granny, too.

The authors deprecate commonsense standards of good: "Designating countries as *undeveloped* or *underdeveloped* implies an evolutionary hierarchy of nations based on wealth, type of economy, and degree of industrialization." Of course it does, you feebleminded idiots.

"Labels such as *feebleminded, idiot, imbecile, mentally defective, mentally deficient, moron,* and *retard* are considered offensive." I mean, you possessors of "a condition in which a person has significantly below-average general intellectual functioning."

Morals are attacked. We are told that "many stereotypical terms that are still found in writing about American Indians" are "highly offensive." One of them being "*massacre* (to refer to a successful American Indian raid or battle victory against white colonizers and invaders)." Ugh, Chief. Log cabins all burn. Heap many scalps. And UN High Commissioner for Refugees got-em all women and children.

And even the idea of normal is condemned: "The term *normal* may legitimately refer to a statistical norm for human ability (normal vision is 20/20) but should usually be avoided in other contexts as . . . invidious."

Thus deprived of all tools of independent judgment and means of private action, the gender-neutral, age-nonspecific, amoral, abnormal *person* is rendered helpless. Or, as *Guidelines for Bias-Free Writing* puts it, "The term *able-bodied* obscures [a] continuum of ability and may perpetuate an invidious distinction between persons so designated and those with disabilities."

We're all crippled. And we're all minorities too, because "A 'minority' may be defined not on the basis of population size, color, or ethnicity (e.g., women and people with disabilities are sometimes described as minorities), but in terms of power in a particular society."

Guidelines then goes about treating these overwhelming minorities with absurd sensitivity. We are warned off "the many common English expressions that originate in a disparaging characterization of a particular group or people"; *Siamese twins, get one's Irish up,* and even *to shanghai* are cited. Nonwhite is "Objectionable in some contexts because it makes white the standard by which individuals are classified." Far East is "Eurocentric. *East Asia* is now preferred." "The expression *ghetto blaster* for a portable stereo (or, more colloquially, a 'boom box') is offensive as a stereotype [the pun goes unremarked in the text] of African American culture." Objection is made to the designation Latin American "because not all persons referred to as Latin American speak a Latin-based language." We are told that "some long-accepted common names for botanical species—Niggerhead Cactus, Digger Pine (from a derogatory name for California native people who used the nuts from the *Pinus sabiniana*)—are offensive and are now undergoing revision in the scientific community." Artwork, also, must be carefully reviewed. "Graphic devices and clip art used by production and marketing staff can be generic and misleading . . . a traditional Zuni design gracing chapter openings in a book about the Iroquois; an illustration of a geisha advertising a press's book on Japan." Law enforcement, too. The word *mafia* is held to be "Discriminatory against Italian Americans unless used in the correct historical sense; not interchangeable with *organized crime*." And we mustn't say anything good about minorities either. "Gratuitous characterizations of individuals, such as *well-dressed, intelligent, articulate,* and *qualified* . . . may be unacceptably patronizing in some contexts, as are positive stereotypes—the polite, hardworking Japanese person or the silver-tongued Irish person."

What's happening here? Is the task force just going to bizarre lengths to avoid hurt feelings? Or is it trying to make those feelings hurt as much as possible? Has the Association of American University Presses crossed the line between petting minorities and giving them—as it were—a Dutch rub? We're all pathetic members of oppressed minority factions, and the whole world—now wildly annoyed by reading *Guidelines for Bias-Free Writing*—hates our guts. And everything, everything, right down to grammar itself, is terribly unfair. Oh, what will become of us? Whatever shall we do?

Some enormous power for good is needed. Government will hardly answer, since *Guidelines* has shown us that even such well-meaning political entities as Sweden and Canada are no better than Cambodia or Congo. Perhaps there is a religious solution. But when we encounter the word *heathen* in *Guidelines* we are told that "uncivilized or irreligious" is a "pejorative connotation." So God is out. And, anyway, He is notorious for His bias in favor of certain minorities and for the gross inequities of His creation. Really we have only one place to turn—the Association of American University Presses and, specifically, the members of its Task Force on Bias-Free Language. Who has been more fair than they? Who more sensitive? Who more inclusive? Who more just?

Sure, the task force seems to be nothing but a rat bag of shoddy pedagogues, athletes of the tongue, professional pick-nits filling the stupid hours of their pointless days with nagging the yellow-bellied editors of university presses, which print volume after volume of bound bum-wad fated to sit unread in college library stacks until the sun expires. Yet the task force will bind the wounds of the world. The very Association of American University Presses itself says so in the position statement adopted by the AAUP Board of Directors in November 1992: "Books that are on the cutting edge of scholarship should also be at the forefront in recognizing how language encodes prejudice. They should be agents for change and the redress of past mistakes."

If the suggestions in *Guidelines for Bias-Free Writing* are followed diligently by the acknowledged cultural vanguard, everything will change, all ills will be rectified, and redemption will be available to us all.

The Task Force on Bias-Free Language shall be our salvation, truth, and light. If you close your eyes, if you open your heart, if you empty your mind—especially if you empty your mind—you can see the task force members. There they are in a stuffy seminar room in some inconvenient corner of the campus, with unwashed hair, in Kmart blue jeans, batik-print tent dresses, and off-brand running shoes, the synthetic fibers from their fake Aran Islands sweaters pilling at the elbows while they dance in circles around the conference table, shouting affirmations.

"Yes! Tremble at our inclusiveness! Bow down before our sensitivity! Culturalism in all its multi-ness is ours! No more shall the pejorative go to and fro in the earth! Woe to the invidious! Behold *Guidelines for Bias-Free Writing,* ye Eurocentric male-dominated power structure, and despair!"

The nurse (either a man or a woman, since it is no longer proper to use the word as a "gender-marked" term) is coming from the university infirmary with their medications.

Max, I shouted to my young assistant, will you put something on my web area?

"Web *site,*" said Max.

10

JUNE 2001

Congratulations!" said my young assistant, Max. "How are Mrs. O and the new baby?"

Howling lustily, I said. The baby, that is. My wife is aglow with the joy of motherhood. Or so she was good enough to tell me.

"I got the kid a Sony PlayStation Two," said my godson, Nick. "I beat the toy-store shortage by fiddling around on my computer."

"This is so cool," said the teenage baby-sitter. "You'll have to reconfigure all your estate planning. The pertinent tax law is right here in my backpack."

"I like it when Mommy has babies," said Muffin, munching on the chocolate cake that Muffin tells me is what my wife always gives her for breakfast.

"Nick and I are going to take Muffin to the Biting and Scratching Zoo in Rock Creek Park," said the teenage baby-sitter.

Biting and Scratching Zoo? I said.

* * *

"Like a petting zoo," said the baby-sitter, "except it teaches kids about real life."

It's a person! I suppose that's the modern thing to say, I said, as I doled out a cigar to the Political Nut, to celebrate the birth of my beautiful—*and* intelligent, capable, and fiercely independent—daughter. I can accept, I said, a few linguistic modifications. But I am a traditionalist at heart. I've bought the requisite box of stogies.

However, as a traditionalist, I'm beginning to wonder about this tradition. None of my relatives, business associates, or barroom pals has given away a corona on the occasion of nativity that I can recall. Everybody's familiar with the custom, but I don't think I've ever seen the customary gesture made. In fact, I believe my entire knowledge of the convention is based on old comic strips, gags from the Pleistocene era of TV comedy, and a couple of dusty boxes of cheroots with pink and blue cigar bands that were in the display case at the drugstore where I had an after-school job in 1964.

I've consulted libraries, etiquette books, and friends who are replete with arcane knowledge. The only thing I've learned for certain is that, at the christening, I should not give a cigar to Father O'Malley. Urban VIII (reigned 1623–1644) wrote a papal bull forbidding priests to smoke cigars.

I called *Cigar Aficionado*—the *Vogue* magazine of the fashion for big smokes—and asked George Brightman, director of business development, why I should be dispensing gaspers. He said he thought it was "rooted in something British—a naval officers' tradition, maybe." Mr. Brightman suggested I call Simon Chase at Hunters & Frankau, Great Britain's most prestigious firm of cigar importers. Mr. Chase said he thought it was "something the English do to imitate Americans. I believe it comes from your side rather than our side." I called Molly E. Waldron at the Tobacco Institute in Washington. No one there knew the answer so Ms. Waldron called Norm Sharp at the Cigar Association of America. The only information Mr. Sharp had was from a seventeen-year-old newspaper clipping saying, "Cigars were so rare and treasured in the late seventeenth and eighteenth centuries that . . . they were used as expression of deep emotional appreciation," and "the birth of a boy was considered a most important event . . . so fathers who could afford to celebrated by giving their friends cigars as a way of expressing happiness." The source named in this clipping was the Tobacco Institute in Washington.

A certain interrogational circularity was setting in. Why do I give a guy a cigar because my wife had a baby? As the most knowledgeable salesman at that best of cigar stores, Georgetown Tobacco, said, "You're not going to give him a lollipop."

I'm probably better off making things up. As I've found out from years of journalism, this is often the case. Perhaps I'm offering cigars to drive away evil. The cigar does seem to be an anathema to ideological types whom I don't want bothering my little darling. Although smoke is not an infallible charm against them. V. Lenin bought cigars at Zino Davidoff's father's store in Geneva. A bill still exists—marked *Not paid,* of course.

Anyway, that theory does not explain why I'm bestowing the gifts. The flow of presents should run in the other direction at blessed- event time—as per three wise men and a newborn babe no doubt almost as adorable as mine. And my wife and I *have* made quite a haul. In fact, if I see one more bootie, blankie, snugglie, jammie, hatsie, pantsie, or shirtsie covered in twee, cloying, dwarfish bears, I'm going to need a bottle myself. Preferably Dewar's. I understand bunnies and chicks, but why bears? Bears are not cute. Bears are bad-tempered predators. Bears eat garbage. Bears smell.

And so do cigars. Maybe the association of cigars with paternity has to do with masking diaper odor. Not that anyone would smoke a cigar anywhere near Daddy's little precious. But maybe cigars are an excuse for fathers to go stand in the garage when diapers need to be changed. A cigar can buy you a whole hour, as opposed to the ten minutes you get from a Camel. Or maybe cigars are a Planned Parenthood policy, a method of spacing births. As long as Dad has cigar breath, the next child is not likely to be conceived soon.

This still doesn't tell me why I'm doing the giving instead of the receiving. There's the obvious Freudian thing. Freud is supposed to have said, "Sometimes a cigar is just a cigar." But that leaves what a cigar is the rest of the time open to Freudian interpretation. By proffering cigars

I'm saying, "I made a baby. Here is an object symbolizing how the deed was done. Let me know if your wife needs a baby, too." Then there's the potlatch aspect. To show what big men they were, Indians of the Pacific Northwest used to give away or burn valuable goods. With cigars you can do both.

A new father is a very big man. He feels like one of those bond moguls of the 1980s. That is, he feels lucky to get out on parole, even if it's only to the garage. But he also feels important and powerful. Cigars are indicators of power and importance. Although I don't know why. Where I grew up they were indicators of old men playing gin rummy. Perhaps it's because a cigar is such a good theatrical device. Light a big one and puff on it, and you're immediately doing an excellent impression of pompous, portly middle age. And when the puffing is done by one of us who actually *is* pompous, portly, and middle-aged, the impression is particularly good.

The cigar as a stage prop to signify plutocracy has been in use at least since Charlie Chaplin's silent films *City Lights* and *The Gold Rush*. And various propped-up stagy plutocrats—Arnold Schwarzenegger, Michael Douglas, Jack Nicholson—are still making good use of it. As did Bill Clinton, who—I have seen photographs that prove it—*leaves the band on his cigar*. I think this says everything that needs saying about the late Clinton presidency.

But I've gotten off the subject. We may never know why a man presents cigars with a birth announcement. But we will know what kind of cigars he's presenting. And here comes the cigar-bore monologue: "The El Fumigatore Malodoro Grande is a big, noisy, wide-bodied smoke. It has an earthy, dirty flavor of wadded-up plant leaves with an undertone of cedar chips from the bottom of the hampster cage and a loud, stupid finish when the exploding device inside goes off." Actually, I don't know how to talk that kind of talk. I'm one of those people who, as I've mentioned before, can't figure out why wine-tasting columns don't mention getting drunk. That *is* the point. Nobody would pay $300 for a bottle of '89 Château Cheval-Blanc if it didn't pack a wallop. And nobody would inhale the fumes of smoldering vegetable matter from a Cohiba Esplendido if the smoke didn't contain nicotine.

The fact of the matter is, I'm distributing drugs to commemorate the arrival of my daughter. This would make more sense if nicotine were a drug that produced uncontrollable impulses to set up trust funds for infants or immunized guests against the noises caused by colic. Nonetheless, the alkaloid $C_{10}H_{14}N_2$ does provide a nice little buzz, the kind of high that allows you to keep your wits about you, so you know just how long to linger in the garage until the nappies are clean and the burping has been administered.

Cigars are a mere narcotic. And I am a democrat—in the small *d* sense—about getting stoned. And yet I confess to a measure of snobbery concerning distinctions among cigars. I can't buy a box of Phillie Blunts. The kind of people who hollow out their cigars and fill them with marijuana are not a presence in my social set. And I can't buy any of the good Dominican and Honduran imports because they're all gone—purchased by au courant types trying to look like Arnold Schwarzenegger, Michael Douglas, or, more realistically, Ronald Perlman. Besides, I have the most wonderful baby on earth. Only the best will do. And Cuba still makes the best cigars.

Maybe it's the soil or the climate. Maybe it's the comely Cuban maidens rolling the cigars on their . . . actually, they roll them on tables. Maybe it's just more $C_{10}H_{14}N_2$. But importing Cuban cigars is illegal. There's a cautionary tale about cigar smuggling in the December 1997 issue of *Cigar Aficionado,* although a possible dodge is mentioned. A customs agent interviewed at New York's JFK airport gives his opinion that body-cavity concealment is "still too extreme for cigars." The mind, however, boggles and so do other parts of the anatomy. This certainly would be a bad way to smuggle lit cigars.

So I didn't get any Cubans. Specifically, I didn't get a box of Montecristo No. 4 coronas. And where I didn't get them—which I can't tell because then I'd not only be committing a crime but engaging in a criminal conspiracy—was from a certain well-known foreign country. An outfit there will ship cigars in a container labeled MADE IN MEXICO, and no lies are being told because the container is indeed Mexican-made.

Finally I possessed some cigars worthy of my fabulous kid. At $13 apiece, they'd better be. And then I faced another problem. To whom should I give them? Although tobacco is very stylish now, many of my friends are still stuck in the outmoded nineties health fad and haven't resumed smoking. As for the chic new breed of puffers I know, I sincerely approve of them. A shared vice is a pleasure. It's also a pleasure to watch a thirty-five-year-old financial hotshot turn pea green as he pretends to enjoy a Romeo Y Julieta Belicosos. And, concerning halitosis among the increasing number of my female acquaintances who indulge, I'm a husband and father and shouldn't be kissing around anyway. But, all that said, giving really scarce, really good cigars to modish neophytes is like casting pearls before debutantes. They'll enjoy it, but I will not.

I can't help suspecting that the trendsetters don't know an El Rey Del Mundo from a White Owl. And seeing four inches of an Havana H. Upmann stubbed out in the ashtray at a martini bar is enough to make a real addict cry (or steal the butt). This leaves, as recipients of my cigar largesse, men with palates as blackened, clothes as smelly, and suit lapels as full of little singe holes as my own. Most of these fellows are older and richer than myself. They already have cigars, they already have children, too, and grandchildren to boot. I've thought it over and decided to hell with them.

I am parting with my cigars very slowly, parceling out just one per day, right after dinner. And every evening, for the next twenty-five nights, you'll find me with a demitasse of good coffee, a snifter of fine brandy, and a celebratory smoke, in the garage.

Hello! I said, as my godson Nick pulled into that garage. [Nick had insisted on driving the teenage baby-sitter home, even though she lives next door. Oh, to be sixteen again and have the ten-minute loan of a car key bring the joy and sense of liberation that could hardly be produced in a man my age by a gift of a month at the Ritz in Paris.]

"The baby-sitter says I should be planning my 401k retirement account now," said Nick, looking a bit deflated. "She says it's important if I'm going to get the kind of surfing and snowboarding opportunities that I want at sixty-five."

Well, I said, I think you can probably let it wait until the end of summer vacation.

"Yeah, summer vacation," said Nick, looking more deflated. "I've got to go to Joy Counseling."

Huh? I said.

"Remember when my football team won the championship? Our headmaster believes that all strong emotions can be deeply psychologically disturbing. Not just grief or fear but happiness, too. The whole team has to go to Joy Counseling. It kind of wrecks summer."

Something always does, I said. For nine long months the memory of summer lays its hold upon me, Nick. Lolling days of sun. Cares brushed away by gentle zephyrs. Pellucid twilights. Sultry evenings—especially when the window AC unit goes out. Madras and poplin and white after Memorial Day. Specifically, white thighs and calves. There's cruising the islands: Mykonos, Ibiza, Staten. That night in Monte Carlo? A Chevy Monte Carlo. I didn't break the bank, but I did back into an ATM machine. What about those merry golf outings? Always bogeyed the eighth hole, the one with the spiral ramp and the windmill. Long walks on the beach. Soft sands, soft promises, and a soft roll of flab spilling over my swim-trunk waistband. Mornings on horseback, or on Lawnboy anyway. The scent of fresh grass clippings. And the smell the electric weed whacker makes when its nylon cord gets snarled. Summer, the fragrant time: flowers, new-mown hay, musk, and whatever else was in that aftershave my high school girlfriend gave me. More long walks on the beach—we never did find the car keys. And, best of all, the famous summer moon. That old lady walking her dog was sure surprised when I stuck my butt out the passenger-side window.

But throw nostalgia aside, Nick. Another summer is here. How did a twenty-five-pound dead raccoon get under the cover of the aboveground pool? The living is easy. The charcoal is damp. We're out of lighter fluid. And we're going to get this summer off to a great start as soon as we get home from the emergency room and the gasoline blaze in the Weber dies down. Summer is for adventure. Summer is the season of sights and sounds. Did Aerosmith always sound this bad? And what a sight they're getting to be.

This summer I'm going to do the things I've always meant to do. Plant a topiary garden. Learn Italian. Read *Middlemarch*. Use the nine mandated days of paid vacation before August or lose 60 percent of accumulated holiday time in the subsequent calendar year. And visit my wife's parents in Des Moines.

I'm going to spend more time with the kids this summer. Like I've got a choice. Muffin has to be taken to tennis lessons at 9, swim lessons at 10, tai kwan do lessons at 11, soccer practice at 1, gymnastics at 2, play date at 3, and a birthday party at a Chuck E. Cheese restaurant in a suburb on the other side of the moon at 4. Don't let me forget to stop and buy a gift. Also, I'll have plenty of time with the kids on the way to Des Moines while they spill grape juice, break the Gameboy, and throw up in the SUV. And, by the time we get back. . . . Gosh, where did the summer go?

More to the point, why are we sad when it's gone? Everybody claims to love this time of the year and yet consider:

Summer school
Summer camp
Summer job
Summer love
Summer rental
Summer reruns
Summer soldiers and sunshine patriots
Summer stock performances of *Annie Get Your Gun*

As an adjective, "summer" is no compliment. The second-rate, the unimportant, the flimsy, and the stupid predominate from June to September.

Summer is the season of big dumb movies and big dumb books and big dumb me turning crab-boil red at the shore. Nature tricks us with its benign looks, and we wander around outdoors unwary as we'd never be in December. Nobody gets chandelier stroke, coat-and-hat-burn, or cool rash. Summer is when we're not paying attention. We get confused about things. Daylight savings versus that 401k of yours. You think you'll retire on a bank account full of extra sunshine after dinner. Temperatures go up, IQs go down. Ghettos do not burn in January and neither do large overfertilized patches of rye grass in my front yard.

The very bliss adults feel at the advent of summer is half-witted. We're forgetting that we're not ten. There comes no lovely day in spring when the doors of America's businesses fly open and employees rush away singing:

Office is out! Office is out!
Management let the monkeys out!
No more faxes! No more phones!
No more taking laptops home!

And, come autumn, adults do not move to a different and perhaps more interesting cubicle where a new and maybe more lackadaisical quality team supervisor will be in charge. Adult life doesn't even have a proper summer. It just has a period of hot weather with more houseguests, more houseflies, and no fewer house payments. Summer is a sham. Summer is a hoax. Summer, if we think about it, is . . .

But let's stop thinking, Nick. It's summer. There may be nobler times of year, but no one's made a movie called *Endless February*. There never was a "Mud Season of Love." And no pop songs have been written about slush and driveway salt.

Summer isn't worthwhile. Bless it. The worthwhile things get on our nerves enough the other three-quarters of the annum. Let's see what Duty looks like in a thong bikini. Let's find out if Honor can water-ski. Summer is inconsequential. But we know what "take the consequences" means. We don't get much done in the summer. But what are we, do-gooders? And, if what we do isn't good, is the world worse off without it? Summer promises us nothing. Couldn't we all use a little more of that in our lives? Summer makes us act foolish. So? How much fun have you had acting serious?

The major religions of the world do not have their high holy days in summer, for good reason. The Goddess of Winter is stern and self-disciplined. The Goddess of Fall is fruitful and wise. The Goddess of Spring is full of hope. But the Goddess of Summer is . . . naked, if we can get her to drink two more Mai Tais.

Summer is pointless. That's the point. Summer is useless. Who wants to feel used? Summer is dumb. And so are you and I. Looks like one more perfect summer, Nick. Better hold on to the car keys. And if you're going out again later, bring home a bag of ice.

* * *

One enormous advantage to being up all night with a baby, I said to my wife, is that we get to watch all sorts of things on television. There are whole segments of popular culture that we never knew existed—except when we were up all night with the previous baby. It's highly instructive.

"You may think so," said my wife. "I'm not allowed to drink until Poppet is weaned."

Let's see, I said, riffling through a copy of *Cable Existence* while mixing an old-fashioned. [Another thing parenting teaches you is how to multitask.] MTV has a new quiz show where all the contestants are members of popular music groups, *Name That Drug*. On VH-1 there's an hour-long special, the story behind Courtney Love's power ballad "I'd Die for Me." The Memoir Channel is featuring Morris Freud.

"Who is Morris Freud?"

Sigmund's lesser-known cousin, also a psychiatrist. He had a theory that there was an aspect to the psyche even more important than the subconscious. He called it "consciousness," the idea being that we sometimes know what we're doing. It's never been proven.

"What's on the History Channel?" asked my wife.

A new look at the Visgoths. Turns out they were sensitive, artistic types—starved for literature, music, drama. They didn't really *sack* Rome. They were just searching for poems. They were sorry if they happened to break some things.

The Disability Channel has a roundtable discussion on handicapped access to Lover's Leaps plus a preview of a new superhero cartoon series that Disney has created for obese children, *The Incredible Bulk*. There's a show on the Paranormal Network about people who've had out-of-auto-body experiences. *Archaeology Tonight* is featuring "The Lost Mall of New Rochelle." There's a live broadcast of the 3 A.M. service at the US Airways First Church of Christ. Or we can watch that Turner Broadcasting show *What If?* It gets five stars out of a possible four: "This week *Moo Sioux*. The Spanish conquistadors brought European livestock to North America, and the history of the West would have been vastly different if their cows had escaped instead of their horses."

"No," said my wife.

How about *Too Rich, Too Thin* on HBO? "A slimmed-down Julia Roberts plays ultra-wealthy American appliance heiress Amana Fridge, who is lured into marriage by a penniless French count (Billy Bob Thornton). After she wills him her fortune he throws her into the Seine from the Pont Neuf and tells the gendarmes that she accidentally slipped through the grating." Here's something even better: *The Great Car Chase,* starring Steve McQueen. He did all his own stunts, you know. We lost one of the true thespian geniuses when he died of lung cancer.

"He should have had a stunt double do his smoking for him," said my wife, as I sneaked out to the garage.

It's the second anniversary of the air war in Kosovo! exclaimed the Political Nut who lives around here [coming in at cocktail hour, when he seems to be most active]. I'm starting an organization of Kosovo War Reenactors, he said. I've got the poster designed already.

Attention Balkans Buffs!!!

Stupendous, Gigantic

WAR IN KOSOVO REENACTMENT!!!!!

Coming This Sunday

to the very government offices and international conference halls where the original conflict was fought

RELIVE THE GLORY OF THE CLINTON ADMINISTRATION AT WAR!!!

The Battle of Brussels

will be staged

By Experienced Kosovo Reenactors

dressed and equipped in every detail with 1990s vintage business suits, briefcases, cell phones, and Washington Post op-ed pieces

SEE

Gifted Actors Portraying

SCENES OF HIGH DRAMA

☞ Madeleine Albright Gets Indignant

☞ The President Bites His Lip and Looks Grave

☞ Gerhard Schröder Waffles

☞ Tony Blair Jumps Up and Down and Squeaks

☞ Sen. John McCain Gets Real Mad

☞ Slobodan Milosevic Lives "La Vida Loca"

★★★★★★★★★★★★★★★★★★★

★★SPECIAL PERFORMANCES★★

PETER, PAUL & MARY

Will Sing Patriotic War Songs

"Where Have All the Peace Creeps Gone?"

"Blowin' in the CNN"

"We Shall Something-Or-Other"

and many more

Berkeley, California's Famous

Left-Wing Ex-Pacifist Draft-Dodger Troupe Will Stage a

GREAT MORAL CONFUSION

A Full-Scale Model of the Proposed

"U.S. KOSOVO VETERANS MEMORIAL"

A Six-Feet-Deep Hole with Nothin' In It

SQUABBLING!! INDECISION!! DELAY!! HALF-MEASURES!!

WATCH

☞ British and American Pilots Fly Off to Someplace and Then Come Back Again

☞ NATO Troops Roll into Kosovo and Stay There Forever

☞ Thousands of Displaced Kosovars Drive Cabs and Open Ethnic Restaurants in Your Neighborhood

(Don't miss the FREE goat-tasting)

★★★★★★★★★★★★★★★★★★★

ENJOY

☞ Collateral Damage

JUST FOR KIDS!!!

Throw Paint at a Mock-Up of the U.S. Consulate in Shanghai!!!

STROBE TALBOTT LOOK-ALIKE CONTEST!!!

Members of the Parma, Ohio, Dead Serbian Civilian Social Club will lie amid detailed rubble

☞ Stirring Speeches At the Cold War Revival Tent

☞ Mock War Crimes Trial

Where perfectly recreated nothing will happen

A KLA DRUG DEALING BOOTH

78 DAYS OF FUN FOR THE WHOLE FAMILY

Admission: $10 billion and counting

Muffin is pretty upset," said the teenage baby-sitter. "Somebody used up all her crayons."

To make a bold political statement, I said.

"I thought Max was going to teach you to use the computer."

I *know* how to use the computer, I said—In theory. But consider this: The Old Testament was composed with a hammer and chisel on tablets of stone. The works of William Shakespeare were limned with a goose quill. Henry James wielded a fountain pen. Jack Kerouac used a typewriter. And John Grisham writes on a computer. You see the pattern. I'm bad enough in crayon.

For millennia the process of communication has been getting easier and more enjoyable. What a terrible idea. The infinitely forgiving monitor is free of eraser burns, white-out puddles, and scribbles in the margin. Various "check" programs spell, punctuate, and correct grammar. The keyboard is as effortless as a Florida ballot dimple. A wrist wiggle and a finger tap deliver the vocabulary of William F. Buckley. Now anyone can put thoughts into words, and—as a glimpse at the Internet shows—almost no one should.

Right here in the November 26, 2000, issue of *Parade* it says . . .

"Mr. O," said the baby-sitter, "my mom thinks you really ought to recycle some of these newspapers. She says you're sitting on the whole Willamette National Forest. She's tinkering with Grandpa's leaf mulcher, so it can do pulp processing and—"

Parade is a valuable research tool, I said. How else can we know what people who collect china figurines think? Anyway, *Parade* says, *Thirteen million older Americans have discovered the home computer.* That includes your grandparents. I rest my case. If one irate phone call from next door about Muffin wearing an I'M THE NRA T-shirt can drive me crazy, imagine thirteen million electronic messages via Internet appliance. But the problem is not limited to pesky old folks with e-mail or idiots your age in chat rooms or management bores "dialoguing" every person in the corporation.

Writers are famously supposed to suffer, and the computer is fun. The difference between writing and the rest of the artistic endeavors used to be that the other artists had toys: saxophones, toe shoes, watercolors and oils. No writer ever sat down to work without feelings of bitter envy toward musicians, dancers, painters. Even the painters redoing the writer's apartment looked like they had it pretty good. As a result, few writers ever sat down to work at all. They would avail themselves of any excuse for missing deadlines: the writer's apartment was being painted. Hence the large number of poets in garrets and freelancers still living at home with their parents. Authors were kept out of the public's hair—itself a good thing. And the author who did author something was almost certain to put the actual writing part off as long as possible, until the piece had been written, rewritten, and polished in his mind. Using your mind is almost as much fun as using a computer—except, of course, computer use is mindless.

Now Amazon.com bulges—or would bulge, if e-commerce enterprises contained anything. Every writer is writing, mostly memoirs. The world is full of quotidian experiences tamely described and tepid ideas lamely expressed.

I was a magazine editor, young lady, when the personal computer first came into use. It was easy to tell, even when articles had been set into type, which writers owned a PC. Their writing was more fun—for the writer. For the reader, the writing seemed to lack a few things, such as a beginning, middle, and end. On a computer, it's so easy to fix those later. But in writing, as in cooking and courting, to defer a decision is to decide.

Computer writing is disorganized, parenthetical, digressive, prolix, and overly casual in tone. We need not alter Lincoln's magisterial phrases to hear how the Gettysburg Address would have turned out if Abe had been noodling on his iMac:

> A great battlefield! Now we are engaged in a great civil war. We have come to dedicate a portion of that field of that war we are met on as a final resting place for those who here gave their lives testing whether that nation (a new nation) so conceived and so dedicated (conceived in liberty and dedicated to the proposition that all men are created equal), or any other nation our fathers brought forth on this continent, can long endure. Hey, 87 years and counting!

And let's not think about Lord Chesterfield's web site for his son, let alone *www.abelard-heloise.com*:

> **Everything fine at the nunnery. Real quiet, tho. Nuns say hi**
>
> **These castration stitches sure itch :(**

Even modern love letters can be spoiled by the computer, if the computer automatically includes the routing:

> To: *jennifer103@aol.com, kkkatie@compuserve.com, suzyq@worldonline.com, fiona@globalnet.co.uk, fred@yahoo.com*

And what if no one had thought to print out the e-mails of Saint Paul to the Corinthians? How would we get through a modern marriage ceremony (written by the bride and groom using Word Perfect™) without First Corinthians, chapter 13, verses 1–7?

> Though I speak with the tongues of men and of angels and have not something, something, something. . . . It was really clever. I've got it in a file somewhere.

No doubt the computer is a marvelous tool, but then so is speech. When humans quit grunting and waving their arms and began to talk, communication definitely became easier and more enjoyable. But we've been speaking for a hundred thousand years and still haven't got it right. After all this time we've yet to learn that what most of us do best when we talk is shut up. Excuse me while I go take a dose of my own medicine, with a brandy, in the garage.

"And I won't say a thing to Muffin," said the baby-sitter, "about what happened to her crayons."

Hello! I said, as my godson Nick pulled into the garage. [He'd been driving the baby-sitter home again, and it seems to take a little more time than backing out of one driveway and pulling into the next usually does.]

"I've been thinking about kids," said Nick.

Not thinking too much about how to make one, I hope.

"No," said Nick, looking a tad crestfallen, "the baby-sitter was explaining Ricardo's Principle of Comparative Advantage to me."

And that got you thinking about children?

"Sort of. I mean it's important to know things—like Ricardo's Principle of Comparative Advantage and whether to ever get married or not."

Definitely, I said.

"Or have kids."

And that, Nick, is the way you really get to know things. Let me tell you what you learn from having kids. You learn you're a total idiot. You experience an epiphany of true and perfect ignorance the moment the scary nurses in the delivery room—masked like Yemeni harem wives—hand you your wet, red, screaming bundle of joy. You learn you don't know a thing about life. Why, here is the most important of all things about life. Here is life itself. And—EEEEE, IT'S ALIVE!!!—you don't even know how to hold it. One hand for the baby's bottom, one hand under its back, and then, with your third hand, you . . . no . . .

The nurses quickly snatch the baby back. You don't know a thing. Maybe you've been to graduate school. Maybe you've been around the world. Maybe you can hack into the company's Human Resources Department files and find out which of the senior VPs is in the federal witness protection program. You're able to pronounce the last names of every placekicker in the NFL. And you don't know an effing thing. An effing thing, literally. You don't know where babies come from. Oh, intellectually you know. But you don't really know until someone near and dear to you has a baby and you are forced by the callous laws of modern male sensitivity to be there when it happens. Babies come from *there*?! Whole babies?! Head and everything?! Ouch.

You learn you're a total idiot, Nick, and then you learn you've married a genius. You thought you and your wife had an equal amount of information about babies. After all, you attended the same birthing classes. (Although she, maybe, wasn't hiding a beer under her sport coat.) As far as you could tell, your wife believed a baby was, mainly, a possible impediment to making partner at the law firm. Suddenly she understands exactly what to do when the baby cries, poops, screams, spits up—actions that babies are capable of performing all at the same time and continuously, if there's an important baseball game on TV.

You've married a genius. In fact, you've married into an entire race of geniuses—women. Aunts, mothers-in-law, female cousins, your wife's sorority sisters, random old ladies from the neighborhood descend upon your house to tell you you're a total idiot. "That's no way to hold a baby!" they say and quickly snatch the baby back. Should you be insulted by this? Or should you watch the Orioles get their bucket kicked? Don't be an idiot.

You probably thought you loved women before. Hah! That was mere admiration from afar—sort of paging through the Victoria's Secret catalog of love, thinking swell thoughts without actually *knowing* women. As a father you learn what these adorable cupcakes are capable of. They're capable of forgiving you for getting them pregnant. What would you do to a person who forced you to spend nine months shaped like a bowling pin? That's a bowling pin that can't have a cigarette or a martini and at the end of nine months has to, basically, pass a kidney stone the size of a cantaloupe. You'd murder him. And consider breast-feeding. Not the earth-mother Madonna-and-child scene of maternal bliss you thought, huh? Here's a wonderful, beloved, helpless little creature depending for its very existence on biting my wife in a sensitive place. And for twenty hours a day.

Then there are diapers and burp cloths and belly button scabs and all the rest of the icky goo of life that women plunge right into, armed with nothing but a Handi-Wipe and a smile. Women can cope with dreadful messes and misbehaviors and turn around and excuse and exculpate the person who made them. This is a wonderful thing. Although, considering the recurrent dreadful messes and misbehaviors in American politics, it also explains why women weren't allowed to vote until fairly recently.

Becoming a father also teaches you that you are, personally, a religious fundamentalist and antiabortion fanatic. This information comes as something of a surprise to those of us who hadn't been to church since, um, my mother got married kind of late and who had always regarded abortion clinics as a sort of emergency date-night resource—where you take a *really* bad girlfriend on the *very* last date. But the first time your little inchoate blob pops up on the sonogram screen and you shout, "He looks like me!" it's all over between you and NOW. Never mind that the baby comes out wet, red, screaming, crying, pooping, spitting up—he (actually, as it turned out, she) looks like me (which, mercifully, she doesn't except for—as my wife points out—the wet, red, screaming, crying, pooping, spitting-up part). What can abortion advocates be thinking? Babies are so soft, so tender, so sweet. . . . Wait, wait, I know, they want to *eat* my baby. Be gone, you imps of Satan. Which brings us to the religious stuff.

A lot of praying goes into becoming a dad, Nick, and it's not just praying for the Viagra to kick in. "Please, God, let my wife be all right. Please, God, let the baby be all right. Please, God, don't forget—ten fingers, ten toes. And, oh, yeah, just one head. And, God, don't let me blow chunks and pass out in the delivery room." By the time it's over, you owe the Big Guy. Not to mention what you owe the hospital and the doctor, plus college tuition is coming up fast—further reasons for prayer.

However, don't be frightened that fatherhood will make you vote for Gary Bauer in 2004. Fatherhood also turns you into a big mush of a liberal. I am, as you know, a Cro-Magnon Republican of long standing. Yet I can now be reduced to a puddle of compassionate tears by *It Takes a Village*. Perhaps I exaggerate. But I did used to think welfare mothers were irresponsible jerks for trying to raise kids without a job, without an income, without a good home, without a husband to blow chunks and pass out in the delivery room. Now I think welfare mothers are irresponsible jerks who should be given the Congressional Medal of Honor. And I am enraged by any government policy that might . . . what do you mean the Reagan administration declared that ketchup counts as a vegetable in school lunches? Don't tell me the guy has Alzheimer's, I'll go out to California and *knock* some sense into his head. These days, I believe the Department of Transportation should require bicycle helmets for children going to bed.

And that, Nick, is what you learn just in the first two days of being a father. This is nothing compared to what you learn later. For instance, when Muffin got old enough to watch children's television, I learned what my hobby is going to be when the kids are grown up and out of the house. I'm spending my retirement years tracking down all the people involved in children's television programming and shoving the Teletubbie with the sexual-diversity issues in their ear. Except Maria on *Sesame Street*. She's still a babe. I've had a crush on her since the show started thirty years ago and my artsy-fartsy MFA friends and I would get together every afternoon and smoke dope and goof hysterically on the Cookie Monster. Which tells you everything about the intellectual level of children's television, not to mention the intellectual level of children.

A child has the same amount of brains as a pot-fumed graduate student. In fact, a child has the same amount of brains as every other member of the nitwit human race. This is why I get *There was a farmer had a dog/And Bingo was his name-O* stuck in my head for a week just the way Muffin does. Except I don't feel obliged to sing B-I-N-G-O out loud all day, although the clapping part is rather compelling: B-I-N-*clap-clap*, B-I-N-*clap-clap*—.

"Stop," said Nick. "Please stop."

Anyhow, all mankind's ideas and interests, all human aims and motives, are exhibited, fully formed, in a three-year-old child. The kid is just operating on a smaller scale and lacks the advantage of having made enormous soft-money campaign contributions to political candidates.

Speaking of whom, no one who is a parent could bear to watch the Bush/Gore debates:

"You did!"

"Did not!"

"Did too!"

"Did not either, you big booger!"

There are plenty of politicians—and business executives and other VIPs—who wouldn't surprise me a bit if they proudly announced to the media, *I made BM!* and then expected to get a Tootsie-Pop for their efforts. Indeed, this is very much how Firestone and Ford handled the death-tire crisis.

Think of the actors, musicians, athletes, models, gossip-column nuisances, people with body piercings, and moron climbers of Mount Everest whose whole lives consist of being a brat on a swing set: "Look at me! Look at me! Look at me! No hands!" Or, in case of the Everest climbers, no fingers.

And then there are all the adults who won't go to sleep at night and then wind up in other people's beds, where they don't belong.

When Saint Augustine was formulating his doctrine of Original Sin, all he had to do was look at people as they are originally. Originally, they're children. Saint Augustine may have had a previous job—unmentioned in his *Confessions*—as a preschool day-care provider. But it's wrong to use *infantile* as a pejorative. It's the other way around. What children display is *adultishness*. Children are, for example, perfectly adultish in their self-absorption. Tiny tots look so wise, staring at their stuffed animals. You wonder what they're thinking. Then they learn to talk. What they're thinking is, *My* Beanie Baby!

I was trying to point out the glories of a sunset to Muffin the other day. Look at all the colors, I said.

"Why?" she asked.

Because they're so beautiful, I said.

"Why?" she asked.

Because the sun is going down, I said.

"For *me*?"

But children are cute when they do these things, an indication of the enormous amount of detailed thought that God put into the creation of the universe. He made children cute so we wouldn't kill them.

Fatherhood teaches you to hate humanity—except your kids, because they're so darn cute, and except everybody else who has kids. You bond with these people immediately no matter who they are and no matter how much you would loathe them under other circumstances—the baby-sitter's single mother, for instance. This parent-to-parent pact is a powerful force. It caused World War II. Roosevelt had kids. Stalin had kids. Hitler didn't have kids. Hey, what's Adolf doing sneaking into the Safeway express line with eleven items while Uncle Joe has Svetlana wrapped around his neck screaming for M&Ms? "Screw that," said Franklin, "I'm invading Normandy."

It's parent solidarity that keeps my wife from leaving me when I spend all day watching the Orioles instead of spooning strained peas, wrangling diapers, fumbling with jammie buttons, and reading *The House at Pooh Corner* over and over and over . . .

"Again!" says Muffin.

. . . until I snap. And then it was hunting season and Christopher Robin shot the stupid bear and skinned him and cooked him and ate him.

"Waaaaaaah!!! Poooooh!!!"

And I am heartbroken. I've just learned one more thing. I'm in love. One pout puts my emotions into a theater full of junior high school girls watching 'N Sync. One smile and I feel like Elvis in a Percodan factory. I knew nothing about being in love before. I thought it had to do with Elizabeth Hurley in a garter belt, maybe. No. True love is feeling absolute, genuine bliss at hearing the words, "I made BM! Can I have a Tootsie-Pop?"

Kids love, too. And here is another example of God's attention to detail. He makes children just stupid enough that what they love is you. They love you with an unalloyed, complete, and trusting love. Even if you did kill Pooh.

Of course, Nick, the kind of love I knew about when I knew nothing about love is still around. This led to me becoming a father for a second time. And then you really start to learn things.

Anybody can have one kid. Having one kid is like owning a dog—albeit a dog that stays a puppy for twenty-two years and never learns to fetch anything but credit card bills and nose colds. But going from one kid to two kids is like going from owning a dog to running a zoo.

It takes about two hours per meal to feed Muffin and Poppet, three hours to get them dressed, with an additional hour for finding lost shoes. It takes two hours to get them undressed, two more hours for bathtub, bath tantrums, and bathroom mop-up, an hour to get them into their Dr. Dentons, and three hours of reading *The House at Pooh Corner* to put them to sleep. By this point it's one in the morning. And yet, in most American families, both parents work. When? And why does America's economy do all right in spite of this?

Don't ask me. I already get enough questions at home from Muffin. Most notably, upon the arrival of Poppet, "Why did you bring home a baby?"

Because I'm opposed to materialism. And having a family cures it. When a one-year-old careens across the living room, knocks over a Waterford crystal vase, smashes an antique Chinese ginger jar lamp, and pukes on the embroidered silk upholstery of the Chippendale settee, what is the reaction of a family man? "Get the video camera! She's *walking!*"

Having kids defines fun down—just in time for middle age when having fun isn't much fun anymore anyway. I used to think booze and sex would bring me joy. Now it's a nap. Or a business trip to a Motel 6 in Akron. Where I can go to the john in peace. Wow, a dry towel. And twenty-six channels to myself.

It's important to have somebody around the house who's in trouble besides me. I rarely miss the toilet bowl. Actually—I'm informed by a reliable source that I'm married to—that's a fib. But I rarely miss with No. 2. There's the absolute and unconditional affection I receive—from the makers of Pampers, Play-Doh, Legos, Fruit Loops, et cetera. I get an excuse to indulge in a longtime private fantasy and build a major Barbie collection. No, scratch that.

The noblest calling in life, Nick, is to shape and form a worthy human character. Mrs. O says that's why she wanted a family too, but so far it hasn't worked on me. And there's the matter of ensuring a kind of immortality. Everyone wants to live forever, and a couple of bored kids can make one rainy Saturday afternoon seem like eternity. Plus I felt I owed it to the world to become a total idiot. Smart people cause so much trouble. I'll bet the folks who invented the atomic bomb weren't taking care of the kids that day. If they had been, the residents of Hiroshima would have been pelted with Pampers, Play-Doh, Legos, and Fruit Loops, instead of radiation and a shock wave.

Actually, by becoming a father I've learned that I'm too much of a total idiot to explain anything, let alone why people have kids. In fact, I'm such a total idiot, Nick, that I'm trying to talk Mrs. O into starting on a third.

11

JULY 2001

Calm down, Dad," said my godson Nick into the cell phone that he was holding a foot and a half from his head. Loud squawking from the device could be heard across the room.

What gives? I asked Nick, who had set the phone on the mantel and was letting his father carry on to the portrait of President Harding over the fireplace.

"My sister Ophelia," said Nick, "has decided to drop out of college and travel through India searching for enlightenment—*after* my dad sent the tuition check to Mount Holyoke."

I'm an old India hand, I said. I was there for ten days in 1998. I'd better write Ophelia a quick note.

"And I'd better tell Dad where Mom keeps the Xanax," said Nick, returning to the phone.

Max, I said to my young assistant, would you mind typing a little something into the e-mail thing?

* * *

Dear Ophelia,

I didn't go to India back in the sixties when I was your age and everyone was going there to get mystical, meditate his or her head off, and achieve the perfect state of spirituality that is embodied even now in Mia Farrow. I guess I wasn't evolved enough to follow my bliss. And, come to think of it, I didn't have the kind of bliss, back then, that you'd care to tailgate.

In fact, I didn't go to India until three years ago. I applaud your decision to go while you're still young and impressionable. You may come back with mystical notions, diarrhea, amazement at the antiquity of civilization, colorful snapshots, outrage over poverty and oppression, a suitcase full of ugly dhurries and cheap brass pots—or you may come back realizing you know nothing about India or anything else. Personally, I attained reverse enlightenment. I now don't understand the entire nature of existence. My conscious mind was overwhelmed by a sudden blinding flash of . . . oncoming truck radiator.

Nirvana, from the Sanskrit word meaning *blow out,* is the extinction of desires, passion, illusion, and the empirical self. It happens a lot in India, especially on the highways. Sometimes it's the result of a blowout, literally. More often it's a head-on crash.

I traveled from Pakistan to Calcutta, some 1,700 miles, mostly over the Grand Trunk Road. The Grand Trunk begins at the Khyber Pass, ends at the Bay of Bengal, and dates back at least to the fourth century B.C. Of the wonders on this ancient route, what made me wonder most were the traffic accidents.

For the greater part of its length, the Grand Trunk runs through the broad, flood-flat Ganges plain. The way is straight and level and would be almost two lanes wide if there were such things as lanes in India. The asphalt paving—where it isn't absent—isn't bad. As roads go in the developing world, this is a good one. But Indians have their own ideas about what the main thoroughfare spanning the most populous part of a nation is for. It's a place where friends and family can meet, where they can put *charpoi* string beds and have a nap, and let the kids run around unsupervised. It's a roadside café with no side to it—or tables or chairs—where the street food is smack dab on the street. It's a rent-free event room for every local fête. And it's a piece of agricultural machinery. Even along the Grand Trunk's few stretches of toll-booth-cordoned "expressway," farmers are drying grain on the macadam.

The road is a store, a warehouse, and a workshop. Outside Chandigarh a blacksmith had pitched his tent on a bridge. Under the tent flaps were several small children, the missus working the bellows, and the craftsman himself smoking a hookah and contemplating his anvil, which was placed fully in the right-of-way. The road is also convenient for bullock carts, donkey gigs, horse wagons, pack camels, and the occasional laden elephant—not convenient for taking them anywhere, just convenient. There they stand along with sheep, goats, water buffalo, and the innumerable cows (all sacred, I assume) sent to graze on the Grand Trunk. I watched several cows gobbling cardboard boxes and chewing plastic bags. No wonder the Indians won't eat them.

The road is the trash basket, as all roads in India are. I saw a dressy middle-aged woman eat a chocolate bar on Nehru Road (the so-called Fifth Avenue of Calcutta). She threw the candy wrapper at her feet with a graceful and decisive motion. And the road is the john. You never have to wonder where the toilet is in India, you're standing on it. The back of a long-distance bus had a sign in Hindi and an elaborate pictogram, the import of which was *Don't crap on the pavement, and wash your hands after you do.*

With all this going on there's no room left for actual traffic on the Grand Trunk. But there it is anyway, in tinny, clamorous, haywired hordes: Mahindra jeeps made with World War II Willys tooling, Ambassador sedans copied from fifties English models, motorcycles and scooters of equally antique design, obsolete Twinkie-shaped buses with trails of vomit from every window like zebra stripes, and myriad top-heavy, butt-sprung, weaving, swaying, wooden-bodied Tata trucks, their mechanicals as primitive as butter churns.

And India had just detonated an A-bomb. The thing must have had rivet heads all over it, big crescent fins, and a little porthole in the door, like Commander Cody's spaceship in *Radar Men From the Moon*.

But nuclear war will be the least of your worries on the Grand Trunk, because all the Tatas, Ambassadors, Mahindras, and whatchamacallits are coming right at you, running all day with the horn on and all night with their lights off, as fast as their fart-firing, smut-burping engines will carry them.

The first time you look out the windshield at this melee, you think, India really *is* magical. How, except by magic, can they drive like this without killing people?

They can't. Jeeps bust scooters, scooters plow into bicycles, bicycles cover the hoods of jeeps. Cars run into trees. Buses run into ditches, rolling over on their rounded tops until they're mashed into unleavened chapatis of carnage. And everyone runs into pedestrians. A speed bump is called a *sleeping policeman* in Jamaica. I don't know what it's called in India. *Dead person lying in the road* is a guess. There's some of both kinds of obstructions in every village, but they don't slow traffic much. The animals get clobbered, too, including sacred cows, in accidents notable for the unswerving behavior of all participants. The car in front of us hit a cow—no change in speed or direction from the car, no change in posture or expression from the cow.

But it's the lurching, hurtling Tata trucks that put the pepper in the marsala and make the curry of Indian driving scare you coming and going the way dinner does. The Tatas are almost as wide as they are long and somewhat higher than either. They blunder down the road, taking their half out of the middle, brakeless, lampless, on treadless tires, moving dog-fashion with the rear wheels headed in a direction the front wheels aren't. Tatas fall off bridges, fall into culverts, fall over embankments, and sometimes Tatas just fall—flopping on their sides without warning. But usually Tatas collide, usually with each other and in every possible way. Two Tatas going in opposite directions ahead of us snagged rear wheels and pulled each other's axles off. And they crash not just in twos but threes and fours, leaving great smoking piles of vaguely truck-shaped wreckage. What little space is left on the road is occupied by one or two surviving drivers camping out until the next collision comes. Inspecting one of these catastrophes, I found the splintered bodywork decorated with a little metal plaque: LUCKY ENGINEERING.

In one day of travel, going about 265 miles from Varanasi to the border of West Bengal, I tallied twenty-five horrendous Tata wrecks. And I was scrupulous in my scoring. Fender-bends didn't count; neither did old abandoned wrecks or broken-down Tatas. Probable loss of life was needed to make the list. If you saw just one of these pileups on I-95 you'd pull into the next rest stop with clutch foot shivering and hand palsied upon the shift knob and say, *Next time we fly*. In India you shout to your car mates, "That's number nineteen! I'm winning the truck-wreck pool for today!"

Approaching the Indian border from Pakistan—even from a distance, Ophelia—it was clear that the land of the unfathomable was nigh. We went down the only connecting road between the two countries, and for once there was nothing on the Grand Trunk. Not even military fortifications were visible, just one company of crack Pakistani Rangers in their jammies because it was naptime. No one was going to or fro. They can't. *Pakistani and Indian nationals are only allowed to cross the border by train,* said my tourist guidebook. This utter lack of customs traffic has not prevented the establishment of fully staffed customs posts on both sides of the boundary.

Getting out of Pakistan was a normal Third World procedure. The officials were asleep, lying on the unused concrete baggage-inspection counters like corpses in a morgue—a morgue posted with a surprising number of regulations for its customers. The number-one man roused the number-two man, who explained the entire system of Pakistani tariff regulation and passport control by rubbing his thumb against his forefinger. He then gave a performance in mime of documents being pounded with a rubber stamp.

"Fifty dollars," said the number-two man. I opened my wallet, foolishly revealing two fifty-dollar bills. "One hundred dollars," he said.

Things were very different on the Indian side of the border. Here they had not just an unused baggage-inspection counter but an unused metal detector, an unused X-ray machine, and an unused pit with an unused ramp over it to inspect the chassis and frames of the vehicles that don't use this border crossing.

Our party consisted of eight people representing four nationalities, in two Land Rovers, with a satellite phone, several computers, and a trailer filled with food, camping gear, and spare parts. The rules concerning entry of such persons and things into India occupy a book large enough to contain the collected works of Stephen King and *The* (unabridged) *Oxford English Dictionary*.

* * *

Ophelia, if you're going to be confounded by India, you can't simply go as a tourist. Tourism is a pointless activity. Pointless activity is a highly developed craft in India. You could spend months touring the country, busy doing screw-all. Meanwhile the Indians are busy doing screw-all of their own. You could accidentally come back thinking you'd caught the spirit of the place. If you intend to be completely baffled, you have to try to accomplish something.

Any goal will do. I was tagging along on one leg of a press junket. The Rover corporation was sending two of its then-new Discovery II products on a drive around the world. The aim of this section of the trip was to traverse India. Then the Land Rovers would be put in a cargo container and shipped to Australia for the next section. The expedition had been meticulously planned. All documentation was in order. The Land Rovers had already passed the customs inspection of twelve nations, including Bulgaria and Iran, without hindrance, delay, or more than moderate palm-greasing.

The Indian officials heard this explained and clucked and wagged their heads in sympathy for the hundreds of brother customs agents from London to the deserts of Baluchistan who had lost an opportunity to look up thousands of items in a great big book. Everything had to come out of the cars and trailers. Everything had to go through the metal detector, even though the detector didn't seem to be plugged in. And everything had to come back through the X-ray machine, which the customs agents weren't watching because they were too busy looking up items in a great big book.

All this took four hours, during which the seven or eight agents on duty met each hint at bribery with the stare you'd get from an octogenarian Powerball winner if you suggested the twenty-year payout option. The fellow who was recording, in longhand, everything inside our passports did take two cigarettes, but he wouldn't accept a pack.

None of the cases, trunks, bags—unloaded and reloaded in 105-degree heat—was actually opened, except for a wrench set. Perhaps there is one size of wrench that requires a special permit in India. The satellite telephone *did* require a special permit, which—meticulous planning or no—we didn't have. The briefcase-sized sat. phone went unnoticed.

(Engine compartments and undercarriages were inspected, but no one looked under the seat.) Our tire pressures must be checked, however, in case the all-terrain radials were packed with drugs. The Indian government tire gauge wasn't working. We offered our own. We were halfway through checking the tires when we realized nobody was accompanying us. I walked around behind the customs building to take a leak and found drugs to spare. I was pissing on a thousand dollars' worth of wild marijuana plants.

By the time we left customs it was late afternoon. The staggering traffic and whopping crowds of India materialized. We still had 250 miles to go that day to stay on schedule. A brisk pace was required. Think of it as doing sixty through the supermarket parking lot, the school playground, and the Bronx Zoo.

This is the India you ordinary travelers never see—because you're in your right minds. And we didn't see much of it ourselves. The scenery was too close to view, a blur of cement-block shops and hovels in unbroken ranks inches from the fenders. Yet my map showed open country with only occasional villages meriting the smallest cartographic type size. There are a lot of people in India, 966.8 million as of 1998. I don't know what they want with the atomic bomb. They already have the population bomb, and it's working like a treat.

Nevertheless India, with a population density of 843 people per square mile, is not as crowded as the Netherlands, which packs 1,195 people into the same space. Nobody comes back from Holland aghast at the teeming mass of Dutch or having nightmares about windmills and tulips pressing in on every side.

Poor people take up room. You may have noticed this when tattooed guys wearing motorcycle-gang insignia come into a bar. And poor people who depend on agriculture for a living, as 67 percent of Indians do, take up even more room than Hell's Angels. If 67 percent of New Yorkers depended on agriculture for a living, someone would be trying to farm the dirt under the floor mats of your Yellow Cab.

Everything is squeezed together in India to keep it out of the picnic-blanket-sized rice field that's the sole support for a family of ten.

Every nook of land is put to use. At the bottom of a forty-foot-deep abandoned well, which would be good for nothing but teenage suicides in America, somebody was raising frogs. The public rest rooms of Calcutta employ the space-saving device of dispensing with walls and roofs and placing the urinal stalls on the sidewalk. No resource goes to waste, which sounds like a fine thing for you to advocate next Earth Day— except, in the real world of poverty, it means that the principal household fuel of India is the cow flop. This is formed into a circular patty and stuck on the side of the house, where it provides a solution to three problems: storage room, home decor, and cooking dinner.

Therefore, what makes a drive across India insane (and stinky) isn't overpopulation, it's poverty. Except this isn't really true either. The reason for those ranks of shops and houses along the Grand Trunk, and for the cars, trucks, and buses bashing into each other between them, is that people have money to buy and build these things. And the reason for the great smoldering dung funk hanging over India is that there's something to cook on those fires.

I don't know how much of this stuff you studied in that ridiculously progressive prep school of yours, but when the British left in 1947, India got itself an economy in the socialist closet, an economy in the political bag. The Indians called it the "license-permit-quota raj." The *Economist* magazine once said, "This has no equal in the world. In many ways it puts Soviet central planning to shame." Indian industries were trapped and isolated by the government. Like an aunt locked in the attic, they got strange. The results can still be seen in the Tata trucks, Ambassador sedans, and motorcycles that Evel Knievel would be afraid to ride. But in 1992, India began to surrender to free-market reforms. Imports were allowed, foreign investment was encouraged, and customs regulations were (amazing as this seems to those who have been through Indian customs) simplified.

In 1998 the Indian economy had been growing for half a decade at about 7 percent a year. As many as 200 million people had been added to the Indian middle class—a number almost equal to the total middle class of the United States. Suppose our entire American bourgeois experience had developed just in the latter years of the Clinton administration. (Bill Clinton probably thinks that's what happened.)

India is still very poor. Small boys with hammers make gravel by the side of the road, an activity that must seem worse than school even to small boys and isn't much of a vocational opportunity either. The people on the Grand Trunk looked in need, but not in wretched misery (until they stepped in front of a speeding jeep). There are plenty of flat bellies in India but few of the distended kind that announce gross malnutrition. And the beggars, whom Western visitors have been taught to expect in legions, arrive only in squads and platoons. A kid selling trinkets in Agra was irked to be mistaken for such. "I'm not a beggar," he said. "You want to buy, you get." Then he named a thievish price.

What is happening in India is what happens every place where an agrarian economy changes into a modern one. The first stage of prosperity is ugly. This is the ugliness that caused William Blake, at the beginning of the Industrial Revolution, to speak of "dark Satanic mills"—dark satanic mills that were giving people cash, social mobility, and an opportunity to escape a hundred generations of chopping weeds with hoes. Hoeing is not as dark, maybe, as working in a mill, but it's plenty satanic, as anyone with the smallest garden knows.

The quaint and orderly India of old is still there, just beyond the clutter of the Grand Trunk Road. In West Bengal we visited a beautiful farm village full of amusing thatch architecture and cute peasant handcrafts. Here the handsome patina of tradition glowed upon lives that were quiet, calm, and as predictable as famine and the dowry needed to marry off the ten-year-old daughter.

The villagers were friendly enough. But what if carloads of French tourists came into my driveway and began taking happy snaps while I was scrubbing down the barbecue grill? I preferred the chaos of the Grand Trunk.

We were driving through the most unattractive part of India at the hottest time of year. The equivalent would be to drive U.S. Route 1 from the outlet shops of Freeport, Maine, to downtown Miami in August. Consider someone who had never been to America before. What would he think, after being Blockbustered, Safewayed, Chevroned, Shelled, Dodged, Nissaned, Wal-Marted, Dress Barned, Gapped, Levied, Burger Kinged, Dairy Queened, and Taco Belled? Would he have a good impression of the United States? No. Would he have an accurate impression? That's another matter.

Of course we did go to a few of the famous tour destinations in India, where international rubbernecks stand agape, getting their tonsils sunburned. (Land Rover needed PR photos with something other than wrecked trucks in the background.)

We took a side trip into the Himalayan foothills to Simla, the colonial hill station that was the summer capital of British rule. It's built at a higher elevation than Kathmandu. The road up is like the Grand Trunk except on the angle of your basement stairs and taking the shape of gift-wrap ribbon after Christmas morning.

Simla is a chutney of concrete and roof tin with only a few colonial-charm leftovers. Along the Mall there's a row of dusty British-era shops that the British—seeing mountains all around them and not knowing what else to do—built in alpine style. The parade ground has views to die for (or die *of* if you lean against the flimsy railings).

Atal Bihari Vajpayee, the Prime Minister of India, was headed to town. Preparation consisted of someone loudly testing the PA system:

> HELLO HELLO HELLO HELLO HELLO HELLO HELLO
> HELLO HELLO HELLO ONE TWO THREE FOUR FIVE
> SIX SEVEN EIGHT NINE TEN MICROPHONE TESTING
> HELLO HELLO HELLO HELLO HELLO HELLO HELLO
> HELLO HELLO HELLO HELLO HELLO HELLO HELLO

For an hour. This was the crowd warm-up. The speech must have been a dilly. Meanwhile, behind handsome batik curtains, tribal women in full native dress, with nose jewelry the size of baby shoes, were repairing the pavement.

In Agra we went to the Taj Mahal, and I recommend you go there too. It's an impressive pile built with public funds while a famine scourged the countryside. The Taj was commissioned by Shah Jahan to memorialize his favorite wife, who died in 1629 giving birth to their fourteenth child. If Jahan had really wanted to show his love, he could have cut back on the ginseng and powdered rhino horn.

We had our first glimpse of the famous monument at sunset, from a heap of trash and offal on the bank of the Yamuna River. Mixed into the garbage around our feet were hundreds of miniature clay images of Krishna. These are tossed into the water by devotees upstream in Mathura, the god's supposed birthplace. The holiness of India is impressive. The ground is littered with divinities.

In Varanasi, to the east, we saw the holiest place of all, where millions of pilgrims descend the steps of the ghats into the Ganges, using its waters to purify themselves of sins and also to dispose of the burning dead bodies of relatives. Everybody but me made a sunrise trip to see these sacred rites. I stayed in bed, believing cremation before breakfast should be limited to toast. Besides, there's the matter of barging in on other people's religious ceremonies: Yo, is that the holy Eucharist? Cool! Can I taste?

And once I got started looking at religions in India, how would I know when to stop? There are Buddhists, Muslims, Sikhs, Jains, Zoroastrians, Christians with a religious heritage dating back almost to the birth of Christ, and 670 million Hindus.

I have to say I was confused enough by the material surface of India and, unlike you, I had no desire to go delving into its metaphysical petticoats. Hinduism is supposed to have 330 million gods. (Disbelieving in all of these must make Indian atheists very busy people.) There's Brahma the creator with five heads; Vishnu the preserver with four arms; Shiva the destroyer with who-knows-how-many appendages; blue-skinned Krishna chasing cowherd girls; Kali dripping blood from her tongue and wearing a garland of skulls; Hanuman, the god who's also a monkey; Ganesh, god of good luck, whose head got cut off by mistake and was replaced with an elephant cranium (lucky him); and so on. No disrespect meant to anyone's depiction of deity—a pious Brahmin coming to my house and seeing a sculpture of a beatnik nailed to a phone pole (courtesy of my Catholic wife) would surely be taken aback. It's just that frequent and lurid representations of these divinities add to the recondite obscurity of India, as do the seventeen officially recognized languages and an intricate caste system that somewhat resembles our ideas about social class except you can't touch Gerald Levine because as chairman of AOL/Time-Warner he's engaged in an occupation involving human waste.

Everything in India is a brainteaser. Just getting dressed is a puzzle contest. This is how to put on a sari: Take a piece of cloth about three and a half feet wide and eighteen feet long and tuck a corner in your underpants. Turn around clockwise once. Tuck the upper hem in your underpants. Make a pleat by holding the fabric between your thumb and little finger, spreading your hand, extending the fabric around your forefinger, and bringing it back to your thumb. Do this ten times. Tuck the top of the pleats into your underpants. Turn around clockwise again, and throw everything that remains over your left shoulder. And I still looked like hell.

Each little detail of India is a conundrum. Painted above door frames you see the Sanskrit character for the sacred meditative *om* bracketed by a pair of backward-facing swastikas. The "swastika" is really just a Hindu symbol for self-energization and the accomplishments of life. (The Nazis bent the arms in the other direction and swiped it for the cool look.) Nonetheless, the message over the doors seems to read, *Sieg heil inner peace sieg heil.*

Which isn't too far wrong. The current coalition government in India—the one that likes atomic bombs—is headed by the Bharatiya Janata Party. The BJP is avidly nationalistic and espouses Hindu fundamentalism, sort of like Pat Robertson with 330 million Jesuses. And the BJP believes in rigid observation of the caste system, so it's like Pat got together with the people who do the Philadelphia social register. Or worse, because the most influential support for the BJP comes from the Rashtriya Swayamsevak Sangh, the RSS, a hard-line and secretive Hindu brotherhood whose half-million members wear matching khaki shorts to early morning rallies and make funny stiff-arm salutes. One RSS leader, K. S. Sudarshan, has said, "We don't believe in individual rights because we don't think we are individuals."

India—which is a little prouder of the title "world's largest democracy" than local conditions would justify—has had icky politics before. Until recently the dominant Indian political organization was the Congress Party, founded by India's first head of state, Jawaharlal Nehru. Congress was supposed to embody the Mahatma Gandhi ethos of tolerance, nonviolence, self-reliance, rule of law, and being a goody two-shoes (or two-sandals) nation in general. Nonetheless India managed to indulge in sectarian violence that killed half a million Hindus and Muslims, get embroiled in three wars with Pakistan and one with China, embrace the Soviet Union as a military and economic ally, and suspend civil rights, jailing thousands of members of the political opposition under Nehru's daughter Indira Gandhi (no relation to the Great Soul in diapers).

So the Congress Party had about as much allegiance to its root principles as political parties usually do. But there are worse things than politicians who say what they don't believe, such as politicians who say what they believe fanatically. Especially when voters agree with them. A *Washington Post* opinion poll, taken in India after the first three A-bomb tests, indicated that 82 percent of India's rural population and 91 percent of city dwellers favored building nuclear weapons. Not that it matters. If India tried to launch an ICBM, the missile would have to stop on its way to Karachi while a team of Indian customs agents looked up warhead exportation in a great big book.

What brought the BJP to power is not hard to understand. The Congress Party had imploded from internal bickering in familiar egghead Democrat vs. no-neck Democrat fashion. Caste-based affirmative action—with as many as 60 percent of public jobs subject to set-aside programs—turned social animosities into institutionalized hatreds. There was corruption, always a reliable campaign theme for nonincumbents. And the BJP played upon the xenophobia that all people exhibit a bit of (me, in this letter, for instance). As K. R. Malkani, vice president of the BJP, put it, "Foreigners have been allowed to come in even with junk food."

However, what the BJP did, once it came to power, was strange. The nukes have no practical value. The major cities of Pakistan are close to the Indian border, and half the year the prevailing winds would blow the fallout back where it came from. Testing the nukes caused international sanctions to be imposed, India's credit rating to flop, Bombay's stock market to plummet, and the rupee to lose 8 percent of its value. And the BJP's budget plan had some bomblike effects of its own. Government spending increased by 13.8 percent. Customs duties on all imports went up 4 percent. Higher excise taxes were imposed on staples such as butter, cheese, milk powder, and packaged tea. The BJP announced a policy of relying on overseas Indians to increase foreign investment in India. This is like your mom and dad relying on you, when you finally move out and get a place of your own, to help with their mortgage. Plus BJP-flavor Hindu nationalism galls India's 105 million Muslims, 22 million Christians, 18 million Sikhs, 6.6 million Buddhists, 4.5 million Jains, and uncountable untouchables. (Which word is now unmentionable—they prefer to be called Dalits, *oppressed,* and now have more reason to say so.)

I'm afraid you're going to find that modern India is, in many ways, an unattractive place. But things could be worse. And the BJP seems determined to make them so. This has been done before. There are ruins all over India—the result of invasions by Greeks, Persians, Afghans, Sythians, Parthians, Huns, Mongols, ancient Aryan hordes, and that modern Aryan horde, the British. Then there are ruins, not very old at all—the result of I don't know what. In Agra I saw an enormous railroad car barn, built with handsome bricks in the ornate style that our immediate ancestors lavished upon industrial buildings. It was empty now and roofless. A monkey was perched on the broken arch over the hulking, rusted gate.

In Calcutta, the seat of the West Bengal state government, the late-nineteenth-century Writers' Building is crumbling and dirty although a row of large, carefully tended potted plants decorates the sidewalk below its windows. Trees, products of less intentional horticulture, grow out of the cracked Edwardian edifice of the nearby Standard Assurance and Life headquarters. Even Calcutta's New Market, built in 1985, seems about to fall down and probably doesn't only because—being nothing but a pile of moldering concrete in the first place—it can't. The whole of India looks as if it were abandoned by its population a hundred years ago, and they've just moved back and are camped in the wreckage of a civilization.

Actually, it's the wreckage of dozens of civilizations. India did not become a unified nation until Independence, and—if you count the bust-outs of Pakistan, Bangladesh, and part of Kashmir—it didn't get unified then. Even under British imperial rule, India comprised thirteen provinces with considerable autonomy, a fluctuating number of anarchic frontier territories, and some seven hundred princely states under greater or lesser colonial control.

India has a population greater than Europe and North America combined. Its land area exceeds France, Germany, Great Britain, Iraq, Japan, Paraguay, and Ghana put together, and its citizens are that similar. They get along as well as everybody at the UN does. India is as complicated as the earth. Indeed, if a person were to claim the nationality of Earthling, there would be a one-in-six chance that the person was Indian. To all this, the Bharatiya Janata Party responds with a slogan: ONE NATION, ONE PEOPLE, ONE CULTURE.

Just when I thought I wasn't getting it about India, I started to get it less. East of Varanasi, in Bihar state, we encountered a communist rally. Hundreds of agitated-looking agitators waved red flags and brandished staves. We were a ripe target for the anger of the masses—eight capitalist prats in Land Rovers with a trailer full of goodies protected only by a tarp. We were ignored. It seems the ideological fury of the Communist Party of India (Marxist-Leninist) is directed primarily at the Communist Party of India (Marxist).

The latter runs Calcutta. According to my guidebook, "They have somehow succeeded in balancing rhetoric and old-fashioned socialism with a prudent practicality. . . . Capitalism is allowed to survive, but made to support the political infrastructure."

Not that you'd know this by driving into Calcutta, where the infrastructure doesn't look like it could support another flea. Certainly the Howrah Bridge over the Hooghly River can't. It carries 60,000 motor vehicles a day, and they were all there when we tried to get across at

5 P.M. Packed along the filthy bank of the Hooghly were temples to scary gods, a ratty colonial fort, a coal power plant barfing cones of smudge, and the dreariest kind of glass-box office buildings. From a distance the city appeared to be an educational diorama: The History of Ugly.

I spent the next four days trying to accomplish something in India again. The Land Rover Discoverys IIs and the trailer had to be put into a cargo container. This would take twenty minutes. Adjusting the clock to Indian Daylight Wasting Time, that's four days.

First the port was closed. Well, it wasn't really closed. I mean, it *was* sort of closed because the port of Calcutta has silted in and is nearly useless. Only about three ships were there. This doesn't keep hundreds of stevedores, shipping clerks, and port officials from coming to work. But there were city council elections that day with attendant rioting. So the police had to suppress voters and weren't available for harassment at the port.

Then the port was closed because it was Sunday.

Then our shipping agents fell into an argument about when to pick us up at the hotel the next day. Not that they disagreed with each other.

"We will go to get them at nine-thirty in the morning," one said.

"Oh, no, no, no, no," said another. "It must be nine-thirty in the morning."

"How can you talk like this?" said a third, stamping his foot. "The time for us to be there is nine-thirty in the morning!"

We had about ten shipping agents. As K. S. Sudarshan of the RSS implied, there's no such thing as hiring an individual in India. In a Bihar village it took the services of two shops, four shopkeepers, and a boy running for change to sell me a pack of cigarettes.

While I waited for the port to open, I wandered the streets of Calcutta. The city is a byword for squalor. Most Americans suppose that to tour its precincts is to flush oneself down the toilet of humanity and amble through a human septic system. This isn't true. There aren't that many flush toilets in Calcutta. Anyway, parts of Washington, D.C., are dirtier (Congress; the White House when the Clintons were there), and Calcutta smells no worse than a college dorm.

The poverty is sad and extensive, but at least the families living on the Calcutta streets are intact families—talking to each other instead of themselves. I did see some people who seemed really desperate, addled, and unclean. But these were American hippies at Calcutta's Dum Dum airport. I was standing in the ticket line behind an Indian businessman who stared at the hippies and then gave me a stern look, as if to say, These are *your* people. Isn't there something you *could do*?

Calcutta's pollution is more visible than it's fashionable for American pollution to be—smoke and trash instead of microwaves and PCBs. The food sold on Calcutta's streets may be unidentifiable, but it's less likely than New York City hot dogs to contain a cow rectum. The crowding is extreme but you get used to it. You get used to a lot of things—naked ascetics, a hundred sheep being herded through downtown traffic, a single file of costumed girls linked by electric wires with one carrying a car battery and the rest having blue fluorescent tubes sticking out of their headdresses.

I was waiting to cross the busiest street in Calcutta when a four-story temple complex on wheels went by, complete with high priest, idols, acolytes, clouds of incense, blazing torches, and banging gongs. And what I noticed was that I wasn't noticing it. Imagine the Pope (and quite a bit of Saint Peter's) coming down Broadway at rush hour and you thinking, *Should I jaywalk or wait for the light*?

There's a certain pest factor in Calcutta, mostly from the touting of roving market bearers. But it's not without its entertainment value. Bearer No. A-49 from the New Market told me not to listen to any of the other bearers because they would get me into their shops and cut my throat. So be sure you get Bearer No. A-49. Accept no other. Lesser merchants, squatting on the street, sell everything from new Lee jeans to brightly colored pebbles and pieces of broken mirrors. The poster-wallah's selection included views of the Taj Mahal, photographs of kittens tangled in balls of yarn, and the gore-faced goddess Kali holding a severed human head by the hair.

In the midst of this is the Oberoi Grand Hotel, with guards stationed at the gate holding sticks to use on touts and beggars. At the Oberoi everything is efficient, crisp, clean, and pukka (except when the electricity goes out). The Indians inside seemed as perplexed by the chaos of India outside as I was. I told Alex, the restaurant manager, about the muddle at the port. "Oh, this country," he said, "there are no two ways around it."

We had parked the Land Rovers and trailer in the hotel courtyard. The shipping agents came by to inform us that everything in the vehicles had to be clean and packed exactly as described on the customs documents. Iain Chapman, who had organized the world trip for Land Rover, and Rover engineer Mark Dugmore and I set about amending 1,700 miles of dirt and equipment disorder. It was 100 degrees in the courtyard. A dozen members of the hotel staff gathered to watch us. I don't think they'd seen Westerners do actual work. (And—as far as my own experiences go in the offices and stores of America and Europe—neither have I.) Removing the trailer tarp, we discovered an ax had come loose from its lashing and punctured a container of beef stew and a can of motor oil. The trailer bed was awash in petroleum and what Hindus euphemistically call *brown meat.*

On Monday we went back to the port, where the customs inspectors ignored everything about our cleanliness and packing except the ax. "What is this?" said the chief inspector.

"An ax," said Iain Chapman.

The officials conferred at length and decided it was so. Then there was a seven-hour delay because of an engine serial-number discrepancy. The customs inspectors were worried that we'd stolen one of the Discoverys IIs from Rover. "*We're* from Rover," said Iain. "These are the only Discovery IIs in Asia, and they can't be stolen because they're both right here." The inspectors returned to their office to ponder this. We sat on the dock.

I asked one of our shipping agents why so many of the Tata truck drivers had decorated their front bumpers with one dangling shoe.

"Oh, for the heck of it," he said.

Finally the Land Rovers were rolled into the cargo container. Things do eventually get done in India. My theory about why they do is that, although making business matters complicated is a great source of fun there, you know how it is with fun. Sooner or later it's time for different fun—such as making family matters complicated. "I am a twenty-one-year-old man involved in a physical relationship with my thirty-six-year-old unmarried cousin for the past six years," read a query to an advice column in a Calcutta newspaper. "It all began when . . . I raped her."

I was sad to see the Discovery IIs go. They weren't wrecked—an anomaly in this land. And they never broke down or exploded, which is more than I can say for ourselves when, leaving the docks, the police tried to arrest us because we had padlocks in our possession.

"What the hell kind of thief comes back with the locks instead of the swag?" Iain asked them. Maybe an Indian one, if it would complicate matters.

I stayed on in Calcutta for a few days, in awe at a dundering muddle of a place that seems in total disorganization but where I couldn't even get lost because everyone with a clean shirt speaks English. And they speak it in a style that is a reminder of India's claim upon the language. There were Indians speaking English when most of America was gibbering in Gaelic, German, Italian, or whatever on the wrong side of the Ellis Island fence. Placards ask that Calcutta's subway be treated WITH RESPECT AND AFFECTION. Street signs say, I USE FOOTPATHS, DO YOU? Yet the country's per capita gross domestic product is only half of China's.

Indian journalist Gita Mehta says India turns out five million university graduates a year. That's four times the number of bachelor degrees awarded annually in the United States, But the ancient guild of scribes still does brisk business outside Calcutta's General Post Office. Scores of men hunker on the sidewalk writing and reading other people's letters. Forty-eight percent of Indians are illiterate, including almost two-thirds of Indian women.

You walk by a newsstand—a news squat, to be precise—and see the Calcutta *Telegraph,* the Calcutta *Statesman,* the *Asian Age,* the *Times of India,* and stacks of newspapers printed in Hindi and other languages. The *Telegraph* ran a Know-How feature on particle physics. A *Statesman* op-ed page had an article on energy efficiency: "The heat rate of the power plant, in layman's terms, refers to how much kilo calorie of heat is required to produce 1 kwp of power." You think you're in a nation of Einsteins until you read the advice columnist's answer to the rapist: "At this stage of life you ought to detach yourself from this cousin to secure a healthy life. . . . Initially your cousin provoked you in the act, and hence it cannot be called rape."

In the midst of Calcutta's street stampede (not a figure of speech, considering sacred cows), there are young hawkers with what look like shoeshine boxes. What's offered for sale isn't a wing-tip buff. The youths crouch in the hubbub, juggle the tiny wheels and springs of wristwatches, and set the timepieces running again. There is a whole street in Calcutta lined with stalls too small and ill-equipped for lemonade sales. Here artisans with flame-heated soldering irons rearrange the logic on the latest computer circuit boards. Then you look up from your newspaper and see a man walking around wearing a bucket upside down over his head.

Good Luck,
Uncle Peej

"Here's a printout of your letter to Ophelia," said Max. "It sounds an awful lot like the article you did for that hippie travel magazine, *National Geodesic*. Don't drop it and break a toe."

My wife lowered *The New York Times* travel section as Max marched off. [He seems a bit grouchy today.] "You know," my wife said to me, "we haven't been anywhere together since we took Muffin to Venice and the pigeons landed on her head. When Poppet is old enough to be left for a long weekend, we should plan a trip. Although India sounds a bit . . . subcontinental. Spain, maybe. Just the two of us."

I'd love to go somewhere with you, my dear, I said. But you know who I'd really like to travel with? *New York Times* travel writers. They're amazing. More than a century after Stanley and Livingstone, they're still discovering unexplored parts of the globe. And when *Times* travel writers disembark in these uncharted regions, they never encounter monsoon floods, clouds of biting flies, or guerrilla war. These writers must be wonderfully knowledgeable about meteorology, entomology, and political science. I know they possess great intellectual resources, because they are able to find mental stimulation in Canadian church architecture and Belgian watercolor artists. The ability to conjure interest in *anything*, no matter how dull, is a trait I wish we had. I also wish we had some of that special American money *Times* travel writers possess. They can go to Paris, find a charming pension next door to the Louvre, have a glorious meal, and take in a brilliant cabaret act, all for about a hundred dollars. I go to Frankfurt, stay at a Novotel, eat one bratwurst at the airport, and I'm out a grand. Also, traveling with *Times* travel writers must be like having a personal bodyguard. I notice they are always treated with courtesy, even in New York, so obviously they're well armed. But most of all I'd like to travel with *New York Times* travel writers because I admire them. While others talk about helping humanity, they take action. Wherever they go poverty, disease and oppression disappear, replaced by vigorous service economies where every native has gainful and satisfying employment—waiting hand and foot on *New York Times* travel writers.

[I don't know if it was something I said, but my wife seems slightly miffed. A getaway would be a nice surprise, and I'm glad I thought of it.]

My dear, I said, everything's fixed. I've bought the train tickets. Poppet and Muffin will stay with Nick's folks. And for our second honeymoon, we'll go to New York and eat at Elaine's.

"For our second honeymoon," said my wife, "we'll go to New York and eat at Elaine's."

Yes! I said. Elaine's is a haven for writers. You know how insecure and timid we writers are. The great thing about Elaine's is the safety. For instance, I'm safe from the food. Every other place in New York seems to be specializing in some horrible gustatory fad: Tibetan dirt salads or Provençal escargot sorbets. God help us if Manhattan restaurateurs ever discover the anthropophagite entrées of the New Guinea highlands. But Elaine never serves me a fish that isn't dead yet or a Bolivian guinea pig terrine. In fact, at Elaine's I'm safe from physical excitement of any kind. Elaine realizes that we writers live our whole lives on paper in the sincere hope of never having to live them anywhere else. There are no fistfights. And anyone who's seen Elaine slam-dunk a paparazzo is unlikely to start one. There is no "pickup" nonsense. If you go home from Elaine's with someone, you're probably married to her—or anyhow someone you know is.

I'm safe from romance and adventure at Elaine's. And, more important, I'm safe from literature. Writers attract bores the way booze attracts writers.

If you're going to the kitchen, could you freshen this up for me, dear?

As I was just going to say, when I was interrupted, I spend ten hours slicing at a Gordian knot of a book chapter, and then I get cornered by the counterman at Starbucks who went to the Iowa Writers Workshop and wants to discuss mimetic distance and objective correlatives. At Elaine's people know better. They're writers themselves. They know what to say. They say, "How much was the advance?"

I should have gone into the time-share vacation condominium business with Uncle Ned. But Elaine doesn't think so. She takes writers seriously; she respects me for being one. I suppose she's been wrong about other things in her life, too, but it's great that there's one place where I'm safe from being thought of as, mainly, a failed time-share vacation condominium salesman. And no matter how much money Uncle Ned makes, he won't be able to get a good table at Elaine's—unless he buys the movie rights to my book.

My wife opened a copy of *Fodor's Guide for Single Women Traveling in the Mediterranean* and said, rather cryptically, "One thing I'll say for you. When life hands you roast beef, diced ham, pared raw potatoes, brown sauce, sliced mushrooms, dry sherry, garlic salt, and a pinch of basil—you make a hash of things."

12

AUGUST 2001

I got an e-mail from Ophelia in Calcutta," said my godson Nick. "She's given up her search for enlightenment and is staying at the Oberoi Grand."

That's good, I said.

"I guess so," said Nick. "She sent an attachment with the e-mail. It's a manifesto."

A Call for Belief Control

It is a tragic fact that guns kill people. But if we are concerned about people getting killed, we must realize that mere gun control will not put an end to shocking violence. During the past thirty centuries, millions of people have died because of the negligent possession of religious beliefs. "And Moses stretched forth his hand over the sea. . . . And the water returned, and covered the chariots, and the horsemen, and all the host of Pharaoh," for example. Then there's the Crusades, the Spanish Inquisition, communal violence between Hindus and Muslims, additional trouble in the Middle East, mass killings in the Balkans, Jonestown, Waco, and the *fatwa* against Salman Rushdie. That is to name only a few examples of what happens when people take religion into their own hands. An international campaign for Belief Control should be a first priority among morally engaged and politically committed persons.

We can start in our own country by advocating a few basic positions that almost all Americans can be expected to support:

- Restrict the import of dangerous and flimsy foreign religions such as Hare Krishna and the Sun Myung Moon Unification Church.
- Ban small inexpensive religions—the so-called Sunday morning specials—practiced by the more obscure televangelists and people who go to church in cinder-block buildings.
- Enforce existing laws, especially those that keep our children safe by making schools and other public institutions "faith-free zones." (Much remains to be done. Too many teachers still end the school day by saying such things as, "God, I need a drink.")

Of course, this is simply a beginning. We need a national system of accountability requiring all spiritual dogmas to be registered with the government lest they fall into the wrong hands the way Christianity did with Jim Bakker and Tammy Faye. Some elements of this program are already in place under Internal Revenue Service nonprofit rules for church organizations. But these rules are threatened by President Bush's "faith-based initiatives" plan. Furthermore, the IRS concerns itself only with the money that churchgoers give. What about the *credence* that people give to their religions? Shouldn't this be audited too?

We also need a nationwide seven-day waiting period for prayer. This would give people time to cool off and reconsider reverence and supplication and maybe call their local social services provider instead.

All religious believers should be licensed to make sure that they are competent to hold opinions and viewpoints and don't believe in just any old thing such as creationism or a flat tax. Perhaps existing state motor vehicle departments could be expanded to provide dogma exams and multicultural sensitivity tests so that intolerance issues such as those between Hindus and Muslims and Moses and Pharaoh will be avoided in the future. And Skepticism Ed classes ought to be required at the grade-school level.

All religions must be made childproof. Our teachers' unions have done good work in this field, K through 12. Delaying first communions and bar mitzvahs until age twenty-one would be another positive step. Religious marriage ceremonies should also be postponed until the children by that marriage are old enough to handle the behavior of their parents in a responsible manner.

Convicted criminals and people with a history of mental illness need to be encouraged to play golf on Sundays.

Easily concealed religions such as mainstream Protestantism should be restricted.

And certain "assault hymns" could be prohibited or modified:

Mine eyes have seen the glory of the coming of the Lord,
He is marching through the vineyards where cabernet sauvignon is stored.

Some will say that America is such a "God-fearing" country that individual religious beliefs can never be contained or eliminated. Yet millions and millions of Americans, in their everyday behavior (not to mention their television viewing habits), show us that this is no longer the case. Nonetheless, we must face the fact that there will be tremendous opposition to even the most commonsensical Belief Control laws. The religious lobby is well funded and well organized (although the National Council of Churches is on our side). We must make our case clearly to the public that we are not opposed to the use of religion for recreational purposes as long as no one is harmed or made to feel guilty or excluded. And we must work hard to counter the false and self-serving argument made by our opponents that all religious beliefs are "protected" by the First Amendment. Take another look, you God-mongering bigots: The First Amendment says, "Congress shall make no law *respecting* an establishment of religion."

* * *

"I've got to show this to my mom," said the teenage baby-sitter. "It'll blow her mind. In 1999, when we lived in Seattle and she was still chained to the Space Needle at Christmas from protesting the WTO in November, she double-chained herself because she could hear Christmas carols while she was on government property and that violated the constitutional separation between church and state. She is such a wack."

"Your mother is a very nice person," said my wife. "And it was sweet of her to bake soybean chip cookies for Muffin."

"No!" screamed Muffin.

"Mind your manners," said my wife.

"Please, please, please, no!" screamed Muffin.

Nick, will you send your sister Ophelia an e-mail letter from me? said the Political Nut who lives around here. I'm rewriting the Ten Commandments for her, as soon as I mix another Bloody Mary.

The Ten Commandments, Version 10.1

And God, after careful polling, and having consulted with focus groups, spake all these words, saying,

I am the Lord thy God, which have brought thee out of the land of Egypt (if you have a Green Card), out of the house of bondage (when the federal appeals court doesn't rule against me *in re* Elián González), and into the longest period of economic expansion in modern history (until NASDAQ flopped).

1. Thou shalt have no other gods before me—but don't say anything about it because it's important to be multiculturally sensitive.

2. Thou shalt not make unto thee any graven image, or any likeness of any thing that is in heaven above, or that is in the earth beneath, or that is in the water under the earth—until you've worked out a licensing agreement for the trademark and the logo. And don't forget who gave the go-ahead. One hand washes the other: for I the Lord thy God am a jealous God, visiting the iniquity of the fathers upon the children unto the third and fourth generation of them that hate me—unless they seek counseling, of course.

3. Thou shalt not take the name of the Lord thy God in vain—except when it's really a career-breaker. And even then you're usually

better off confessing the truth up front and giving yourself maximum spin time. It's always the cover-up that gets you.

4. Remember the sabbath day, to keep it holy. Holey-in-oney, is what I say. Ha-ha. Six days shalt thou labor—no, make that five. Casual dress on Fridays and all week during August. For in six days the Lord made heaven and earth, the sea, and all that in them is, and rested the seventh day: wherefore the Lord blessed the sabbath day, and hallowed it—and, wouldn't you know, got stuck for five hours in traffic coming back from the Hamptons anyway.

5. Honor thy father and thy mother—or the whole bank balance is going to the brains-in-her-bra cocktail waitress Dad just married and the busboy on Mom's Bermuda cruise.

6. Thou shalt not kill. But if you have humanitarian intentions and Tony Blair is in favor of it too, something like the air war in Kosovo is okay as long as there are no NATO casualties. P.S. Don't kill whales.

7. Thou shalt not commit adultery. On the other hand, you'd be a fool not to buy Pfizer stock.

8. Thou shalt not steal—not when you can form a corporation for zilch, rake in the venture capital, swing a big IPO, and effin' *print* money.

9. Thou shalt not bear false witness against thy neighbor—or bear true witness either, for that matter. Look what happened to Mark Furman and Ken Starr. Key thy neighbor's Lexus instead.

10. Thou shalt not covet thy neighbor's wife, nor his manservant, nor his maidservant, nor his ox, nor his ass—and certainly not all five without getting an agent and a book contract, a slot on Ricki Lake, and a major made-for-TV movie deal, at the very least.

And all the people saw the thunderings, and the lightnings, and the noise of the trumpet, and the mountain smoking: and when the people had finished selling their home videos of this to *Fox News*, they said unto Moses, Speak thou with us, and we will hear: but let not God speak with us, lest we never get him to shut up.

And Moses spake unto the people, saying, I've got the ACLU on this. Don't worry about a thing.

* * *

My young assistant, Max, came in just then. "Great news, I've got a real job," he said to my wife. "No offense," he said to me.

"Good for you," said my wife. "What will you be doing?"

"I'm the new editor of *Elephant in the Living Room,* the monthly magazine of the Fairfax County Republican Party."

Excellent! said the Political Nut. You can run my article "Evil, Stinking Democrats." I begin by proposing that we Republicans take a step back from our partisanship and give a moment's thought to the decent, well-meaning, intelligent people who oppose us—and how there aren't any.

Then I show how Democrats suck. Consider what they believe—such as anything Yasir Arafat says. And when a mother sacrificed her life in a desperate attempt to free herself and her child from a totalitarian dictatorship, Democrats believed this was a great opportunity to show Fidel Castro's family values. Fidel probably does have family values, of the Democrat type, about abortion for instance. And there is ample indication that Fidel is a big supporter of Right to Die legislation.

Democrats believe in killing babies and old people, and, to judge by their various plans to modify American medical care, they believe in killing everybody else too. Except for murderers. Murderers will get a time-out and a chance to speak at the graduation ceremony of a prominent liberal arts college.

Assuming that a few of us (who haven't been lucky enough to murder somebody) make it to old age, Democrats believe we should spend those declining years (until Dr. Kevorkian has an appointment opening) in poverty. Democrats believe in the bankrupt Social Security system on the simple and forthright grounds that privatizing the nation's pension fund would give people money.

Being rich is no fair. Democrats believe in fairness. If you're right-handed, that's no fair either. You should chop some fingers off your right hand and sew them on your left. That way your arms will have equality. And Democrats believe in equality—except equality for minorities. Democrats believe minorities are stupid and helpless (no fair counting Jews or Orientals). Democrats believe affirmative action programs are necessary for all minorities except minorities that use yarmulkes or chopsticks; those minorities need quotas to keep too many of them from getting into Berkeley. Otherwise, say Democrats, we'll never have true equality in an America where everyone has the same opportunity—to be a Democrat.

But although Democrats don't believe that blacks and Hispanics are as good as a Kennedy, Democrats do believe that the rain forest is almost equal to Ted (and not just in how damp, vast, and icky it is). Democrats believe trees and rocks and animals on the endangered species list have souls. However, Democrats are not sure the developer who built your ranch house does. Anyway, that developer's kids have no business praying in school. And neither do yours. Democrats believe kids shouldn't pray in school, especially not during moments of silence, because silence can lead to thinking and if people get to thinking they might become Republicans.

Actually, Democrats believe kids shouldn't even *be* in school, at least not in anything that could properly be called a school—where children learn to count and read and don't get shot at recess. Without playground gunshot injuries, there might not be sufficient public outcry in support of nationalized medicine. Thus Democrats do not believe in school vouchers.

And yet Democrats do believe in gun control, even though playground gunshot injuries are a proven vote-getter. This is because Democrats believe that gun owners want to keep their guns mostly in case they need to shoot Democrats. It happened in 1861 and it could happen again. Plus National Rifle Association PAC money is used for nothing except screwing Democrats. Democrats believe this is something that should only happen literally. Maybe sex education can overcome people's natural repugnance in this matter. Democrats believe in sex education.

But what Democrats believe in most is politics. If you scrutinize Democrat beliefs one by one you'll get a mere random catalog of insanity. But if you examine Democrat beliefs as a whole, you'll discover an underlying, unified, systematic worldview that cannot be treated with psychopharmaceuticals, therapeutic chats, or a "long rest" at MacClean's. The world still awaits a cure for politics.

Every doctrine and tenet of the Democrats entails an increase in political power and a decrease in the power of conscience, religion, tradition, civil society, the free market, mothers, and (if there are any left around—and in many Democrat strongholds, like Beverly Hills, there aren't) fathers.

Why? Why would anyone want a society organized around appearing on *Hardball* in preference to a society organized around raising kids, working hard, making money, going to the VFW hall on Saturday night, going to church on Sunday morning, and obeying the scout's oath? It's important to remember that Democrats aren't just crazy, they're evil. Democrats suspect—with considerable evidence to support them—that they aren't very good at those things I just mentioned. Democrats need a field of endeavor where they can yak and blabber their way to the top without displaying any virtues. (And apparently, in light of Bill Clinton's remarkable sexual incompetence with Ms. Lewinsky, Democrats don't even need to master vices.)

But America has a representative form of government. Is it so wrong to seek political power in free and fair elections? Yes, if you're a Democrat. I say this with confidence because of an article that appeared in the house organ of the Democratic Party, *The Washington Post,* on June 5, 2000. The text of the piece concerned, allegedly, an obscure type of chimpanzee called the bonobo. But the subtext was not hard to decode. It tells us everything about the America we get when we elect Democrats, and in particular, that she-ape from New York State.

> The animals live in extremely peaceful, egalitarian, close-knit communities "that are held together not by male domination but by female bonds," according to Congolese scientist Inogwabini Bila Isia.
>
> They work out most conflicts through elaborate social interaction rather than fighting, and they distribute food evenly throughout the group. They are very sexual, engaging in constant genital rubbing and other sexual behaviors with the same and the opposite sex. The primary role of sex is usually social rather than reproductive. . . .
>
> "They show us what we could be. They make us ask, Why do we have to have a violent male-dominated society?" said Gay Reinartz, a bonobo researcher and conservation coordinator at the Zoological Society of Milwaukee.

The noble bonobos have just one problem. And you guessed it correctly. They're about to become extinct.

"Shh . . . ," said my wife. "I just got Muffin to sleep."

That was quick, I said.

"I read her one of your books."

Where's Nick?

"He's out on the screen porch with the baby-sitter."

"What Ricardo's Principle of Comparative Advantage means," I could hear the baby-sitter saying, "is that: Let's say I'm better at kissing and you're better at hugging. But I'm better at both than you are. Should I do all the kissing and hugging?"

Nick said something I didn't catch.

"Let's say," continued the baby-sitter, "that I'm three times as good at kissing and twice as good at hugging. And I can produce six kisses per minute or I can produce two hugs. That means you can produce two kisses or one hug. And let's say each hug or each kiss equals one unit of net production. So, if I spend half my time kissing and half my time hugging and you don't do any of either, I'll produce three kisses and one hug, which equals four units. But if I spend all my time kissing and you spend all your time hugging, I'll produce six kisses and you'll . . ."

My wife handed Poppet to me and marched toward the screen door. "Ahem, you two, it's gotten awfully quiet out there."

"You know," said my wife to the Political Nut, "I sent an e-mail message of my own to Nick's sister. I tried to talk to her sensibly about religion, about how it's the nature of faith to encompass the miraculous and so forth. I guess I shouldn't have mentioned the Shroud of Turin."

What did Ophelia say? asked the Political Nut, bouncing Poppet on his knee.

My wife sighed. "She instant-messaged, 'For God so loved the world that He gave His only begotten Son—and a fitted sheet.'"

Well, they're horrible at that age, said the Political Nut. And why not? I'm horrible at my age. I've been thinking about this. And I've decided to apologize.

"To whom?" asked my wife.

I don't quite know yet. At first I was going to apologize for things I'd done personally.

"That works," said my wife, "when accompanied by gifts of jewelry."

But, continued the Political Nut, it dawned on me I could also apologize for things that cannot be blamed on a specific individual—such as me—but that a specific individual—such as me—can get credit for regretting. So I apologize for racism, sexism, religious bigotry, and discrimination based on age, physical ability, and whether people are wearing any little lacy items under their three-piece suits. I apologize for poverty, crime, social injustice, damage to the Amazon rain forest, and inhumane treatment of farm animals. I apologize for certain harsher aspects of Hammurabi's code.

Then I was reading in the newspaper that the government of Poland had apologized for a massacre that had taken place almost sixty years before in a village that's now part of Russia. And I realized there's all sorts of terrible stuff done long ago and far away by people who are dead, and I can apologize for that. I'll become a better person. We all know apologizing makes you a better person. But I'll be safe from anybody asking me to do anything about what I'm apologizing for. So I apologize. And, while the men who actually sold slaves and killed Indians burn in hell, I get to enjoy jazz and soul food and buy a summer place on the Vineyard without being attacked by Narragansettes.

"Except," said my wife, "we can't afford a summer place on the Vineyard."

I apologize, said the Political Nut.

I'm excited about becoming a better person by apologizing, said the Political Nut, a few days later. And now that I'm a better person, I'm going to do something nice for Democrats, something to make up for all the hurtful things I've said about them over the years, especially the true things—those must have really hurt. I've written an "Open Letter to Democrats." I already gave a copy to the teenage baby-sitter to take home to her grandparents.

Open Letter to Democrats

I suggest that you members of "the party of Jefferson" do something that Jefferson would have done—I don't mean make like William Jefferson Clinton with Sally Hemings—and stop and think for a minute. *Why* are you a Democrat? Are you a Democrat because you're poor? Poor people vote for Democrats. Rich people vote for Republicans. Do you think the bigwigs in the Democratic Party don't know this? When was the last time Al Gore called you with a hot tip on Occidental Petroleum stock?

Are you a Democrat because you're a union member? Then why, after eight years of Bill Clinton, did some Chinese guy in Guangdong province have your job? Plus, it's the same with the union high muckety-mucks as it is with the Democratic Party pooh-bahs. Notice it's called "organized labor," not "organized you're-the-boss." Have you ever heard your union president say, "Look at the loot we've got in our pension fund and all the swell rackets we're in on with the mob guys—let's just effin' *buy* General Motors?"

Are you a Democrat because you're a woman? Then how come you're married to a Republican? Most women are. Face it, you were afraid that a two-Democrat family might cause the kids to grow up to be liberals—forty years old, still wearing nostril rings and living at home, clomping around the house in Doc Martens with no job yet except volunteer work on Nader presidential campaigns.

Are you a Democrat because you're gay? Come on, do you really think Republicans hate gays? You've been to Republican homes. Do they look like they were decorated by the Christian Coalition? What are interior design firms going to do with Democrats, go rearrange their bowling trophies? Who appreciates Karl Lagerfeld, Nancy Reagan, or Barney Frank? What kind of ballet does the UAW sponsor? Imagine *La Scala* sung by Snoop Dogg.

Are you a Democrat because you're part of a minority group? Forget about it. Mexicans, Blacks, Jews, Italians, Irish, Puerto Ricans—you guys hate each other. Become Republican and at least you'll be allowed to admit it—after three drinks. "Wall Street? I'll tell you what's wrong with Wall Street. Ever since that sonofabitch Joe Kennedy, the goddamned shanty Irish have been running Wall Street. Say, Patrick, another G and T and make it snappy. Hey, what's in this? *Arrrrrgh!*" (Drops dead.) Although even Republicans have to watch their mouths sometimes.

Anyway, don't be fooled by affirmative action. It's just another trick the Democratic Party uses to keep you poor even after you get a law *and* a medical degree. Affirmative action makes employers think, "Black woman nuclear physicist? Hah! Probably let her into Harvard 'cause they were looking for a twofer. Bet she got Cs in high school practical math. Give her a job in personnel." Meanwhile, the same guy is thinking, "Whoa, male, Japanese, and Jewish—he must have been *really* good to get into chiropractor school."

You see, it's actually Republicans who favor racial and ethnic diversity. Just look at the people who are cleaning Republican houses, mowing Republican lawns, cooking Republican meals, and caring for Republican children—black, brown, yellow, you-name-it. And every single one of these people is in this country illegally. I mention that in case you are a Democrat because you're a criminal. You'd be a lot better off as a Republican. Republicans know crime. Would you rather swindle corporate shareholders out of billions or knock over a convenience store?

What Americans don't understand about Republicans, and what causes a lot of Americans to continue to be Democrats, is that Republicans don't *want* anybody to become Republican. This is because it's already hell getting a tee time. And that's why Republicans insult gays, attack feminists (like Sandra Day O'Connor is a Stepford Wife), support Confederate flag flying (as if Robert E. Lee voted for Lincoln), make bigoted remarks, threaten everybody with "law and order," and pretend to love born-again religious ding-dongs. It's to put you off. It's so Republicans can take five hours to play a doubles match while half in the bag from afternoon gin rickeys without some parvenu former Democrat coming up and saying, "Vernon Jordan and I reserved this court."

But I'll tell you a little secret. If you want to join the Republican Party, we have to let you in. There's nothing we can do about it. I mean, if we'll take Al D'Amato, we'll take anybody.

* * *

Being as I'm such a better person, said the Political Nut, I'm also going to do something nice for Republicans. You know what Republicans need? Excuses. Republicans are always short on excuses for who they are and what they do. So I've drawn up a list of excuses for Republicans. It can be printed on a handy three-by-five card and carried in a suit pocket or slipped in a golf bag.'

Taking the Fifth

I. FIVE EXCUSES FOR REPUBLICAN CIGAR SMOKING

1. I can identify my clothes by smell. That way, when I'm getting dressed in the dark, I don't accidentally wind up in a Norma Kamali skirt and a pair of Joan & David lizard pumps.
2. Cigars produce more secondary smoke. Thus antismoking types are killed off faster.
3. I'd feel like a jerk serving brandy and Freedent.
4. Tell the following anecdote: Years ago I was on the porch of a little inn on the coast of Maine. An old lady was sitting in a rocker. I asked would she mind if I smoked a cigar. "Young man," she said, "when I was a little girl my mother told me never to object when a man lights a cigar. 'Where there are cigars,' said my mother, 'there's money.'"
5. Cigars are the way I relax and unwind. They're better for my health than drinking.

II. FIVE EXCUSES FOR REPUBLICAN DRINKING

1. If I stopped drinking and smoking, it would add ten years to my life. But it would add them to the wrong end.
2. "I was drunk" is a better excuse than "I was stupid."
3. Weddings, funerals, divorces, hostile takeovers, bankruptcies, tax audits, drops in the NASDAQ, weekends with the family—I'm an occasional drinker.
4. When you've been through as many weddings, funerals, divorces, hostile takeovers, bankruptcies, tax audits, drops in the NASDAQ, and weekends with the family as I have, you've got some memories you'd like to lose. Drinking causes memory loss.
5. There's another excuse, but I forget it.

III. FIVE EXCUSES FOR REPUBLICANS DRIVING SPORTS CARS THAT COST MORE THAN THEIR FATHERS EVER MADE IN A YEAR

1. A high-powered executive in a high-pressure job may not have time to sail his yacht or fly his plane, but driving a fine performance vehicle is a way for him to relax and unwind twice a day just going back and forth to work. (The president of Porsche once actually said this in an interview. Claim he said it to you.)
2. When I was in high school I promised myself that someday I would get one of these babies. Lots of people abandon their youthful ideals.
3. When a thing gives you honest unalloyed pleasure, you can't think of it in terms of monetary expense.
4. It's really an investment.
5. Anyway, it's cheaper than marrying a woman half my age.

IV. FIVE EXCUSES FOR REPUBLICANS MARRYING WOMEN HALF THEIR AGE

1. Because I can.
2. She loves me for my money—and that's true love.
3. She believes my stories about the sixties.
4. If she tries to screw me in the divorce, I'll fire her dad.
5. She's mellow. She's laid-back. She doesn't care if I smoke, drink, drive like hell, and stay out all night.

V. FIVE EXCUSES FOR EVERYTHING ELSE REPUBLICAN

1. My wife won't let me.
2. I'm in the middle of a terrible divorce.
3. After I gave up smoking and drinking and sold the Porsche and quit running around with women half my age, I had to do *something*.
4. One thing I've learned in all my years of experience—never make excuses.
5. I used to be a Democrat.

An integral aspect, I remarked to my wife, of Hegel's philosophy is *don't put jelly beans up your nose!*

"It's difficult to have a serious conversation with a toddler in the room," my wife said, handing Muffin over to the teenage baby-sitter. "Anything interesting in the *Sunday Times*?"

The Japanese, I said, want sumo figure skating to be a demonstration sport at the Salt Lake City Olympics. The Tampa Bay Devil Rays have traded for a fellow who's been rookie of the year nine times. And Oprah is starting a professional Women's Emotions League with teams in six cities. There's an exhibit of Republican folk art at the Met—wrist corsages, hand-knit mittens for golf club heads, and a rare Philadelphia Main Line needle-point throw pillow stitched with the motto A FOOL AND HER MONEY ARE SOON MARRIED. The magazine has a story about a human child, abandoned at birth, who was raised to adulthood by New Yorkers. Someone has genetically engineered an oak tree with foliage that resembles McDonald's cheeseburger wrappers so that, in the autumn, falling leaves will blend with the environment. A California gynecologist is offering drive-through pap tests. An international tribunal is being established in The Hague to conduct Peace Crime Trials, prosecuting people who committed capitalist atrocities between 1945 and 1989. Vermont will experiment with low-sodium driveway salt this winter. And a Million Girlfriend march on Washington is being planned, which will focus on the issue of—

"Commitment," said my wife.

"What is man's place in the universe?" I heard the baby-sitter ask Muffin. They seemed to be playing some kind of board game.

"Um, I dunno," said Muffin.

"Okay," said the baby-sitter, taking another card from the top of a stack. "If God is just, why does evil exist in the world?"

"Um, I dunno," said Muffin.

What are you two doing? I asked.

"We're playing Significant Pursuit," said the baby-sitter. "My mother invented it. Muffin's doing really well. She said that if a tree falls in a forest and nobody's there, everybody will hear about it if it falls on Pooh and kills him."

"That game might be a little old for Muffin," said my wife.

I'm feeling a little old myself, I said. There's an article in the Book Review—do you realize it's been thirty years since Hunter Thompson wrote *Fear and Loathing in Las Vegas*? Seems like yesterday.

"I'm sure it does," said my wife. "You can't remember anything about yesterday, either."

Well, I said, not much happened yesterday. But, then again, not much happens in *Fear and Loathing*. That's the truly amazing thing about the book. Here is a famously colorful era's finest specimen of the picaresque—a genre that, according to William Rose Benét, "deals sympathetically with the adventures of clever and amusing rogues"—and what gives? The rogues aren't clever. Amusing is not the word for them. They accomplish little roguery. The author shows them no sympathy. And of adventures they really have none. Two men in early middle age visit Las Vegas while intoxicated. They frighten a few people (mostly each other), are rude to bystanders, and astonish a cleaning lady. Two rental cars and several bedrooms and bathrooms are left the worse for wear. A couple of large corporations are cheated of modest sums. As for serious malefaction, there is possession of controlled substances, a (poorly) concealed weapon, possible sexual contact with a woman who may be underage, and a skipped hotel bill. In a century marked by countless unspeakable crimes, we may speak of these, and they don't count.

Fear and Loathing in Las Vegas is a bloodcurdling adventure where no one is murdered, robbed, imprisoned, or hanged. The only hair's-breadth escape is from a speeding ticket and DWI citation. And at the end of the story comes, not triumph or tragedy or revenge or contrition, but status quo ante like a TV sitcom. But Hunter is such a genius that it's a thrilling saga. A thrilling saga in which nothing much happens—a fitting example of the picaresque for the Now Generation. One of the things Hunter did in this book was write a coda to, an obituary for, the nonsense of the 1960s. It's important to recall that in the 1960s nothing much happened.

"Could be," said my wife. "I was in preschool."

Well, the war in Vietnam was widely and vigorously protested, I said. And nothing happened, the war went on. Blacks rioted in the slums. Nothing happened, the slums are still there. Mysticism was practiced, psychedelics were ingested, consciousness was everywhere raised. Nothing happened. Hundreds of thousands of people gathered at Woodstock. Nothing whatsoever happened. And we were all freed from sexual prudery and repression. And nothing happened—at least nothing very splendid, though there were plenty of illegitimate children, venereal diseases, and hurt feelings.

We see the protagonists of *Fear and Loathing* in 1971, in the wake of this great generational blow-off, wallowing in the inanity of the times. It would be a masterly period piece if Hunter had decided to go no further. But Hunter is nothing if not a gone cat. Instead, the book is an entire description of all life as complete senseless idiocy.

Good and evil are a ridiculous mess. We hear much about the "vicious," "twisted" "swine" who control American society and who threaten Raoul Duke and his three-hundred-pound Samoan attorney. But the only people we see being vicious or twisted or swinish are that attorney and Duke. Authority is described as nasty and corrupt. And nearly all the ancillary characters in the book, even the hotel clerks, are portrayed as authority figures. Yet these people are largely honest, forbearing, even hospitable. "Let's have lunch!" says one hotel clerk as Raoul Duke absconds.

Threats are, indeed, made to Duke and the attorney, but only by innocents such as the carload of Oklahoma tourists who've had "Shoot! Scag! Blood! Heroin! Rape! Cheap! Communists!" screamed at them. And when we encounter actual "pigs"—as Duke calls law officers—they turn out to be, at worst, bemused. "What the hell's *goin' on* in this country?" a small-town Georgia DA quite reasonably asks when Duke and the attorney tell him narcotics addicts are everywhere, working in pairs and slitting people's throats. And when Duke is apprehended drunk, stoned, and driving at 120 mph, the California highway patrolman is downright kind. And has a sense of humor: "I get the feeling you could use a nap."

There is a terrific loneliness throughout the book. The protagonists are not friends. Duke shows occasional protective impulses toward the attorney. He forgoes an opportunity to electrocute him. The attorney threatens to carve a **Z** in Duke's forehead. Duke locks the attorney in a bathroom. No explanation is given for these two being together. But neither mentions any other emotional bond. The only romance is when the attorney seduces a runaway who obsessively draws Barbra Streisand and has come to Las Vegas to present her portraits to the star. This, it hardly needs saying, comes to a bad end.

Duke and the attorney profess no moral, religious, or philosophical principles. The attorney makes no statement of conscience except to call Duke a "filthy bastard" for proposing to prostitute the Barbra Streisand artist. And Duke seems actively opposed to belief. He goes so far as to blame the failure of 1960s utopianism on "the desperate assumption that somebody—or at least some *force*—is tending that Light at the end of the tunnel." The only credo in *Fear and Loathing* is freedom in its most reductive and alienated sense, "a gross, physical salute to the fantastic *possibilities* of life in this country."

Hunter gives us a harrowing portrayal of the human condition as absurd. This is anomie writ wide and deep. Compared to *Fear and Loathing in Las Vegas,* Albert Camus's *L'Étranger* is a lame jailhouse whine, and Samuel Beckett's *Waiting for Godot* is a puppet-theater skit about idleness and boredom. Thompson alone captures the—how else to put it?—fear and loathing that are at the root of the contemporary essence.

And he makes us laugh at it. This is something we're unlikely to do during *Waiting for Godot* performances, even if we're as high as Raoul Duke. Hunter takes the darkest questions of ontology, the grimmest epistemological queries, and just by posing them sends us doubled over in fits of risibility, our sides aching from armpit to pelvic girdle, the tops of our legs raw from knee-slapping, and beer spitting out of our noses.

Hunter performs this philosophical legerdemain by creating a pair of empty clowns who seem to have the brains of marmosets but who speak with the mouths of poets. They are utterly insensitive, lawless creatures who are nonetheless agonized by the dilemmas of being and nothingness. It's as if two of the Three Stooges had discovered Søren Kierkegaard and William Butler Yeats.

Then Thompson fills his clowns with drugs. Drugs let us see things differently. Drugs give us new viewpoints. Drugs provide us with alternative perceptions, thousands of alternative perceptions, all of them wrong. Thus we see the futility of relying on the mind when facing the abyss. Contort the mind however we will, it cannot do the job. What's more, drugs are all about the self. Thus we see the futility of ego. Drugs are potent agents of change, but they only change me. They have no effect on the outside world. So there everything is, just the way it's always been, and I'm all changed—like somebody who shows up at a wedding dressed for an orgy. And Thompson fills his clowns with drugs so they can be clowns while also, presumably, being normal (well, more or less normal) men. If you want a truly frightening idea, consider Raoul Duke and the three-hundred-pound Samoan attorney doing all the things they do in *Fear and Loathing* sober.

Hunter Thompson takes two fools, incapacitates them, sends them on a farcical quest after a material manifestation of something—the American Dream—that has an immaterial existence, and sends them to look in the wrong place besides. After two-hundred-odd pages of perfect and lyrical writing about that "nothing much," which twentieth-century hipsters insisted on thinking was the central fact of reality, the fools are back where they started.

Like all true comedy, *Fear and Loathing in Las Vegas* is a cautionary tale. Live in a universe that stops at the end of one's nose, and this is the life one will lead. Lead a life where one believes in nothing, and this is the universe one will live in.

"Maybe," said my wife. "But when I read *Fear and Loathing,* it just sort of tickled me."

You know, I said, there's a theory about tickling. The theory is that a tickle is halfway between a blow and a caress. The victim doesn't know whether to kiss you or run and lock himself in the garage. I think this explains most laughter. Laughter is an automatic response to unexpected contradictions and absurdities, a means of expressing sudden upset and confusion. And it's more attractive than the only other means of expressing sudden upset and confusion that I can think of. Compare laughing to vomiting out loud, vomiting up your sleeve, getting the last vomit, vomit and the world vomits with you. . . .

"All right, all right," said my wife, "but even if the Samoan attorney does vomit a lot, I don't think you can call *Fear and Loathing* a comedy."

Why not?

"Because real comedies end in a marriage," she said, cuddling up next to me on the sofa. "Or is it vice versa?"